MW00680301

DIASPORIC CHINESE VENTURES

Wang Gungwu is an eminent and prolific writer whose work spans a great number of themes and approaches. Over the past 50 years he has made an outstanding contribution to the scholarly and political debate in several disciplines, bringing his unparalleled knowledge of the histories of East and Southeast Asia to bear on urgent contemporary social, political and cultural issues. As doyen of studies on the Chinese diaspora and China's relations with Southeast Asia, for the last half-century he has been at the very heart of this emerging field of scholarship.

This collection of essays by and about Wang Gungwu brings together some of Wang's most recent and representative writings about ethnic Chinese outside China. It illuminates key issues in Asia's modern transformation, including migration, identity, nationalism and cultural reconfigurations. In addition to providing an intriguing assessment of Wang's own political and scholarly influences, the book collects interviews, speeches and essays that illustrate the development and direction of his scholarship on the diasporic Chinese.

Diasporic Chinese Ventures is an ideal introduction to the often complex field of ethnic Chinese studies and essential reading for students embarking on it. Readers already familiar with Wang Gungwu's writing will find in this collection a useful map of the evolution of his opinions over time and a mirror onto the political and scholarly influences that shaped his thinking.

Gregor Benton is Professorial Fellow in Chinese History in the School of History and Archaeology at Cardiff University. **Hong Liu** is Associate Professor in the Department of Chinese Studies at the National University of Singapore.

CHINESE WORLDS

Chinese Worlds publishes high-quality scholarship, research monographs, and source collections on Chinese history and society. "Worlds" signals the diversity of China, the cycles of unity and division through which China's modern history has passed, and recent research trends toward regional studies and local issues. It also signals that Chineseness is not contained within borders – ethnic migrant communities overseas are also "Chinese worlds".

The series editors are Gregor Benton, Flemming Christiansen, Delia Davin, Terence Gomez and Frank Pieke.

THE LITERARY FIELDS OF TWENTIETH-CENTURY CHINA
Edited by Michel Hockx

CHINESE BUSINESS IN MALAYSIA
Accumulation, ascendance, accommodation
Edmund Terence Gomez

INTERNAL AND INTERNATIONAL MIGRATION
Chinese perspectives
Edited by Frank N. Pieke and Hein Mallee

VILLAGE INC.
Chinese rural society in the 1990s
Edited by Flemming Christiansen and Zhang Junzuo

CHEN DUXIU'S LAST ARTICLES AND LETTERS, 1937–1942
Edited and translated by Gregor Benton

ENCYCLOPEDIA OF THE CHINESE OVERSEAS
Edited by Lynn Pan

NEW FOURTH ARMY
Communist resistance along the Yangtze and the Huai, 1938–1941
Gregor Benton

A ROAD IS MADE
Communism in Shanghai 1920–1927
Steve Smith

THE BOLSHEVIKS AND THE CHINESE REVOLUTION 1919–1927
Alexander Pantsov

CHINAS UNLIMITED
Gregory Lee

FRIEND OF CHINA
The myth of Rewi Alley
Anne-Marie Brady

BIRTH CONTROL IN CHINA 1949–2000
Population policy and demographic development
Thomas Scharping

CHINATOWN, EUROPE
An exploration of overseas Chinese identity in the 1990s
Flemming Christiansen

FINANCING CHINA'S RURAL ENTERPRISES
Jun Li

CONFUCIAN CAPITALISM
Souchou Yao

CHINESE BUSINESS IN THE MAKING OF A MALAY STATE, 1882–1941
Kedah and Penang
Wu Xiao An

CHINESE ENTERPRISE, TRANSNATIONALISM AND IDENTITY
Edited by Edmund Terence Gomez and Hsin-Huang Michael Hsiao

DIASPORIC CHINESE VENTURES
The life and work of Wang Gungwu
Edited by Gregor Benton and Hong Liu

DIASPORIC CHINESE VENTURES

The life and work of Wang Gungwu

Edited by Gregor Benton and Hong Liu

RoutledgeCurzon
Taylor & Francis Group
LONDON AND NEW YORK

First published 2004
by RoutledgeCurzon
11 New Fetter Lane, London EC4P 4EE

Simultaneously published in the USA and Canada
by RoutledgeCurzon
29 West 35th Street, New York, NY 10001

RoutledgeCurzon is an imprint of the Taylor & Francis Group

Editorial matter and selection © 2004 Gregor Benton and Hong Liu;
individual chapters © the contributors

Typeset in Baskerville by Wearset Ltd, Boldon, Tyne and Wear
Printed and bound in Great Britain by MPG Books Ltd, Bodmin

All rights reserved. No part of this book may be reprinted or reproduced or utilized in any form or by any electronic, mechanical, or other means, now known or hereafter invented, including photocopying and recording, or in any information storage or retrieval system, without permission in writing from the publishers.

British Library Cataloguing in Publication Data
A catalogue record for this book is available from the British Library

Library of Congress Cataloging in Publication Data
Benton, Gregor, 1944–
Diasporic Chinese ventures : the life and work of Wang Gungwu /
Gregor Benton and Hong Liu.
p. cm.
Includes bibliographical references and index.
1. Wang, Gungwu. 2. Scholars—Australia—Biography. I. Title: Life and work of Wang Gungwu. II. Liu, Hong, 1962– III. Title.
CT2808.W365B46 2004
950′.04951′0092—dc21
2003013094

ISBN 0–415–33142–0

CONTENTS

ACKNOWLEDGEMENTS

The editors would like to thank Wang Gungwu for helping to track down elusive texts and solving some enigmas that arose along the way. Throughout the editing, he was always available to answer our questions and to help sort out issues of copyright and bibliographical citation. We should add that the responsibility for choosing titles and planning the overall structure of the volume is ours alone.

We would also like to thank Stephanie Rogers, Zoe Botterill, Sarah Coulson and Zeb Korycinska for their expert help in bringing this book out.

The texts are as they originally appeared, except that we added references (marked as ours) on terms and names that might not be familiar to the non-specialist reader.

The editors and publishers would like to acknowledge the following for permission to reprint copyright material: Chapter 6: Taylor & Francis; Chapter 9: Centre for Asian Studies, Hong Kong University; Chapter 10: Times Publishing Group; Chapter 11: The Social Science Research Council, New York.

Every effort has been made to contact copyright holders for their permission to reprint material in this book. The publishers would be grateful to hear from any copyright holder who is not here acknowledged and will undertake to rectify any errors or omissions in future editions of this book.

Wang Gungwu at Hong Kong University, 1987

Wang Gungwu with his mother, 1951

INTRODUCTION

Hong Liu and Gregor Benton

This collection of essays by and about Professor Wang Gungwu serves two main ends, biographical and conceptual. By bringing together in one volume some of Wang's most recent writings concerning ethnic Chinese outside China, we hope to provide readers with a deeper understanding of Wang's views on an abiding element in Asia's modern transformation, migration. Most of the essays by Wang collected here were originally given as keynote speeches at meetings and conferences in Asia, Europe and North America. By grouping them under a pair of focused themes, we aim to highlight the historical and geographical settings in which Wang developed his ideas and to illustrate their evolution over the past 50 to 60 years, years that witnessed not only the political transformation of colonies into nation-states but the emergence of regionalism and globalization. In that sense, Wang's biography reflects the turbulent times through which he has lived. His observations, based largely on active participation in the events he comments on, form an historical commentary in their own right on the postwar and postcolonial world.

Like his multi-faceted and wide-ranging publications, Wang Gungwu's life can be observed from several different angles. He has been, variously or at once, a Chinese overseas, a scholar, an administrator, and a political activist. He was born in Surabaya in the Netherlands East Indies (today's Indonesia) in 1930. His father, Wang Fo-wen (1903–1972), one of a small minority of first-generation Chinese immigrants to receive a college education, was a respected educator well versed in traditional Chinese culture. He taught in Singapore, Kuala Lumpur, Malacca, and Surabaya before serving as an inspector of Chinese schools in the Malay State of Perak.[1] The son attended Anderson School in Ipoh, a mining town in British Malaya, where he was taught in English and studied the history of the British Empire and Commonwealth. At home, starting at the age of three, he received an education in Chinese from his father and his mother Ting Yen (1905–1993). In addition to this basic training in the mother tongue, "they also imparted to their only son a love for China and things Chinese".[2] Later, he learned

Malay and picked up some other European languages besides English, as well as Japanese.

As a Chinese living outside China, he personally – in common with the great majority of Chinese in Southeast Asia after World War II – experienced the transition from sojourner (before 1945) to settler, and is therefore a prime example of one of his own main research topics. This passage is summed up in the Chinese phrase *luodi shenggen*, "falling to the ground and striking root", a description of the accommodationist project, which includes permanent settlement abroad, the renunciation of Chinese citizenship, and public adjustment to the majority way of life, while privately preserving a Chinese lifestyle and cultural values. He has lived and worked not only in Asia but in Europe and Australia. (Delivering the Commonwealth Lecture at Cambridge in 2002, Wang remarked that he has lived all but 3 years of his life "in countries that are, or were, parts of the British Empire and Commonwealth".)[3] He therefore has first-hand experience of migration and settlement in several contexts and historical periods, an experience his scholarship reflects. It is hardly surprising that he should have demonstrated an enduring interest in the fate of Chinese outside China and their political and existential choices (which, more recently, have included remigrating from Southeast Asia to North America, Australia, and Western Europe).

Wang's training in different cultures in various parts of the world helps explain the range of his scholarly interests and his remarkable achievements in numerous fields. Before the war, under the influence of his father but also by personal inclination, he described his infant self as "a Chinese, who intends to return to China". He spent a year at the National Central University in Nanjing between 1947 and 1948, at the height of the Chinese civil war. This visit gave him first-hand experience of Chinese migration and of the background to China's social and political transformation under the then impending People's Republic. In making this journey to China, Wang followed in the footsteps of many young ethnic Chinese males of his generation. This act of "homegoing" is encapsulated in another well-known phrase, *luoye guigen*, "fallen leaves return to their roots", a reference to those Chinese who remain loyal to their native places and wish (usually in vain) to return to them. Even so, he had no difficulty in understanding his father's decision, taken sorrowfully in the 1950s, to give up his Chinese nationality and become Malayan, a step that he himself found less painful.[4]

Upon completing his three-year undergraduate studies at the University of Malaya in 1952, Wang Gungwu had the choice of pursuing his degree at honours level in any one of the three fields he had studied – economics, English literature, and history. He opted for history, under the influence of his history professor, C. N. Parkinson,[5] and embarked on a career that led him to probe deeply the vicissitudes of the time. From

1954 to 1957, he studied at London's School of Oriental and African Studies under D. G. E. Hall (1891–1979), a pioneer in the then young field of Southeast Asian history, and the Tang historian Denis Twitchett. He wrote his PhD on a topic in Chinese imperial history, the Five Dynasties, which he later published in Malaysia and the United States.[6] His sinological training lent a new and rare dimension to his work on Chinese migration and settlement overseas, and is among its greatest strengths.

After completing his PhD in London, he returned home to the University of Malaya (then located in Singapore), where he became Dean of the Arts Faculty in 1962. He was promoted to a full professorship in 1963, a remarkable achievement in the highly racialized political climate of post-independence Malaya. In his research and teaching, he set about exploring contemporary issues of nationhood and ethnicity in the newly independent and ethnically complex Federation of Malaya. This tack towards the social and political sciences was no temporary excursion but the start of a lifelong engagement with issues relevant to community and the body politic. He rejected the communalist project, popular in some Malay and ethnic Chinese circles, and strove instead to help create a society based on the idea of liberal pluralism and cultural tolerance. Even so, he continued to take the longer view, by embedding his analysis of the present day in its historical context.

He subsequently extended his research interests to the new nation states of Southeast Asia. Again, this switch of focus supplemented rather than supplanted his commitment to writing history, his first and in many ways best love. In particular, he turned his attention to the historical evolution of Southeast Asia's ethnic Chinese communities. His solid grounding in Chinese history and his first-hand acquaintance with China gave him a strong angle from which to view Sino-Southeast Asian interactions. In his work on the dynastic period, he concluded that China's relationship with Southeast Asia was overwhelmingly commercial in nature and only marginally political or "imperial". Chinese traders adapted of necessity to the regimes of their Southeast Asian hosts, a practice followed by subsequent generations of Chinese migrants and their descendants and a good example of how (in the contemporary period) to accommodate asserting ethnic Chinese identity with postcolonial nation building. Where Chinese dealt successfully with indigenous elites, "intermarriage and assimilation were common".[7] Interventionist campaigns by mainland Chinese state representatives and political campaigners to harness the Chinese in Southeast Asia to the cause of China's self-strengthening and modernization in the late nineteenth and early twentieth centuries awakened fears among Malay political leaders that a Chinese Fifth Column would form in the region. Wang's historical studies helped weaken the indigenous perception of ethnic Chinese as clannish and potentially disloyal.[8]

In the mid-1960s, John Fairbank, doyen of Chinese studies in North America, invited him to contribute to a volume on the Chinese world order alongside Yang Lien-sheng and Benjamin Schwartz, leading China scholars of the day. Fairbank called Wang Gungwu's "Early Ming Relations with Southeast Asia: A Background Essay" a "masterly study" and "the broadest survey of the evidence concerning pre-Ch'ing [Qing] tribute relations that has yet been made". Together with a couple of other essays on similar topics,[9] this study on early Sino-Southeast Asian interactions is one of Wang's favourites, since it "gave me a valuable perspective that has helped me look back to the formative centuries of Southeast Asia as well as forward to the centuries of dynamic transformations, and that has helped me better understand history".[10]

In later studies, Wang emphasized ethnic Chinese accommodation to local circumstance and drew a distinction between Chinese ethnic pride and Chinese national identity in Southeast Asia. Calls from the north for loyalty to China were damaging from the point of view of ethnic Chinese relations with other peoples in their Southeast Asian homelands; and usually unworkable in the long term, given the distinctive evolution and deepening local roots of Chinese communities across the region. Ethnic Chinese resisted China's patriotic efforts to resinicize them, but they also resisted local assimilation. Some adopted new identities, which often incorporated versions of Chineseness that did not necessarily depend on a knowledge of the Chinese language. In so doing, they stretched the definition of Chineseness in unpredictable ways, by creating new niches and cultural amalgams. Wang's exploration of the variety and autonomy of Chinese communities overseas and the multiplicity of their identities again helped to demonstrate that they are no menace or liability but an enrichment of the societies they inhabit.[11] Thus his scholarship is characterized by a high-minded sense of social responsibility.

Wang is not a historian in the traditional definition, despite his training in and affinity for history. Partly because of his own approach to scholarship and partly because of the very nature of ethnic Chinese studies, which cover many fields and regions, his work straddles disciplines and perspectives. He is keenly aware of paradigm shifts in the social sciences and their ramifications. He suggests that unlike universities in the West where such shifts come from "academic and intellectual activity", in Asia they are "more situational, much more influenced by contemporary political and economic developments".[12] In terms of spatial concerns, his simultaneous engagement with China and Southeast Asia equips him to stand above isolated events and processes and glimpse their interconnections. His methods prompt an analogy with Chinese painting, which strives to depict objects and landscapes from several different angles and thus to convey a sense of the wholeness of things, unlike Western perspective drawing, with its fixed "scientific" viewpoint. His work reflects many of the strengths of traditional Chinese historiography, including its attention to texts and sources, but ultimately it shatters the sinocentric (and the colonial) view of Asian history and has created the conditions for ethnic Chinese studies to emerge as a field of scholarship in its own right.

In 1968, Wang was appointed Professor and Head of Department of Far Eastern History at the Australian National University (ANU), the first person of non-European origin elected to that position. Since then, he has published a great many articles and books on various aspects of Asian and Chinese history and on Chinese migration. His scholarly achievements are reflected in his membership of a number of prestigious scholarly institutions worldwide, including the Australian Academy of the Humanities, Taiwan's Academia Sinica, the American Academy of Arts and Science (of which he is a Foreign Honorary Member), and Beijing's Chinese Academy of Social Sciences.

His impact on the scholarly fields whose directions he helped shape has been profound. He is universally acknowledged to be the most influential scholar in the study of Chinese outside China and the Chinese migratory experience. His commitment to ethnic Chinese studies, a sub-field at the interface between the humanities and social sciences, has been lifelong. In 1955 he wrote *The Nanhai Trade,* which deals with early Chinese migration to Southeast Asia, part of a general switch in pre-independent Malaya in the 1950s away from a colonial and metropolitan focus and towards Asian history. A recent example of his intellectual leadership of the field is his keynote speech to the 4th International Convention on the Chinese Overseas (organized by the International Society for the Studies of the Chinese Overseas, of which he is chairman, held in the Academia Sinica in April 2001), in which he called for a historical and comparative understanding of the recent phenomenon of Chinese new migrants (see Chapter 18 in this book).

He has often spoken of his passionate objection to the terms "overseas Chinese" (*huaqiao*) and "Chinese diaspora", which he believes have invidious political connotations. Instead, he favours the more neutral "Chinese overseas". His objection is partly that these words suggest transnational cohesion and homogeneity, whereas Chinese overseas commonly adapt to local environments. More importantly, he is aware of the terms' emotive power in Southeast Asia, where unconscionable politicians draw attention to them in order to scapegoat ethnic Chinese and raise doubts about their loyalty. His call has been positively received. It is echoed in several recent major works on ethnic Chinese, including the *Encyclopedia of the Chinese Overseas*[13] and *The Last Half Century of the Chinese Overseas.*[14] China scholars such as Philip Kuhn and Prasenjit Duara and Southeast Asia scholars such as Anthony Reid have also paid close attention in their writings on ethnic Chinese to Wang Gungwu's conceptual formulation. Wang's studies on

Sino-Southeast Asian historical relations and the Chinese overseas are classics in their field.

Although he has paid less attention of late to Chinese dynastic history, his book on the Five Dynasties continues to be cited as a crucial reference work, nearly 40 years after its publication.[15] In a review of Wang's *Community and Nation: Essays on Southeast Asia and the Chinese* (1981), G. William Skinner wrote:

> Professor Wang Gungwu enjoyed a solid reputation as a political historian of medieval China and has made important contributions to Chinese history of more recent centuries. The volume under review, however, displays only those of his wide-ranging concerns that touch on Southeast Asia. Even within this restricted scope, three scholarly personae are evident: the sinological historian, the pundit of Malaysian affairs, and the expert on the Nanyang Chinese.[16]

As an academic administrator, Wang Gungwu has been deeply committed to improving the scholarly environment in the Asia-Pacific region. His administrative appointments, including Director of the Research School of Pacific Studies at ANU (1975–1980), Vice Chancellor of Hong Kong University (1986–1995), and Chairman and Director of the East Asian Institute in Singapore (1996–present), provided him with a rare opportunity to influence the course of educational development in the region. While at Hong Kong University, he pushed for greater research funding from the government in both the humanities and social sciences and the natural sciences and succeeded in creating a healthy research culture, reinforced by a graduate student population that shot up during his period of tenure. For his administrative accomplishments (while serving, for example, as Executive Councillor to the Hong Kong Government, as Chairman of Hong Kong's Advisory Council on the Environment, and as Chairman of the Council for the Performing Arts in Hong Kong), he received a CBE.

Wang's administrative activities have been largely mainstream and conventional, but at various times he has played an active role as an oppositionist to established authority. As part of his political work, he strove to popularize scholarship that he felt threw light on current issues of concern to ordinary citizens. From the mid-1950s to the mid-1960s, he gave radio and television talks on a wide range of topics about the new Malaysian nation and the role of ethnic Chinese in the region.[17] In early 1968, at a time of great political change in Malaysia, he was one of the six founding members of the Parti Gerakan Rakyat Malaysia (Malaysian People's Solidarity Movement, popularly known as Gerakan). The Gerakan, which represented one of three major approaches to Malaysian

Chinese politics, pledged support in its formative years for "multi-racialism, moderate socialism and parliamentary democracy".[18] But Gerakan was unable to turn back the communalist tide and made little headway. In the 1970s in Australia, he supported the protest movement against the Vietnam War and joined demonstrations. He has not only sought to give Asian people a voice by recording their thoughts and feelings but has fought hard to improve their everyday living. His campaign to upgrade Hong Kong's university system and promote its bilingual status can also be seen as a political act, intended to protect and strengthen the territory while at the same time preparing it to play a useful role after its return to Chinese rule in 1997. As a scholar-administrator of Chinese descent living outside China, he has participated in processes of change at all levels.

Wang's persona embodies the seemingly contradictory ideals of "intellectual" in both the Chinese and the Western senses. He himself points out that "the intellectuals in imperial China, for about two thousand years until the beginning of the 20th century, were distinguished by their identification with the Confucian state which they had a key part in shaping and developing".[19] In the Western tradition, on the other hand, intellectuals are mainly seen as "the critics of power" who stand outside the establishment, ever vigilant and sceptical.[20] They are often regarded as "social critics", "political intellectuals", or (to borrow Foucault's phrase) "thinker[s] with a public voice".[21] The journey between these two traditions is not easy, and the complexity of the non-Chinese environment has made it even more challenging.[22] Yet with his multi-cultural upbringing and sensibilities as well as his training in the Chinese and Western traditions, Wang Gungwu has been in a position to create a remarkable new synthesis. He has been aided in this endeavour by his personal philosophy. As Philip Kuhn has shown, at the heart of Wang's academic and social concerns is "a liberal idealism" that forcefully rejects narrow communalism in any shape or form.[23]

Although by no means a complete record of Wang Gungwu's life and scholarly contribution, this collection of essays reflects not only his multi-dimensional career as viewed by his colleagues and students but many of his recent scholarly concerns in various fields. The first part, "Encounters", comprises six interviews and profiles. They touch on his family background, his youthful days in colonial Southeast Asia and war-torn China, the impact of the Chinese tradition (and its classic genre of historical writing) on his thinking, his involvement with Nanyang University, the only tertiary institution outside China, Hong Kong, and Taiwan that used Chinese as the main instructional language, his experiences in Australia, and his recent reflections on the controversial concept of "diaspora". Collectively, they tell us much about the profound impact that this past half century has had on his life and career as well as his intellectual evolution. The second part, "Reflections", is devoted to his recent writings. (Some, for example Chapter 14, are autobiographical.) The sole exception is an essay written by Wang at the age of 16 (titled "Confucius the Sage"). Written for a high-school publication, it sets a precedent for several of his subsequent concerns, including the impact of culture and tradition on the Chinese both in China and abroad. Unlike his earlier studies, which are meticulously documented and based on detailed case analyses, his recent writings (selected from a far wider opus)[24] are understandably more concerned with conceptual formulations, theoretical frameworks, macro-perspectives, and grand patterns, as well as with possible future directions that the field might take. These essays, which form a small but representative component of Wang Gungwu's wide-ranging scholarship, dissect with penetration and critical discernment issues at the heart of the contemporary world, including diasporic transformations, identity, nationalism, and culture.

Notes

1 On Wang Fo-wen's life and career, see Wang Gungwu, ed., *Wang Fowen jinian ji* (Wang Fo-wen, 1903–1972: A memorial collection of poems, essays, and calligraphy), River Edge, New Jersey, and Singapore: Global Publishing Inc., 2002.

2 Wang Gungwu, *Anglo-Chinese Encounters since 1800: War, Trade, Science*, Cambridge: Cambridge University Press, 2003, p. 3.

3 Ibid., p. viii.

4 Wang Gungwu, "Zai lun haiwai huaren de shenfen rentong" (Reassessing overseas Chinese identities), in Hong Liu and Huang Jianli, eds, *Haiwai huaren yanjiu de dashiye yu xin fangxiang: Wang Gengwu jiaoshou lunwen xuan* (Macroperspectives and new directions in the study of Chinese overseas: Selected essays of Wang Gungwu), River Edge, New Jersey, and Singapore: Global Publishing Inc., 2002, pp. 97–116.

5 Cyril Northcote Parkinson (1909–1993), born in Durham, was professor of history at the University of Malaya (1950–1958). His books include *Britain in the Far East* (1955), *The Evolution of Political Thought* (1958), and *British Intervention in Malaya, 1867–1877* (1960). He achieved wider renown by his seriocomic tilt at bureaucratic malpractice in *Parkinson's Law: The Pursuit of Progress* (1957).

6 *The Structure of Power in North China during the Five Dynasties*, Kuala Lumpur: University of Malaya Press, 1963 and 1968; and Stanford: Stanford University Press, 1967.

7 Wang Gungwu, *The Chinese Overseas: From Earthbound China to the Quest for Autonomy*, Cambridge, Mass.: Harvard University Press, 2000, p. 55.

8 See, for example, Wang Gungwu, *The Chinese Way: China's Position in International Relations* (Nobel Institute Lectures 1995), Oslo: Scandinavian University Press, 1995; and Wang Gungwu, *China and Southeast Asia: Myths, Threats, and Culture*, Singapore: World Scientific and Singapore University Press, 1999.

9 "The Opening of Relations Between China and Malacca, 1402–1405", in J. S. Bastin and R. Roolvink, eds, *Malayan and Indonesian Studies: Festschrift for Richard Winstedt*, London: Oxford University Press, pp. 87–104; and "China and Southeast Asia, 1402–1424", in J. Chen and N. Tarling, eds, *Social History of China and Southeast Asia*, Cambridge: Cambridge University Press, pp. 375–401.

10 Wang Gungwu, *Community and Nation: China, Southeast Asia and Australia*, St Leonard's, NSW: Allen and Unwin, 1992, p. vii.
11 Wang Gungwu, *Don't Leave Home: Migration and the Chinese*, Singapore: Times Academic Press, 2001.
12 Wang Gungwu, *Shifting Paradigms and Asian Perspectives: Implications for Research and Teaching, Research Paper Series*, Singapore: Centre for Advanced Studies, National University of Singapore, 1999, p. 4.
13 Edited by Lynn Pan, Richmond: Curzon, 1998.
14 Edited by Elizabeth Sinn, Hong Kong: Hong Kong University Press, 1998.
15 Endymion Wilkinson, *Chinese History: A Manual*, Cambridge: Harvard-Yenching Institute, revised and enlarged edition, 2000, p. 822.
16 *Asian Studies Review*, vol. 6, no. 2, 1982, pp. 74–78.
17 One of these radio talks was subsequently published as *A Short History of the Nanyang Chinese*, Singapore: Donald Moore, 1959, which is one of the first treatments of the history of the ethnic Chinese in the whole region from a Southeast Asian nationalistic perspective.
18 On the history of the Gerakan and its place in Malaysian Chinese politics, see "*Gerakan*: Its History and Struggle", in Leong Kam Yun, ed., *Gerakan 1968–1988*, Kuala Lumpur: Gerakan Rakyat Malaysia, 1988, pp. 24–31; and Lee Kam Hing, "Three Approaches in Peninsular Malaysian Chinese Politics: The MCA, the DAP and the GERAKAN", in Zakaria Haji Ahmad, ed., *Government and Politics of Malaysia*, Singapore: Oxford University Press, 1987. Wang's personal participation in Malaysian Chinese politics had a direct impact on his scholarly writing, including analysis of the different factions of Malaysian Chinese politics. See, for example, his "Chinese Politics in Malaysia", *The China Quarterly*, 43, 1970, pp. 1–30.
19 Wang Gungwu, *The Chinese Intellectual: Past and Present*, Faculty Lecture, Faculty of Arts and Social Sciences, National University of Singapore, 1983, p. 1.
20 Richard Hofstadter, *Anti-Intellectualism in American Life*, New York: Knopf, 1964, p. 429.
21 See for details Richard A. Posner, *Public Intellectuals: A Study of Decline*, Cambridge, Mass.: Harvard University Press, 2001, pp. 22–24.
22 As Wang himself has noted, "Being Chinese in China is in itself a complex problem, but being Chinese outside China has several additional complicating features.... Many mirrors, some less distorting than others, intervene when a Chinese living abroad constructs his composite image of what it means to be Chinese." See Wang, "Among Non-Chinese", *Daedalus, Journal of the American Academy of Arts and Sciences*, Spring, 1991, pp. 135–157.
23 Philip A. Kuhn, "Wang Gungwu: The Historian in His Time", in Billy K. L. So, John Fitzgerald, Huang Jianli, and James K. Chin, eds, *Power and Identity in the Chinese World Order: Festschrift in Honour of Professor Wang Gungwu*, Hong Kong: Hong Kong University Press, 2003, pp. 11–31. This book came to our notice when the final version of our manuscript was being prepared. With the exception of the Kuhn essay, all the other essays in this book are written by Professor Wang's former students.
24 For a complete list of Wang Gungwu's writings, see the Appendix to *Power and Identity in the Chinese World Order: Festschrift in Honour of Professor Wang Gungwu*, pp. 408–427.

Part I

ENCOUNTERS

1

LOOKING FORWARD, LOOKING BACK

An interview with Wang Gungwu[1]

Hong Liu

Liu Professor Wang, thank you for granting me this interview opportunity. How did your family circumstances affect your early years?

Wang My father Wang Fowen (1904–1972) was born in Taizhou in Jiangsu. He graduated from Nanjing's Dongnan University in 1925 and then went south. He worked as a teacher in Chinese schools in Singapore, Kuala Lumpur, and Malacca. At the age of 25, he was appointed head of the first Chinese school in Surabaya in Indonesia, where I was born in 1930. Later, during the economic slump, the school was forced to close and we returned to Malaya, where father became deputy school-inspector in Perak. So I was brought up in Ipoh and received my education at Anderson School, through the medium of English.

Liu Given your English education, how did you develop an interest in Chinese culture and history?

Wang It came through my parents. When I was still an infant, no more than 3 or 4 years old, my mother taught me Chinese characters. I learned texts off by heart and copied them out. Later, my father taught me classical Chinese, starting with the *Three-Character Classic.* However, he knew that fathers rarely find it easy to teach their sons so he set up a special class at home and arranged for me to study Chinese alongside the children of his friends.

Liu Did you ever go to China as a child?

Wang My father was always keen to return to China, but his salary at Surabaya middle school was too meagre to allow him to get beyond Singapore. Later, in 1936, he took me back to China with him. His relatives in Taizhou said that war with Japan would soon break out and that we would do better to stay abroad, from where we would be able to help the family economically. After the Japanese surrender in 1945, he again wanted to go back, but he decided to wait until I'd finished my education. I was quite good at English, so I skipped a year and went straight into the senior Cambridge class. In April 1947, I graduated from middle school. Father retired and took me to Nanjing, where I sat the entrance exam for the National Central University (the then new name of Dongnan University).

Liu How did you fare in the exams?

Wang I had no problems with English and Chinese, but maths and science were quite a challenge. We'd done maths and science in English in Malaya, so I had to work hard to acquire a new specialized vocabulary. I spent little more than a year at the National Central University, in the Foreign Languages Department, but Nanjing started to descend into chaos after the Communists launched their Huai-Hai Campaign in October 1948. In November, the university closed down. Most teachers and students went home, just a few of us remained. Everyone expected the fighting would soon reach Nanjing.

Liu So your family decided to return to Malaya?

Wang Back in China, my father had started teaching in the middle school attached to the university, but he could not get used to the Nanjing climate and his health was poor. I remember I sometimes used to help him mark exam scripts after arriving home in the evenings. At about that time, some educationalists in Ipoh invited him to return, so in 1948 both my parents went back to Malaya. They were heartbroken. They knew they'd never get another chance to return to China.

Liu So you were left in Nanjing by yourself in 1948?

Wang That's right. My father used to send me eighteen Hong Kong dollars a month. Every time I needed money, I'd change one dollar. Inflation raged because of the fighting, so I was a millionaire, at least on paper. I was an only child, so my parents were particularly worried about my safety and urged me to rejoin them. Actually, I couldn't care less at the time whether I studied or not. The university had closed down, so there was nothing to study anyway. In late 1948 I donated my books to the library, gathered together the bare necessities, and boarded the train for Shanghai, like a refugee. (I didn't even have to buy a ticket.) I then returned to Malaya by way of Xiamen, Jilong (in Taiwan), and Hong Kong.

Liu I suppose returning to Malaya was a decisive turn in your life. How did you manage to blend in and adapt?

Wang In early 1949, I taught for a few months in Ipoh. After that, I enrolled at the University of Malaya in Singapore to do literature.

In my three years at the university, I studied three subjects: English literature, history, and economics. I was offered the chance of doing honours in all 3. My actual interest was literature but I decided to do history, because it seemed to me that the history professor was a good scholar.

Liu In 1954 you went to London to do your PhD. After getting it, in 1957, you returned home to teach at the University of Malaya. Malaya was then in the midst of the transition from colonialism to independence. What influence did that have on you?

Wang Those were indeed highly volatile years. In 1948 the British Government declared the Emergency. The struggle against imperialism and colonialism flared up, and I joined in activities on the campus. Subsequently, many of my fellow students became leading lights in Malaysian society and politics. Through the optic of Malayan anti-colonialism and British-style socialism, I acquired a new national identity. That was the first step from being a sojourner to self-consciously deciding to settle outside China. I wasn't sure where I'd finally end up, but I felt that being a citizen of the Federation of Malaya was a start. Even so, I still felt a sense of responsibility towards China. I needed to finish what I had begun, to understand the unacceptable byways along which that ancient civilization might stray while at the same time realizing that China nonetheless had a future. I discovered that being an ethnic Chinese was no obstacle to completing the switch from sojourner to settler. On the contrary, it was a support. So it was the most natural thing in the world for me to turn towards studying Chinese history.

Liu In 1968 you were appointed professor and Head of the Department of Far Eastern History at Australian National University. Later you headed the School of Pacific Research at ANU, and in 1986 you became Vice-Chancellor of Hong Kong University. What is your deepest impression of your years in Hong Kong?

Wang At the time of my appointment, the Sino-British Joint Declaration had already been signed. I felt that my biggest challenge was to ensure that Hong Kong University was equipped both to adapt to the new postcolonial situation after 1997 and to preserve its scholarly tradition, which was quite unlike that of China's other universities. I stressed two points in particular. (1) If the university was run well, China would surely value it; the main thing was to keep up standards, so the students could make a contribution to society after graduating. (2) From China's point of view, Hong Kong's role was to assist it internationally, in all sorts of ways. After Deng Xiaoping took charge of the reforms, Hong Kong's role was even more essential. In that respect, I supported a dual-language policy for Hong Kong.

Liu Was there any opposition to that policy in the run-up to 1997?

Wang Many people proposed elevating Chinese above English, the colonial language. Actually, regarding Hong Kong's role and position, that was a bad idea. From the point of view of Hong Kong University and its students and of Hong Kong's role in the future development of China, a dual-language policy was of the utmost importance. Perhaps that position was misunderstood politically. I discussed the issue with students, parents, and leading figures in Hong Kong society. Basically, they backed me. I'm not against mother-tongue education, but if you turned Hong Kong University into a Chinese-language institution, in what way would it differ from China's internal universities? How would that help China? I told the students, after the retrocession your Chinese will never be better than that of the students in China. You'll be lucky even to match their mastery of that language. But if your English is also good, at least there'll be some things you can do. So I urged them to learn good English. I know it was controversial to say so, but that was my policy and I stuck to it.

Liu How would you rank teaching and research at Hong Kong University in Asia-Pacific and world terms?

Wang Quite good. The foundations have been laid, especially in medicine and physics, where research at Hong Kong University bears international comparison. The same might also be said of engineering and law. The situation is a bit more complicated in the humanities and social sciences. When I joined the university, the biggest problem was a lack of research funding. Neither the government nor industry was prepared to help. Their view was that if you wanted to do research, you should go abroad and do it. My own view was that a university with insufficient research funding would never prosper. So I actively canvassed the government for funds. My predecessor, Rayson Lisung Huang, had already done his best: I took up where he left off.

Liu With what results?

Wang By 1988, the government had realized the seriousness of the situation. Unless something was done, the brain drain would accelerate. The main reason why most of Hong Kong University's best students failed to come home after getting their PhDs abroad wasn't the salary level or the political situation but the lack of research funding. I produced statistics to show the government the extent of the problem. I said, if the majority of our talented young people fail to return, what future will Hong Kong University have? Relying on foreign scholars is no solution. The government saw my point and research money began to flow. Suddenly, you could ask for funds with confidence.

Liu What other important changes took place during your nine and a half years at Hong Kong University?

Wang Research saw the biggest changes. When I first arrived, few of the teaching staff really did research, and the level of the research they did do was rather low. By the time I left, four out of five of the staff were doing research, often of top quality. What's more, the humanities and social sciences had made some progress. In our appointments, we paid more and more attention to research results. Needless to say, this trend is international. Another important thing: I did everything in my power to recruit research students. In the old days, we'd relied mainly on Hong Kong students, but they provided a fairly small pool of researchers, and getting jobs in other spheres was relatively easy. So we started welcoming research students from the mainland and abroad. As long as they came up to scratch, we gave them scholarships – that was especially true of applicants in science and engineering. During my period of office, the number of research students shot up from just a few hundred to around 3,000. I considered that a cause for great satisfaction, for such students will play a major role in promoting future teaching and research.

Liu You have dozens of scholarly books and scores of articles to your name. You're a fellow of Taiwan's Academia Sinica, a senior honorary researcher of Beijing's Academy of Social Sciences, and a foreign honorary member of the American Academy of Arts and Sciences, to name just three of your numerous academic distinctions. What would you say have been your chief scholarly contributions?

Wang My starting point is Chinese history. From the point of view of China, I imagine that my contribution would lie in that direction. My personal background is that of a Southeast Asian Chinese, but my main field of study has been Chinese history. From the point of view of my own personal history, I ought to take as the theme of my research the experience of ethnic Chinese in adapting to local conditions as seen against the background of local transformations. After all, that's my own experience. All the same, I took Chinese history as my starting point. In my opinion, the two aspects can be combined: one's point of departure cannot be reduced either to a pure China or to a pure Southeast Asia. That's the special feature of my work. I do not completely accept the standpoint either of Southeast Asia or of China. I think that makes me relatively objective. I have feelings for both, but neither gets the upper hand.

Liu Could you tell me about your methodology?

Wang I was never tempted to adopt Maurice Freedman's and Bill

Skinner's approach, which is to use the results of studying Chinese outside China to explain Chinese society. I've never stressed the numerous historical and contemporary examples of Chinese assimilation, nor do I agree with the present trend just to study the ethnic Chinese response to Southeast Asian nationalism. Instead, my research has always moved between two wishful but ambiguous positions. One is China's hope – eventually to view all ethnic Chinese outside China as sojourners, as members of the great Chinese family, whose loyalty and patriotism can be counted on in troubled times. The other is the hope of the Chinese migrants and settlers – that their sons and daughters will, to some degree, remain culturally Chinese and ensure the lines of descent, at least for a few generations.

Liu How is it that you started looking at the issue of ethnic Chinese in Southeast Asia while at the same time pursuing your study of Chinese history?

Wang The construction of nation-states is a subtle process that requires new historical approaches. When I started working with colleagues at the University of Malaya to promote the study of Malayan history, we were particularly keen to nurture from among our students a new generation of national historians. As for myself, I put my main effort into researching the history of the Chinese of Malaya, for they had already made the transition from sojourner to citizen, they knew what it meant to be Malayan. In 1959, I published a series of radio talks under the title *A Short History of the Nanyang Chinese*.[2] That was my first research treatise on the Chinese of Southeast Asia. My research on Chinese history enabled me to narrate and reach new conclusions about the early history of relations between China and Southeast Asia – the Nanyang trading scene,[3] Zheng He's fifteenth-century naval expedition, the defensive nature of tributary relations between China and Southeast Asia, the coolie trade, Nanyang trading networks, and the rise of Chinese patriotism among the overseas Chinese. I immersed myself in local publications and historical documents and paid even greater attention to new scholarly works on the changing nature of the ethnic Chinese community, especially social-science works of the 1950s. At the same time, this nation was in the throes of a dramatic evolution, including between 1961 and 1965 the incorporation into the new Federation of Malaysia of a number of former British colonies with sizeable Chinese communities. That marked the beginning of my comparative research into the efforts of the various ethnic Chinese communities to come to terms with the new political realities. I feel that my work has been rather objective even though, unlike Westerners (and despite my Australian citizenship), I consider myself someone of overseas Chinese background.

Liu Despite your heavy administrative duties in Hong Kong, you still managed to carry on your research and to publish a stream of influential articles. How did you succeed in balancing these two activities?

Wang To tell the truth, it wasn't easy. However, conditions at Hong Kong University were very good, chiefly because colleagues set great store by research. Hong Kong people are used to making the most of their time. I've always admired their spirit of initiative and their attention to efficiency, and I did my best to follow their example. Moreover, apart from my year and a bit in Nanjing I've spent my whole life outside mainland China. Hong Kong is half Chinese, quite a rare place. One of the reasons I love Hong Kong is its proximity to China. You can see the changes as they happen, your observations and research are made practically at first hand. For me personally, my nine and a half years in Hong Kong were of great significance. China changed enormously in those years. The changes I witnessed touched me greatly.

Liu What will be the main issues confronting ethnic Chinese in the new century?

Wang Globalization will be the main issue – not just politically and economically, but in terms of information. From now on, the migration experience will be quite different from what it used to be. Migrants' lives will never again be the same. On the one hand, they can take part in local activities and adapt to local circumstances. On the other hand, they will be able to sustain their ties to China, to Chinese culture, and to ethnic Chinese traders and manufacturers in other places. To do so will be both easy and convenient. Similarly, the old notion of the nation-state will be subject to revision. It will be seen as less important.

Liu So how should ethnic Chinese confront that challenge?

Wang They will be active in every sphere. They will fight for their rights, especially in the context of the struggle for a state ruled by law. In the course of their participation in politics, they will win for themselves the rights due to an ethnic minority in a multiethnic society. That's a new challenge. When I was young, it was all very simple, it was a case of nationalism and patriotism, China was very weak. In future, however, China will undoubtedly grow in strength and talk of nationalism among ethnic Chinese overseas will acquire a new meaning. To put it another way, it's essential that ethnic Chinese maintain their dignity as Chinese, so that others respect Chinese culture and China's position in the world. In my view, that's possible; but we must never cause non-Chinese to fear China, that would be to no one's advantage.

Liu Lee Kuan Yew said recently that China would be among the world's economic superpowers by the year 2030. From your many years of observing China, what direction do you think that country will take, from a social and economic point of view?

Wang As the economy develops, political life will stabilize. There will be progress in political institutions, the legal sphere, and the rule of law. Democratization is inevitable, and universally desired in China. The reason people caution against a too rapid democratization is because they fear chaos and instability. One can see their point. But if the economy develops and people become prosperous and politically stable, freedom and democracy will become realizable ideals.

Liu What might be the intellectuals' role?

Wang Principally, to attain world standards of knowledge and build up their own intellectual capacity. To lead the world in terms of scholarship should be a realizable goal. To do so, we need society's support and encouragement, in terms – for example – of funding and resources, so that intellectuals can move their scholarship and science forward. If you just pay attention to saving money and ignore levels of scholarship, you'll never reach world levels.

Liu Could you tell me something about your family and your leisure activities?

Wang I met my wife Margaret Lim Pingting at the University of Malaya, where we both studied. She was in the year below me, studying English literature. Ours was a love match, no one interfered. We got married in London in December 1955. We have a son and two daughters, professionals resident in Singapore and Australia. I like to relax by listening to music, reading good books, and going to the cinema or the theatre. Music and reading are my main leisure-time pursuits.

Liu One final question. From your rich experience of life over the 52 years since you first went to university, what would be your advice to young people today?

Wang [after a long pause] Bend every effort to the things you love. Scholarship cannot be forced or artificially sustained. If you truly love it, if it is truly in accord with your nature, then you will never experience it as an imposition and you will find it endlessly interesting. Don't give yourself over to the pursuit of wealth and comfort, they're of scant interest in the long term. Develop your strengths and do your best to build on them. I must stress, however – I know this from my own experience – that circumstances are important: whatever your predilections, you must adapt. Personally, I've been most fortunate. My life as a scholar has been free of constraints, not everyone can say as much. I know many good scholars who were unable to nurture their talents because of external hindrances, which is a great pity. That's why I especially admire those people who produce first-class scholarship under adverse conditions. Personally, I've been able to work to the best of my ability under good conditions.

Translated by Gregor Benton

Notes

1 First published in Chinese in the *Depingxian yuekan* (Hong Kong), no. 1, 2000 [eds].
2 Wang Gungwu, *A Short History of the Nanyang Chinese* (Singapore: Donald Moore, 1959).
3 Nanyang, "the Southern Ocean", is a Chinese name for Southeast Asia [eds].

2

HOW READING THE *HISTORICAL RECORDS* (*SHIJI*) HELPED SET WANG GUNGWU ON THE ROAD TO BECOMING A HISTORIAN[1]

Xiao Li

"I'm no longer young, I've read too many books; and every book I've read has influenced my study to some extent, however big or small. But learning is a matter of stages, and the books you read at different stages differ in their impact. For example, the books I read when I was young had quite a different import from those I read now." After pausing for a moment, Wang Gungwu continued: "All I can say is, the book that influenced me most, in terms of my career as a historian, was the *Historical Records*".

Wang Gungwu read the *Historical Records* "when he was young", meaning after the age of ten. Wang Gungwu after the age of ten had already developed a great appetite for his father's vast library. As a small child under his father's tutelage, he had read the *Anthology of Classical Prose*, the *Tang Poems*, and the *Selections of Refined Literature.* This reading gave him quite a deep knowledge of classical Chinese literature and was the foundation upon which he later read the *Historical Records.*

He had already come across excerpts from the *Historical Records* while reading *Guwen guanzhi* (*The finest of ancient prose*). Some of the stories had given him endless food for thought. Subsequently, at middle school, he pored over the rest of the *Historical Records*, which kindled in him an interest not unconnected with his later love for history.

A love for biography

Even today, Wang Gungwu still recalls his youthful encounter with the *Historical Records*: "They not only taught me early Han history but introduced me to the writing of the period. The book has literary value." He particularly liked the biographic sketches of historical figures such as Xiang Yu, Gao Zu, and Qin Shihuang, and passages such as the *Hereditary*

Household of Chen She and *Biography of Lianbo Nixiangru* with which we are all familiar. "These biographical sketches are marvellous to read, they're like a novel. They're rich in materials. By reading them, you can learn much about pre-Han Chinese history." Wang also said:

> There were many famous people in Chinese history before the Han. But Sima Qian manages to select from more than one thousand people just a few hundred to represent the entire period. Like *Hereditary Household of Confucius*, the *Biography of Boyi*, and the *Biographies of Qu Yuan and Jia Sheng*.

Although his thirst for knowledge drove him to read other works in those early years, the *Historical Records* influenced him far more than any other book.

> After reading the *Historical Records* from cover to cover, I never had any difficulty in reading other history books. By reading books like the *Comprehensive Mirror for Aid in Government*, I gained a basic understanding of Chinese history and my interest in it gradually deepened.

In this way, one book launched Wang Gungwu on his scholarly career.

Wang Gungwu threw himself into history, including cultural history, for which he developed a great passion. "Many people think that Chinese culture is frozen and immutable, but in my view it changes frequently." He also said:

> The post-Confucian Daoists had a demotic disposition, they reflected the grievances of the lower classes; and the Buddhists had the same sort of influence on China as does Western culture today. Where did Buddhism come from? India. So can we really say that Chinese culture is immutable?

Karl Marx's influence

These views on cultural history derive mainly from Wang Gungwu's reflections on his later reading and research. Needless to say, his readings progressed far beyond the *Historical Records*.

"Given my interest in history, I naturally read many books on historical research, in order to master its methods and objectives", he said. Three authors in particular made a big impression on him. One was Arnold Toynbee, author of *A Study of History*, another was Robin George Collingwood, the English historian and philosopher, author of *The Idea of History*. Finally there was Karl Marx, author of *Das Kapital*, who created Marxism and deeply influenced today's socialist countries.

"Toynbee proposed a theory of history based on a cyclical analysis of the rise and fall of civilizations. He taught me to explore the civilizations of the entire world." With great gusto Wang remarked:

> In terms of his research methods and attitudes, Collingwood was the opposite of Marx, he argued that history is a branch of knowledge in which people re-experience the past in their own soul; only when they strike deep into the psychological activities that underlie events and relive the past within the bounds of their own experience can historians discover the principal patterns and dynamics of a culture and a civilization; whereas Marx took the economy as his starting point, arguing that the economic base is more important than the superstructure.

Culture is more influential than economics

Although Wang Gungwu's wide reading greatly broadened his field of vision, he continued to believe that while economics is important, it is never all-important. "In the history of a nation and its progress, the cultural background is important. Look for example at the sudden rise of Southeast Asia. Economics cannot by themselves account for it, profound cultural factors were at work."

That passage is an illustration of Wang Gungwu's scholarly depth, a reflection of the process by which he advanced from reading to research. In the course of his maturation, his encounter with classical literature stimulated in him an urge to read the *Historical Records*, which in turn nurtured in him an interest in history and its research. In his endeavour to master historiographical methodology, he turned to the works of Toynbee, Collingwood, and Marx, including *A Study of History*, *The Idea of History*, and *Das Kapital*.

On this basis, he also read numerous other books relevant to human civilization, including Toynbee's *Change and Habit: The Challenge of Our Time* and *Mankind and Mother Earth: A Narrative History of the World*, Collingwood's *Essay on Metaphysics* and *Essay on Philosophical Method*, Joseph Needham's *Science and Civilisation in China* and Marx's *Communist Manifesto*.

In Wang Gungwu's opinion, *Change and Habit* can be likened to an historical equation: its theses permit the charting of a nation's rise and fall.

Although he is now engaged in historical research and no longer reads such books, the influence on him of the *Historical Records* cannot easily be erased.

Translated by Gregor Benton

Note

1 First published in Chinese in *Mingbao* (Sunday edition), 12 March 1995.

3

A MOMENTOUS DUTY IMPOSED BY HEAVEN[1]

Te-Kong Tong[2]

A new star has come to prominence, my old friend and fellow student Wang Gungwu, the internationally renowned newly appointed Vice Chancellor of Hong Kong University. Given Wang's reputation at home and abroad, it is not surprising that some journalist friends, aware that I have the honour (though it is one of which I am actually quite unworthy) to count myself among Wang Gungwu's acquaintances, should compel me to write an article along the lines of "Wang Gungwu as I knew him". Strictly, such an article would need to be short, for although Wang and I both attended National Central University on the mainland, I was several years his senior. Moreover, Central University in those days was an important national not to say international seat of learning, to which students flocked from all over China and the world in search of learned masters. Gungwu, a Nanyang Chinese, did not reach Central University until after the war, and he never got to know the arrogant gang of "old-timers" to which I myself belonged. Although I never made his acquaintance at university, I nevertheless feel that we Central University students of that generation share the same cultural background. We are cast in the same mould, so we naturally share qualities in common; that I should write an article about "Wang Gungwu as I knew him" is therefore not necessarily unthinkable.

First impressions on meeting Gungwu in London

I first got to know Wang Gungwu not at Central University in the 1940s but in London in the early 1960s. In the early 1950s, historians on the mainland had started a debate about the "sprouts of capitalism" theory in Marxist historiography. Foreign sinologists quickly responded, and in 1963 a large number of veteran sinologists of the period met in conference in London to discuss contemporary Chinese historiography. Riding on their coat-tails was the author of this article, then but a comparative youngster. Gungwu also took part in the conference, and we got on well together.

The conference was held not far from Oxford University, in a stately home belonging to a British aristocrat. It went on for a whole week. The stately home was in a park in the suburbs. With carved beams and painted rafters, it was amazingly luxurious. Jokingly, the pair of us called it the "imperial leisure lodge". Sinological giants of the day – men and women like Professor Yang Liansheng – recorded their stay in verse. In a youthful attempt to ape these refined and sophisticated people, I penned my own appalling doggerel. I still remember two lines: "The passers-by admire the leisure palace. Do they recall the reduction of the Yuanming Yuan to ash?"[3]

The conference-goers were locked up in the "leisure lodge" for an entire week, like monks sunk deep in meditation. The participants – especially we overseas Chinese – were confined to each other's company day and night, and Gungwu and I became close friends. The main speakers were all prominent European and American scholars. They all knew each other and were *au fait* with one another's sinological theories. Each understood what the other was saying without having to be told. At the time, I was in charge of the Chinese Library at Columbia University, and I was also assistant professor in the Columbia East Asian Research Institute, where I was professor of "catalogue studies". There was not one of the ladies and gentlemen present at the conference whose particulars my "catalogue" did not embrace, so as a "lecturer in catalogue studies" I was ideally qualified to make a fair assessment of the attainments of each and every one of them. Only a handful of talented budding young scholars escaped my prior attention. Most budding of all the young people in attendance was Gungwu, to whom I naturally paid exceptional attention. When I discovered that he was, like me, an alumnus of Central University, my feelings of warmth and curiosity naturally intensified.

My four years at Central University had been unforgettable. Never at any other time in my adult life have I been so conscientiously devoted to learning, so cheerful and light-hearted – and so oppressed by hardship and bad health. Half a century on, the man who I had predicted would become an "outstanding individual of his age" had not disappointed me, and we were once again joined by ineffable feelings of warmth and friendship. But the Gungwu I had met in England had excited in me not only affection and comradeship but an intense curiosity. For he was one of Central University's "Nanyang Chinese", who along with the university's recruits from Korea, China's border regions, and elsewhere in the world formed part of its rich tapestry of scholarship and talent.

The impression Gungwu gave me in England was that of a combination of the casual and elegant disposition of the Confucian scholar of the sort associated with Central University and the sedate ways of the young

English gentleman-scholar. He spoke a pure form of British English and accent-free Mandarin. He was also fluent in Malay, and more or less at home in other European languages. He brimmed with talent. Elegant in demeanour and uncommonly dignified, he instantly reminded me of Judge Wellington Koo,[4] then at the Hague International Tribunal, whose "oral history" I was recording at the time. It occurred to me that this young man could be a second Koo, a diplomat of the first water; or one of China's leaders of light and learning. Sadly, however, he was born into the wrong people – a people engaged in mutual slaughter, which squanders its best talent; a people that makes it necessary for a young man like Gungwu to go to England to attend some stuffy "sinological conference" with a bunch of old men and women academics – it troubles me to picture Gungwu's rare talent in such circumstances; a people that is incapable of employing talent on behalf of the nation – but it is too late for regrets and lamentations.

A second meeting in Beijing

After the Oxford meeting, I heard that Gungwu had moved from Singapore to Australia – he was still working at university, doing sinology and Chinese history (which were anyway second nature to him). I always felt in my heart that Gungwu could have been a great general or a university principal, that his talents were on a par with those of China's ambassadors to the superpowers. The thought of him pushing chalk alongside the rest of us – indifferent teachers, old soldiers, retired veterans – was too humiliating to bear. He should have taken his place at state banquets to eat his fill of delicacies from land and sea rather than mingle with the rabble in the rowing boats beneath the Red Cliff.

It had been 20 years since we first took leave of one another in England. Then, in the early autumn of 1985, the mainland hosted a meeting to celebrate the 200th anniversary of the birth of Lin Zexu.[5] Several Chinese academics working in North America – Têng Ssu-yü, Ho Ping-ti, Jerome Chen, and myself – were invited to Beijing to take part. In Beijing, I suddenly bumped into Gungwu. It is always a delight when old friends meet. More than two decades had elapsed since our previous encounter, and Gungwu had greyed a little. Normally, the ravages of time excite distress, but all such thoughts evaporated when I observed how gracefully Gungwu had negotiated the transition to middle age, with an elegance of speech and deportment that put even his bearing and demeanour in more youthful times into shadow. As an ambassador, he would have been the doyen of the diplomatic corps. Surely a man of such elevated gifts could not end his working days at the blackboard, alongside the great mass of us, with our mediocre talents? I continued to sigh on his account – not just because he had talent for the use of which he lacked the opportunity, but because of the tragedy of our people, which casually leaves a man of such distinction unemployed, like an awl abandoned in a sack.

But not long after the Beijing meeting, news came that Gungwu had accepted an invitation to become Vice Chancellor of Hong Kong University. I could not but raise my hat to the members of the search committee, to whom the highest respect is due.

The reason why the English-speaking countries, even British colonies like Hong Kong, are so stable and prosperous in today's world is that they follow the precept independently expressed by Sun Yat-sen in advising Li Hongzhang: "Make full use of people's talents and the advantages of geography, have the goods freely distributed among the consumers." Top-ranking university principals and industrial managers in North America and Western Europe are chosen with meticulous care. All considerations other than sheer ability – for example, ties of blood or friendship – are scrupulously discounted.

I am not saying that top-ranking university principals in Britain and the USA do not include the occasional good-for-nothing. Columbia University's Dwight David Eisenhower was a prime example of such a rice-bucket. But that appointment was a result of momentary negligence on the part of the search committee, of a temporary lapse into the cult of personality, rather than of the exercise of selfish or nepotistic motives. Mr Eisenhower's mediocrity and incompetence escaped the notice of the lady and gentleman appointers. Usually, however, the right people are installed. Wang Gungwu's appointment as the Vice Chancellor of Hong Kong University is an example of China's modernization. The back door has been slammed firmly shut. Let us learn from this precedent!

A night-time conversation in Cuiheng

In November 1986, Gungwu and I unexpectedly met again in Cuiheng, Sun Yat-sen's native village. Our wives were also present. (Gungwu's wife is a distinguished English teacher who whiles away her time correcting the English of private and official documents.)

Gungwu's talent had been recognized, although the awl by no means protruded from the sack. I congratulated him on having achieved his destiny. A scholar of talent and virtue, his gifts would enable him to execute his assignments speedily. How could the contribution of such a man be weighed?

Wang Gungwu's appointment, this long overdue recognition of his ability, is an illustration of the true meaning of Mencius' dictum that "Heaven has entrusted this man with a heavy duty". In taking the burden of Hong Kong University on his shoulders, Gungwu will not only promptly discharge the duties of his new office but may even write an epoch-making new page in the 3,000-year history of Chinese education.

While we were sipping coffee one evening in the Cuiheng guesthouse, Gungwu modestly opined that the task he was assuming was an extremely heavy one. He added that he very much wanted my advice, as an old friend. Other friends had told him that China would soon have one thousand universities and that in 10 years' time Hong Kong would revert to the motherland. Hong Kong University would then be part of the Chinese state system of universities. Wang should therefore "go with the times" and gradually introduce Hong Kong University into the "mainstream", so that in a decade's time, after "the fallen leaf had returned to the root", it would chime in easily with the prevailing circumstances.

I advanced a contrary opinion. Instead of going with the stream, Gungwu should boldly and resolutely seize the opportunity to produce in the 10 years available a modern university for China that truly matched up to international standards, and thus light the touch-paper for the comprehensive reform of China's system of higher education. He had the training, the vision, the resolve, and the opportunity to bring about the modernization of Chinese university education, truly a heavy duty with which Heaven had entrusted him!

It seemed to me that in the course of its 20 years' rule (excluding the Cultural Revolution) the Chinese Communist Party had still not succeeded in establishing a "mainstream" in its universities. In the light of today's "four upholds",[6] how can China hope to create a mainstream to guide thinking in its institutes of higher learning?

During the Cultural Revolution Mao Zedong said: "When I say we need universities, I mean colleges of science and engineering".[7] He asked Huang Yongsheng[8] how many years he had studied. When Huang told him 6 months, Mao was delighted, and made him chief of the general staff of the People's Liberation Army. Can Mao's theory that study has no point still claim to be the mainstream? Does it still guide China's system of university education?

Restore dignity to China's seats of learning

In a nutshell, the future of China's universities lies in restoring dignity and integrity to its seats of higher learning and in preventing their contamination by party politics. The representative structures of today's Western civilization rest on Europe and America's top-class seats of learning, which boast a history of hundreds of years of dignity and integrity.

Although China's universities are young by comparison, people of talent and high moral standing have come forth in large numbers in them. I have every confidence that Principal Wang Gungwu will take up the mantle of Cai Yuanpei, Hu Shi, Fu Sinian, and Ma Yinchu,[9] important past Chinese leaders of bookish distinction, and transform Hong Kong University into a contemporary model for the rest of China, so that the country's universities can break from their present rigid mould and be reborn with the strengths of both the Chinese and the Western traditions of education.

Translated by Gregor Benton

Notes

1 First published in Chinese in *Baixing* (Hong Kong), no. 145 (1987).

2 Te-Kong Tong (Tang Degang), born in Hefei, Anhui Province, in 1920, studied history at the National Central University in Chongqing in 1943 and went to the United States in 1948. After studying at Columbia University in the 1950s, he taught at Columbia and the City University of New York. His many publications include *United States Diplomacy in China, 1844–60* (University of Washington Press, 1964) and *The Memoirs of Li Tsung-jen* (Westview Press, 1979) [eds].

3 The reference is to the destruction wrought in Beijing in 1900 by the imperialist armies sent in to crush the Boxers [eds].

4 Wellington Koo (1888–1985), born in Shanghai, received his PhD from Columbia University in 1912. He was the Minister of Foreign Affairs and China's Ambassador to France, the UK, the United States, and the United Nations in the 1930s and 1940s. He served as Judge at the Hague International Tribunal from 1956 until his retirement [eds].

5 Lin Zexu (1785–1850) was a late Qing official who ordered that opium imported into China by the British be thrown into the sea [eds].

6 The four basic principles that underlie China's political system: upholding the people's democratic dictatorship, upholding Marxism-Leninism-Mao Zedong thought, upholding socialism, and upholding the leadership of the Communist Party of China [eds].

7 Quoted from *Mao Zedong sixiang wansui* (Long live Mao Zedong thought).

8 Huang Yongsheng, born 1906, was a leader of the Lin Biao clique and became Chief of the Military Staff of the People's Liberation Army in 1968 [eds].

9 Cai Yuanpei (1868–1940), a leading educationalist; Hu Shi (1891–1962), a scholar and philosopher; Fu Sinian (1896–1951), a nationalist historian; Ma Yinchu (1882–1982), an economist and educator [eds].

4

WANG GUNGWU ON THE NANTAH INCIDENT[1]

An interview

Yuan Yaoqing et al.

Question In what capacity did you join the committee to examine the Nantah curriculum[2]? Were you connected with the government in any way?

Wang It's important to bear in mind that Singapore had just entered the Federation of Malaysia. As a result, Singapore had to accommodate in all respects to Malaysia's needs – in regard to education, labour, trade, economic administration, and public order. It was all very complicated. Singapore became part of Malaysia in 1963 and in late 1964 the Singapore Education Department and Nantah got down to thinking about what steps to take to adapt to the new political circumstances, so someone proposed setting up a committee to reform the curriculum. Why they chose me I don't know, since I was not a Singaporean. I was brought up in Malaya and was teaching at the time in the University of Malaya. After they'd decided to form this committee, they needed someone to chair it and they chose me. They needed someone relatively familiar with Malaya, and I fitted their requirements.

In early 1965, we held a meeting, the first of many. In May, I finished writing the report and submitted it to the authorities. At the meetings, our main concern was the future of Nantah's teaching staff, students, and graduates (who were politically very active at the time, both in the People's Action Party and the opposition parties, they were a constant source of criticism and opinions). We felt that Nantah was being discriminated against, that it was being treated unequally. Malaysia had only two universities, the University of Singapore and the University of Malaya. Both were supported by the government, both were privileged. Nantah, on the other hand, suffered active discrimination. Its graduates failed to find employment, neither government was prepared to recognize them, and their opportunities were extremely limited. The committee sympathized with them absolutely. We set great store by equality. We felt that it was not enough to look just at the curriculum, we should also review the treatment of Nantah staff and students, we should compare their treatment – I'm talking about the principal, the staff, the workers, and the students – with that of their counterparts in the other two universities. After we had discussed the issue, I wrote a report along those lines, submitted it to the authorities, and returned to Kuala Lumpur, whereupon the committee was wound up.

Later, two things happened that I had not foreseen. In August 1965, Singapore withdrew from Malaysia. Although the two sides had always been in some respects at loggerheads, Singapore's withdrawal was a grave blow to the Chinese in Malaya. Within Malaysia, Singapore was a boon to the ethnic Chinese. From a demographic point of view, they swelled ethnic Chinese numbers, with a population of getting on for one million. That was important electorally and politically. So the Chinese in Malaya were overjoyed when Singapore joined the Federation. Singapore's withdrawal was a big tragedy, for in talking about Nantah's unequal treatment we were also alluding to the unequal treatment of the Malaysian Chinese. More than half of the students at Nantah were from Malaya – Singaporeans made up no more than around 40 per cent. Nantah played a crucial role in the Malayan Chinese schools, so Singapore's withdrawal was an enormous blow. Lee Kuan Yew[3] was heartbroken. He was in tears when he went on TV to proclaim the establishment of the Republic of Singapore. All of us were heartbroken.

Given Singapore's withdrawal, it seemed to me at the time that the report should be torn up, since its main purpose had been to deal with the new political circumstance of Singapore's entry into the Federation of Malaysia. After the withdrawal, everything had changed, the report was no longer relevant in an independent Singapore. Its subject was Nantah within the Federation of Malaysia. Two further points need making. (1) Not long afterwards, Singapore stopped allowing Malaysian students to enter. This measure was a big blow to Nantah. Don't forget, three out of five students were graduates of Malaysian middle schools, some of which were stronger than their counterparts in Singapore. After independence, Nantah relied entirely on the support of Singapore's own Chinese schools. That made a big difference. (2) For some reason not altogether clear to me, the new government did not declare our report invalid and no longer relevant. Perhaps they had their reasons, I'm not Singaporean, so they were unlikely to ask my opinion. The report was submitted in May and the withdrawal happened in August. Throughout that period, the report remained unpublished. After a few days, the new independent government suddenly declared that it intended to implement the report's recommendations, but it never actually did so. If you carefully compare the report with Singapore's policies on Nantah, you'll see that its recommendations were not followed.

The report aimed at achieving equal status with the other two universities for Nantah, equal treatment. Also, I harboured various ambitions. I was still young, inexperienced, and rather idealistic. I'd always thought that overseas Chinese had many special characteristics. Most them were rather intelligent, culturally knowledgeable, diligent, industrious, and courageously prepared to face up to almost any difficulty, so I was full of confidence in them. As a result, we didn't only want Nantah to be equal to the other two universities, we wanted it to be better, at least in some ways. Thinking back, we were perhaps a little immature. We wanted Nantah to leap ahead and Singapore to join Malaysia. Many of the Malaysian students had good Malay but poor English, and those from Indonesia spoke even better Malay. Malay rather than English is Malaysia's mother tongue, so it was not a colonial issue, for Malaysia was already independent. Since some Malaysian students had good Malay, the committee proposed setting up a Malay Department at Nantah. We wanted Nantah students to be trilingual. Looking back, we were too idealistic. You can't expect everyone to operate in three languages. Students who were not so good at languages could at most be expected to know two, either English and Chinese or Malay and Chinese. (Everyone had been to a Chinese middle school so Chinese would be no problem, that was our view at the time.) However, the problem was how to fit in with the situation as it then was, both commercially (where English was probably the main language) and politically, where Malay was very strong and could not be ignored. At the time, we thought that Nantah graduates would need English for trade and industry and Malay for intellectual, cultural, political, and social purposes. But we also had great faith in Chinese. Everyone had been to a Chinese school and had a good foundation in the language, of that there could be no doubt. By proposing that Nantah set up a language centre, we hoped to encourage everyone to perfect their knowledge of one or two additional languages. Were that to happen, Nantah students would be at an advantage over the two other universities. Their English and Malay would be on a par, and then they'd have Chinese. It would give them an edge when they graduated into society.

Question What competencies did the committee have? What was the source of its powers? In what ways was the report carried out?

Wang The committee had no powers whatsoever, it was simply a question of gathering together a few people to make a report on the situation in education. We wanted to achieve equality for Nantah, so we inevitably touched on issues beyond that of the university itself. It wasn't just an internal question, we were trying to gear Nantah up to compete with the other two universities, to make it equal with them. Many of the members of the committee were local experts, I was imported as the chairman. We discussed the issue and interviewed people, but we lacked authority. Once we had submitted our report, we disbanded. Regarding its implementation, it seemed to me that the most obvious thing was that after Singapore's withdrawal from the Federation the report was no longer directly relevant. However, I had no authority to intervene, and I had nothing whatsoever to do with the Singapore Government. The committee had nothing to do with the People's Action Party, it had absolutely no political colouring. The reason they approached me was because I was an outsider, I had no political ties.

Question You just said that the report espoused two principles. It aimed to achieve equality and it hoped to promote bilingualism or trilingualism among Nantah's staff and students. But some people say that after the report was published there was a clear shift at Nantah away from a Chinese people's university or a university dedicated to preserving Chinese culture to something approximating a British-style university, from a university in which Chinese was the language of instruction to one in which the bulk of the curriculum was taught in English. Moreover, this influenced the development of Singapore's independent middle schools or Chinese middle schools. What was your view of Chinese education and a Chinese people's university?

Wang That was not the report's intention. The report saw Chinese as the principal language of instruction, but we strove for a bilingual education, this was a very difficult question. We were rather idealistic in those days, we thought that if we worked hard enough at it, we could overcome the difficulty. But we were absolutely committed to preserving Chinese as Nantah's basic language, the report said as much. We even proposed abolishing the English Department, we thought it was wrong to give English too much weight. We wanted Chinese as the main language, plus a Malay Department to encourage the students. Lots of people knew English in those days, it was taught in the Chinese schools, so we could see no reason to worry about the students' English. But Malay was another question. It received far too little attention, so we thought it best to encourage students to take Malaysia's national language seriously. We definitely didn't throw out Chinese and promote English at its expense. What happened subsequently is another question. Don't forget, Singapore had withdrawn from the Federation. Within Malaysia as a whole, it would have been no problem, because there had been no fundamental change in the Chinese schools in Malaysia, they still have independent middle schools. However, Singapore's educational policy after independence is another question. That's something we failed to foresee. The report was written with the Federation of Malaysia in mind. Malaysia had such an abundance of Chinese schools that we had every confidence, there was no way that the government of the time could have brought pressure to bear.

Question But from what I've heard, even before the publication of the report the committee had already issued two announcements proposing reforms at Nantah. On another issue, sources suggest that even in the very early days Nantah encountered numerous obstacles. According to Lim Ho Hup,[4] the government was against the setting up of Nantah. What's your response?

Wang I have no doubt that Lim Ho Hup knows more than I do. After all, he's Singaporean, whereas I'm far from clear about the Singapore Government's attitude to Nantah. Don't forget, there were Nantah graduates in the government and in the leadership of the People's Action Party, I hardly think that they can have been antipathetic to Nantah. But I should point out that many Nantah students supported the opposition, though I can't say I'm well up on Singapore's internal political struggle. I don't doubt that the old colonial government had no good feelings for Nantah, but the situation in the People's Action Party was more complicated, different members had different views. Some of the English-educated didn't understand Chinese and some weren't even Chinese to start with. However, some Nantah graduates were even more authoritative and energetic, they edited a whole series of publications and were not without influence.

Question The committee's remit was to look into the curriculum, but the report proposed reforming the university's entire system of study. Was that not overstepping its competencies?

Wang No. You can't look at the curriculum in isolation from the broader system. As soon as you start looking at equality, you have no choice but to look at how the degrees are viewed after graduation, so other issues get dragged in, they're all part of the same debate. But we definitely didn't propose switching to a three-year system, that never once cropped up. At the time it was still a four-year system, but it was different from the four-year system in Hong Kong. It was three years plus one, which has now been changed to three years for an ordinary degree and a fourth year for honours, i.e. four years in all. So it seems to me that the four-year system is quite natural, it's just a matter of how you use those four years, that's something that merits further discussion.

Question According to some critics, the report adduced insufficient evidence to support its proposal for language changes and its criticism of the future prospects of Nantah graduates. How did the report view these two issues?

Wang Basically, Nantah students were saying that they encountered difficulties. Potential employers were prejudiced, or the students were unable to match up to language requirements, we often came across such opinions in the course of our discussions. We also made our own investigations, and we carried out quite a few interviews. Naturally, some particularly talented individuals went abroad. Quite a few took their PhDs at foreign universities. But as Lim Ho Hup pointed out, the quality of the students was very high at the outset, he was quite right in that respect.

Before and after the war, Singapore and Malaysia's good graduates went to China for further study – I too went to China to read for my degree. After 1949 it was no longer easy to go to China. The Malaysian Government was fiercely opposed to students studying in China, if you went you were unable to return. So parents were no longer keen for their children to do further study, and many of the better students headed for Nantah. At the same time, many parents sent their children to British universities, that trend was already apparent. Some students at Nantah in the early years were therefore relatively old. Moreover, there was quite a backlog of middle-school graduates who applied to Nantah once it started up, so the quality of applicants was on the whole extremely high and they included many people with work experience, for example in teaching or journalism.

Later, starting in 1949, parents gradually started sending their sons and daughters to British universities, since China seemed a dead end. The same was true of Hong Kong and

Taiwan. Hong Kong didn't even have enough university places for its own students. But the Chinese schools were still comparatively strong. Many people supported them and were willing to help fund them, it's still the case today. Later, however, many of the students at the Chinese schools transferred to English-language schools when they reached senior-middle level. In the final two or three years, many students with a background in Chinese transferred to English schools for their advanced studies. In the last analysis, it seems to me that the gravest blow to Nantah was the exit from Malaysia. Once Malaysian students were no longer admitted, there was no choice other than to concentrate on the graduates of Singapore's Chinese schools, which naturally represented a big step backwards.

Question The report very much gives the impression that its overriding aim was to prepare students to meet the needs of society, that its main purpose was to train graduates. Did it actually think through the issue of creating a new spirit of learning at Nantah?

Wang In my view, the situation at Nantah was quite different from the situation in Hong Kong, I see few similarities. Nantah was a discriminated university, we did everything we could to bolster it up, to help it achieve equal status with other universities. I've always thought that universities should strive to meet social needs. When it comes to the university's own teaching system, the aims are very much the same. However, the situation in any two places can never be identical. It was essential to consider the needs of the day, and to avoid retreating into an ivory tower. It seemed to me that some of the outsiders at Nantah in the early days, the non-Southeast Asians, were not necessarily familiar with local conditions, it was as if they wanted to run the university from behind closed doors, regardless of how things were on the ground, so all sorts of problems arose. It's my belief that a university should not be run along such lines.

Question Why do you think the Singapore Government merged the two universities?

Wang That happened in the 1970s. I'm not quite sure of the exact details, but I recall that Lee Kuan Yew's Government discussed this matter at great length with Nantah's board of directors. Lots of materials appeared in the press, that's where my information came from, for the most part. Lee Kuan Yew published a number of his letters to Nantah's board of directors, and later the correspondence from both sides was published. Much of it was critical of the government's decision and put forward a whole number of good arguments. But the Singapore Government pointed out that Singapore's best middle-school graduates didn't want to go to Nantah, they wanted to go to the University of Singapore. As a result, Nantah's students were seen as rejects of the University of Singapore. I seem to remember that the Singapore Government urged the University of Singapore to accept the best students and had no intention of distributing the students equally across the two campuses. That was a policy decision. As a result, Nantah graduates found it even harder to get jobs. They were viewed as second class and their degrees were condemned as worthless. This influenced parental choice. More and more people wanted their children to attend English-language institutions and to sit exams for the University of Singapore. That had nothing to do with the findings of the report. Generally speaking, the Singapore Government of the day was intent on its own survival in Southeast Asia. It had its own difficulties and viewpoints. This policy started roughly in 1975. After a few years, no one any longer wanted to go to Nantah. What's the point of good teachers if the students are not up to scratch? The basic principle of our report was that Nantah should be equal, but the Singapore Government failed totally to accept it.

Question What was the relationship between the report and the closing down of Nantah, and what was the effect of comments by outsiders?

Wang I mentioned a moment ago that it was not until 15 years after 1965 that the government merged Nantah with the University of Singapore. Many things happened in the meantime, none of which had anything to do with the report. Actually, Nantah's two principals in the years after the report was published were Rayson Lisung Huang and Hsueh Shou-sheng,[5] I think you will have heard of them, they worked at Nantah for a good many years and to quite some effect, I'm sure you will agree. They went to great lengths to build up Nantah. Whether the right decisions were taken in the end is a matter for Singapore to decide, it had to do with the government, or perhaps with some lobby within the government, I don't know. But what I do know is that all Nantah's workers, from the principal and the teachers down to the students, did their utmost to preserve Nantah, so I sympathized utterly and greatly regretted the decision to merge it with the University of Singapore.

Question Twenty years on, how do you evaluate the report? Others have commented on this question in articles. How do you view their comments?

Wang In some respects the report was too idealistic, too immature. Now that I'm 20 years older, I view some issues differently and am informed by different experiences. Basically, I feel that the main thing is that people should understand that the situation in Malaysia in those days was very complicated, to a degree that you could not now imagine. The merger was regrettable, but it was hardly my responsibility. The report supported Nantah, it wanted Nantah to succeed, but whether it succeeded or not was nothing to do with me. I had no authority. Lee Kuan Yew was hardly likely to follow my advice. I say again, our report was written in the context of the Federation of Malaysia, whereas it was implemented after Singapore went independent. The responsibility for what happened belongs to them.

Question You said a moment ago that twenty years ago you had an ideal vision of how Nantah should be reformed. Under the different social circumstances of today, might the values you espoused in those days have any relevance for your future policies?

Wang Of course. But before I set about trying to influence developments in Hong Kong, I must first acquaint myself better with the situation here. It will be a while before I set about trying to solve concrete problems. Today, we seem to have spent rather a lot of time talking about the past, perhaps on another occasion we can talk about the future. I look forward to reading students' criticisms and proposals, I'm sure they will be a source of help and inspiration.

Translated by Gregor Benton

APPENDIX: INTRODUCTION AND CONCLUSION OF THE NANYANG UNIVERSITY CURRICULUM REVIEW COMMITTEE REPORT

Chapter one

Introduction

1. The terms of reference of this Committee are: "To review the current organization of courses of study and contents of individual courses in Nanyang University and to recommend to the University revised courses of study adapted to the needs of our society."
2. We examined in detail the present degree structure, all courses of study and the examination system, and made recommendations on all aspects of the curriculum as well as on matters concerning the teaching staff relevant to our recommendations on the curriculum. The contents of the Prescott Report and the Gwee Ah Leng Report on the University were noted and all relevant documents pertaining to our review were closely studied. Three academic sub-committees were set up to study the curriculum of

each of the colleges and one other sub-committee to study matters concerning the teaching staff. We met several key members of the staff and, as most of our meetings were held at the University itself, there was ample opportunity to see the existing facilities for ourselves.

3. It appears to us that the University has so far served only a limited purpose. Attention has been paid to producing large numbers of graduates without adequate consideration of the prospects of employment for the graduates, or of high standards of teaching and research, or of the fundamental objectives of higher education in a plural society. It has so far catered only for students from the Chinese-medium schools in the country. We feel that this function is too narrow and a great deal can be done to re-orientate the University towards serving our society as a whole.

4. We feel that the nature of our society must be reflected in any institution of higher learning which purports to serve that society. In order to achieve this, the courses of study in the University must be adapted to ensure that students from all streams of education in the country may benefit from the University's existence.

5. Our society is greatly concerned with the prosperity and peaceful development of our new nation of Malaysia. In this context, there is an urgent need for people with a deep, rational and sympathetic understanding of the multi-racial basis of the country. The University should produce graduates able to guide the course of the country's development, and trained to administer the public services and manage the growth of commerce and industry, and specially equipped to meet the nation's need for rapid modernization.

6. We therefore believe that particular attention must be paid to the problem of necessary language skills. It should be the aim of the University to produce graduates who are at least bi-lingual, if not tri-lingual, in the languages relevant to the development of the country.

7. We also came to the conclusion that the degree structure itself should be revised in order to bring out the best in all students and to produce the kind of graduates needed.

. . .

Chapter ten

Summary of conclusions

115. We revised the curriculum and recommended a new degree structure consisting of a pass degree and an honours degree.

116. We believe that the University should open its doors to students from all streams of education in the country.

117. A Language Centre serving the whole University should be immediately established.

118. A Department of Malay Studies should be established in the College of Arts.
119. The Department of Modern Languages and Literature, the Department of Education, and the Department of Chemical Engineering should be abolished.
120. The Department of Political Science should be reorganized and renamed the Department of Government and Public Administration.
121. The Department of Industrial Management and the Department of Banking and Finance should be merged into one department called the Department of Industrial and Business Management.
122. The requirements of the relevant professional bodies must be kept in mind if courses in the College of Commerce are to be of an acceptable standard.
123. Staff of high academic quality must be obtained as soon as possible; it is particularly important that each Department should have a strong Professorial Head.
124. New salary scales should be immediately introduced in order to attract and retain good staff.
125. Opportunities and facilities for research must be adequately provided.
126. For future staff, facilities must be provided for the training of the University's own graduates. Plans should now be drawn up to offer higher degrees.
127. None of our recommendations concerning the new degree structure will be meaningful unless salary scales for teaching staff are revised and made comparable to those of other universities in Malaysia.

Notes

1 This interview was conducted by a group of Hong Kong University students on 14 August 1986, in Chinese, and was not formally published [eds].

2 Nantah (Nanda) is the abbreviated Chinese name of Nanyang University, founded in 1956 in Singapore. On 20 January 1965, the Nanyang University Curriculum Review Committee was formed, chaired by Wang Gungwu. The Report of the Committee was formally submitted to the Vice Chancellor of Nantah on 14 May 1965. It was approved by the University Council on 12 September 1965, more than one month after Singapore's separation from Malaysia on 9 August 1965. Nanyang University merged with the University of Singapore in 1980 to become the National University of Singapore. The introduction to and conclusion of this report, often called the Wang Gungwu Report, are included at the end of this interview as an appendix. For historical accounts of Nantah and the full report, see *Nanyang University Tenth Anniversary Souvenir, 1956–1966,* edited by the Ad Hoc Editorial Committee, Nanyang University (Singapore: Nanyang University, 1966); Edwin Lee and Tan Tai Yong, *Beyond Degrees: The Making of the National University of Singapore* (Singapore: Singapore University Press, 1996); and Li Yeling, ed., *Nanyang daxue zhouguo de lishi daolu* (Selected historical sources on Nanyang University), Kuala Lumpur: Nanyang University Alumni Association of Malaysia, 2002, pp. 323–362 [eds].

3 Lee Kuan Yew (1923–), political leader who led Singapore to independence and was Prime Minister from 1959 to 1990 [eds].

4 Lim Ho Hup, a graduate of the University of Malaya and classmate of Wang Gungwu, directed the Singapore Economic Development Board (EDB) and was one of the six members of the Nanyang University Curriculum Review Committee [eds].

5 Rayson Lisung Huang (1920–), born in Shantou, China, was educated in Hong Kong and Oxford. He taught at the University of Chicago before joining the faculty of University of Malaya in Singapore in 1951. He was Vice Chancellor of Nanyang University (1969–1972) and of Hong Kong University (1972–1986). Hsueh Shou-sheng (1926–), born in Wuxi, Jiangsu, received his PhD from the University of Geneva in 1953 and taught at Hong Kong University, the University of the Philippines, and Nanyang University. He was Vice Chancellor of Nantah (1972–1975) and founding president of East Asian University of Macao (1981–1986).

5

WANG GUNGWU IN AUSTRALIA[1]

Stephen FitzGerald[2]

I once said to Wang Gungwu, over dinner and only partly in jest, that he would make a good Prime Minister of China. He demurred.

Perhaps the job he is going to as Vice Chancellor of the University of Hong Kong is more important. At least for the survival of the idea of intellectual freedom. In that part of China. And to some extent in all the rest of China. And therefore in our region.

Wang Gungwu's eighteen years in Australia have been important for this country, and also a preparation for what he is about to undertake. There is a connection between these two, in broader regional, cultural terms, which has to do with where Australia and Asia now stand in relation to each other in matters less tangible than war or commerce. Wang Gungwu in Australia has been an Asian "contribution" to Australian life and society. That much is obvious. What he can do in Hong Kong is, perhaps less obviously, an Australian as much as an Asian contribution to that part of the world. And, I think not too fancifully, what he does in Hong Kong affects both our futures, Australia's and Asia's.

What did Australia do for Wang Gungwu? Above all, it gave him a place in which he could pursue his intellectual interests in an environment of great intellectual freedom, and develop his skills as a scholar administrator free from political interference. Born in one colony (the Dutch East Indies), raised in another (British Malaya), his early education – largely at home – in a country under armed occupation, by an Asian dictatorship (Japanese) and his induction to higher learning under another Asian dictatorship (China's Guomindang), he finished his education in Britain and went back to teach in colonial Singapore and independent Malaysia. But the place he came to, and the place in which he has spent more years than anywhere else, was Australia.

In fact, he did not seek it. And to the best of my knowledge he was not even looking for another place to go to, or a haven where intellectual freedom was not under threat. He was actually sought out, by the Australian National University, as a fitting replacement for the great C. P. FitzGerald in the Department of Far Eastern History, perhaps the first occasion on which an Australian university had so solicited a non-European for a prestigious chair (and one of the many perceptive contributions to Australia of Sir John Crawford).[3] He was reluctant. Malaysia, under the impact of the dramatic events of its early post independence years, was showing signs of setting itself against some of the more liberal traditions of British Malaya. Wang Gungwu was a participant. He had been involved in the foundation of a new political party which sought to break out of the pattern of racially based parties, and embrace all ethnic groups. Friends were importunate. So was Crawford. The scholar in Wang Gungwu, the professional, the historian and teacher, prevailed over the politician.

So? In relation to his new appointment in Hong Kong, it could just as well have been Britain or the United States, you say. In logics, yes, but in fact, no. It was Crawford who sought him out; because he was not merely a young China historian of established repute but also because he was a Southeast Asian, a North Asian, a "European" Asian, a scholar whose cultures defied the gaps. Crawford understood the point even if few others did. But for Wang Gungwu also, there was a logic to Australia. If he had to follow the professional opportunity outside Malaysia, then it needed to be the right place, for his psyche as well as his profession. For the former, Australia was in his region, and just starting to recognize that. It was remote, but not like Europe or North America. Singapore to Sydney is in fact about the same as Singapore to Tokyo. In Australia, one might still feel caught up with Asia and its issues. For the latter, there was the prospect of the study of Asia in Australia at the point of take-off, culture-bound Australia at the threshold of potentially dramatic change, through education, in attitudes to the region. For an historian of Asia there was a further element, already important and to become increasingly so during his time in Australia, enlargement of his research interest from Chinese history to the history of both China and Southeast Asia and the relationship between the two.

In the event, the period of Wang Gungwu's tenure at the Australian National University has been a difficult one for that part of Australia which is Asia-oriented or which would like Australia to be. The promise has been largely unfulfilled. To be sure, we are in general more accepting of a future in this region and we are to a limited extent more substantially engaged with some of the countries of the region. But there is still an alarming degree of hypocrisy, lip-service and bravado on the part of politicians, business people, academics, teachers, journalists and others who profess an Australian closeness with Asia.

The traditional Australian commitments to isolationism, cultural Eurocentricism, monolingualism and economic protectionism, and plain laziness in responding to new and difficult challenge, remain predominant. You don't have to disagree with Hawke[4] to observe the frailty of an engagement with Indonesia which could be so easily upset by a critical newspaper article. You don't have to like Japanese business practice to be concerned at how sour Australian business opinion is about Japan. In Australian universities, protectionism has taken on new meaning in the defences thrown up against the highly competitive and intellectually successful Asian students in their midst and the rising opposition to the export of education services intended to benefit Asian countries. And if you had any doubts about underlying hostility to Asian people, recall how easily and quickly a wave of anti-Asian poison spread across Australia in 1984, in the Geoffrey Blainey[5] immigration debate.

The occasional and casual Asian encounter of the politician, businessman or academic might be more meaningful if over the same period the study of Asia in our schools and universities had broadened and deepened. Sadly for Australia, that process has almost come to a standstill. Witness the depressing figures recently released by the Commonwealth Department of Education, which show that only a little over 14 per cent of Australian children study foreign languages at school, and that, of the languages studied, French and German, the imperatives of Britain's geopolitical situation at the time of their transplant into Australian education a century ago, remain predominant.

Wang Gungwu can hardly be blamed for this situation. If he were a person given to depression, he would be depressed by it. Because he has done as much for the cause of Australia's consciousness of Asia over these 18 years as any other Australian academic and more than most. Although not born in Australia, he took up the Australian cause with a passion and dedication which left many of his Australian-born colleagues behind. Still the participator, he became involved. He marched in the Vietnam protests. Not for communism in Indo-China, not for dogmas, not for most of the "anti's" of that movement, but for reasoned understanding of Asian societies and Asian issues, for the rights of Asian societies to be heard and to determine their own futures, for informed and intelligent decision-making about Asian societies on the part of the governments of non-Asian countries. He attended the Whitlam[6] rallies of 1972, fired, as we all were, with enthusiasm at the prospect of an Australian government which would come to terms not only with China but with all of the Third World. He took part in the early abortive attempts to create associations of one kind or another for Asian Studies, and in the successful movement which led to the creation of the Asian Studies Association of Australia. He accepted appointments with the Australian Government, first as a member of the Australia–Japan Coordinating Committee, and then as Chairman of the Australia–China Council, the first ever occasion, I think, that an Asian has been appointed to head a semi-governmental authority in Australia. He talked, he taught, he broadcast, he appeared on television. He did 5 years as Director of the Research School of Pacific Studies at the

Australian National University, which as everyone knows is a position which seems inimical to the serious pursuit of research. He tried to reform the Australian National University. Or at least some of its rigidities in postgraduate training. He was President of the Asian Studies Association of Australia, and for good measure President of the Academy of the Humanities. He entertained, he went to concerts and the theatre. He collected Australian wines. He watched Aussie Rules on television and drank beer.

What's that to do with Asian Studies, you ask. Everything, I say. We talk about getting inside the minds of Asian people. Wang Gungwu has been about getting inside the minds of Europeans. He wrote poetry in English in Malaya, he knocked about in London, he has spent the last 18 years getting inside the thinking of the people of his adopted country. With that, he has been more effectively armed to take up the fight for the study of Asia in Australia. For he does this not as an Asian in Australia saying "you" ought to understand us, but as an Australian saying "we" have to study and understand these societies. Perhaps only a Southeast Asian could have done that.

Wang Gungwu has not contributed a great book in this period. His contribution has been different. It is an intellectual contribution which has been felt throughout the community of Asian scholars, and beyond, into the community at large. He has been a teacher, a direct communicator of ideas, an intellectual catalyst for the thinking of those he has taught, postgraduate student, undergraduate, public service trainee and Western Suburbs rotarian alike. His impulse to teach has been reflected in the pattern of his work. Unselfish of his time, he has spent much of it over the last 18 years lecturing, teaching and talking outside his own university department. He has given lecture courses in most Australian (and many overseas) universities. No matter who wrote and asked him to talk, how small the country town, how lay the audience, he has always been prepared to respond. This is his impact, and it is far broader and far more profound than that of most of his colleagues in the field.

The pattern of Wang Gungwu's writings over the period, however, and the drift of his academic interests, reveal what has been in gestation. The articles and lectures and seminars and conference discussions are part of a broad historical exploration of China in Southeast Asian history and Southeast Asia in Chinese history, from the earliest times until the present. His ideas are already mapped out. Whether they are brought together in one historical blockbuster remains to be seen after he has finished his stint at Hong Kong University. But that they have prepared him for that stint as almost no other could have been is not in doubt.

The University of Hong Kong, although in a colony, enjoys intellectual freedom as universities do in Australia. Universities under the government of the People's Republic of China do not. The assumption of control over Hong Kong by that government will not be a simple turn of the switch in

1997. It will happen gradually and is happening now. The guidelines are being set, the "indirect directives" are being felt, the influence is there. The next 5 years will be the testing period for the future of intellectual life and the independence of the two universities. If that intellectual independence is circumscribed, subverted and perverted, that will be tragic for the people of Hong Kong. But also for the people of China. Because if it does become the case that Hong Kong is treated by the People's Republic of China as a laboratory for social experimentation, and if intellectual freedom in the universities were to prevail, there would be hope for greater intellectual freedom in the universities of China. That is one issue which the present leadership in China has not been able to come to terms with and yet, it seems to me, intellectual freedom is as critical to the success of the reforms they are trying to implement as the responsibility system in economic management. Without the former, it is really impossible ever to attain the latter. And if intellectual freedom were to grow in China, that would have its influence on China's neighbours; if it does not, that will make things very difficult for us all. From his own life, and from history, Wang Gungwu understands that in no country to our North is there a tradition of intellectual freedom in the way that it is understood in our society.

So Wang Gungwu goes into an interesting situation. He is a Chinese. He speaks the Chinese of the mandarins. He also speaks the Chinese of Hong Kong (to the astonishment and delight of the student representative group which met him last year). He is an historian of Chinese history, of its political and institutional history and its foreign relations. He is also Southeast Asian. He speaks Malay and Indonesian. He is an historian not only of Southeast Asia but of the Chinese in Southeast Asia and of China in Southeast Asia. And much of his writing has been on the contemporary aspects of these issues. He is perhaps a politician *manqué*, but certainly a scholar administrator. He is a diplomat. He is a man of universal intellectual curiosity.

He is also an Australian. He speaks English as fluently as he does Chinese. He is in his intellectual interests if not in his writing an historian of Britain and Europe. He understands from his sojourn in Australia and his adoption of that country the importance of the issues in Hong Kong to the whole of our region.

He goes into an historically unique situation in which, by negotiated settlement, without the exercise of force, an Asian population enjoying intellectual freedom and very considerable freedoms in other ways, is to be handed over by a European government to an Asian country in which most of those freedoms do not exist. Some in the Chinese Government would like to see them in China. Some would not. One man alone, even as Vice Chancellor of Hong Kong University, could hardly be expected to resolve that problem. But if there is anyone equipped in the whole of the academic world, East or West, to understand the issue, to know what is right to do, and to do it, I know of no one remotely comparable with Wang Gungwu.

There's plenty of time later on for the historical blockbuster.

Notes

1 Originally published in the *Asian Studies Association of Australia Review,* vol. 10, no. 1, 1986.
2 Stephen FitzGerald (1938–) received his PhD from the Australian National University. He was Australia's first Ambassador to the People's Republic of China (1973–1976) and was concurrently Ambassador to North Korea. He was the founding editor of the *Australian Journal of Chinese Affairs* (1979–1986) and president of the Asian Studies Association of Australia (1982–1984). He is currently Chairman and Professor at the Asia–Australia Institute at the University of New South Wales [eds].
3 C. P. FitzGerald (1902–1992), China scholar; Sir John Crawford (1910–1984), Director of the Research School of Pacific Studies and professor of economics, Australian National University (1960–1967), Vice Chancellor (1968–1973) and Chancellor, ANU (1976–1984) [eds].
4 Bob Hawke (1929–), Australian labour leader and prime minister from 1983 to 1991 [eds].
5 Geoffrey Blainey (1930–), Australian historian [eds].
6 Gough Whitlam (1916–), Australian politician and lawyer [eds].

6

THE PROBLEMS WITH (CHINESE) DIASPORA[1]

An interview with Wang Gungwu

Laurent Malvezin

Malvezin A mountain of books has been written about the so-called Chinese diaspora in Asia. Do you think it deserves such attention?

Wang The word diaspora, as I understand it, implies nowadays, both business acumen and wealth among a dispersed population, and the success of the early Chinese merchants in the early days reminded many of a similar social position achieved by the Jewish merchants elsewhere. However, the Chinese merchants moved to Southeast Asia a long time ago[2] and today, such a view is of little relevance to the realities. For the last two hundred years, the Chinese who left China by the millions were not for most of them traders or businessmen. They were poor, and very much in the situation of the journeymen today leaving the countryside for urban areas in hope of a better future. They were far from wealthy, rather the opposite. I cannot associate such a migration with the word diaspora, which has the opposite meaning.[3]

Malvezin Nevertheless, we can associate the word with a large social group which is self-centred and which derives its strength not from the individuals but from its cohesion.

Wang Of course, diaspora also has such a connotation, but then it is assumed that all the overseas Chinese are involved and that there is a cohesion. Such a view is very misleading. The fact is that the Chinese, wherever they go, are easily influenced by their environment. They adapt to new circumstances and thus become very different from other groups of Chinese living elsewhere. I don't see much cohesion.

Malvezin To a foreigner, it does not look like that at all. Chinatown is very much a Chinese city, and a foreigner tends to see them as being all over the world very much Chinese.

Wang The Chinese get together for their festivals and Chinese New Year. They will also look for a new business partner among their community as a matter of convenience, but really, all the overseas communities have their own characters, they can rarely communicate with one another, and there is a myriad of them. To me, instead of saying there is one big Chinese diaspora, which brings negative commentaries, it would be better to look at the way they were able to adapt in order to survive and what sort of strategies they developed over time to fit into their new environment. We will see that each one is in fact unique.[4] Look at the Chinese who have gone to the Philippines. They are very different from the Chinese who settled in Thailand. Both are very different from those who left for Brazil, Argentina or the United States.[5] Each of them had to find ways and means to adjust accordingly.

Malvezin Yet they remain, for essential purposes, Chinese.

Wang Of course they keep their Chinese culture and what goes with it in their social relations. But that behaviour is not central to their purpose. They will do whatever is necessary to improve their standard of living. It is true that most of them are successful, but today the interesting question is to see whether the new emigrants, no longer poor and uneducated people, but rather better educated people, are as successful as their poor predecessors.

Malvezin If we look at the Hong Kong people who went to Canada and are now coming back, there are fewer and fewer success stories among fresh emigrants. Why?

Wang All those people from Hong Kong, Taiwan and China are in fact facing a much more challenging task than the poor coolies or the merchants of the past.[6] They have a very different experience and what they need is some professional opening, it means competing directly with local professionals. It requires a different strategy. If you have no skills, and just want to be a waiter, it's somehow much easier because you don't have to fight with anybody or to compete very hard with others, but to be a lawyer, an engineer, an accountant or a doctor with an established clientele is another matter.

Malvezin But qualification can also be seen as an asset that the poor did not have.

Wang Yes, but then you have local professionals. They have very powerful ways of keeping you out of their business. They won't make things easy for you and you must find ways of coping with them.

Malvezin You can't deny that the industrialized countries do offer a lot of opportunities.

Wang That is the paradox. The countries that are welcoming the new better educated emigrants from China, Hong Kong or Taiwan give them a lot of credit when it comes to their dedication, professional skills and qualifications. They certainly have a better chance of getting in. But being admitted is one thing, to have a job in your profession and make a good living out of it is quite a different matter. Ultimately, many of them have to do other things, hold minor jobs just to survive. How then can they fit into the concept of a wealthy and powerful diaspora? Most of those people are just strenuously trying to make a living, sometimes surrounded by a hostile environment.

Malvezin Why, if that is the case, have scholars been writing mountains of books about the influence and the power of the Chinese diaspora? Is it all a myth?

Wang There is a political dimension in the word and the meaning people are trying to convey with it. If the analysis were only descriptive and the terms generic, it would not capture the headlines. But it does make headlines. It is only because it fits some people's prejudice or reinforces a pre-judged view.

Malvezin Such as the existence of a Chinese threat?

Wang One has to look at the context in which the term diaspora is used to see it is not innocent. For instance, the term diaspora normally covers a specific social content. As such, it can be applied to any group that fits the social content and one can make various comparisons from one diaspora to the next. But it is only an academic exercise valid in a narrow social context. If you lift the word out of its context, it is another matter. In the media or in the context of public affairs, it becomes politicized and it is then used by politicians who have an agenda. In such a case, we have to ask ourselves, what was the purpose? Are we trying to demonize some social groups?

Malvezin Then, let's ask the question. Are we trying to demonize the overseas Chinese and if yes, why?

Wang The word diaspora is in itself an oversimplification and I find it personally very alarming that people talk commonly of a Jewish diaspora, an Indian or a Chinese one, as if the world consisted of a few "leagues". It is simply not true but unscrupulous people can use such a description to build up the image of a new yellow peril. Some people are going even further, saying that China is behind it, sending out people and contacting people all around, acting like an enormous octopus, spreading its tentacles and building up its network. Such nonsense is bound to be believed when one is using out-of-context words like diaspora. With a lot of imagination, one could even end up saying: "The Chinese are coming, the Chinese are coming!" So, I would say that it has to be scrutinized, even by the scholars. I hope they will come out and say: "Hey! That's not what you mean, you use that word for this political purpose and that is not legitimate."

Malvezin What can be done to stop this nonsense?

Wang The scholars must be careful and thorough. When the word diaspora is used out of context, they must denounce it and point out that it is not used legitimately but for a political purpose. If a concept is being abused by other people for other purposes, scholars must definitely take a stand and expose whoever has a political purpose. After all, such overuse is totally against what scholars do through scientific studies. The tragedy is that some scholars don't even know what damage they are doing, abusing this term or another. After all, is there any justification to use the word to imply that there is some kind of international conspiracy or network of Chinese all over the place acting as one force? Are all these people acting as if they were responding with very sensitive antenna to each other against the rest of the world, with China behind it? No, it's sheer nonsense.

Malvezin Probably, but there is this lingering feeling that the Chinese have no real sense of belonging where they live. Why?

Wang Most of them identify themselves with the country where they live. A Chinese in Thailand is first of all a Thai. The confusion is that if you ask them, they tell you that they find it useful to learn Chinese to do business or, it is a way to regain some pride in their culture, to try to understand who their ancestors were. But such an attitude does not translate into a political identification. The confusion for some is that, in Asia, the concept of a political identity and a cultural identity has to be understood as being two different things and they are not exclusive.

LM Can you really identify with your country of residence if you try hard to keep a different cultural identity than the prevailing one?

Wang That is the question and I think the answer is yes. It is now better understood. When you are in France, you may say I'm Parisian, while saying I'm European when you are in Asia, and you feel like it, because perhaps in Asia, you want to differentiate yourself from the Americans. So each one of us can, depending on where and when, use different labels.

Malvezin We can probably separate the political from the cultural, but at some point you have to belong somewhere and to adhere to a common ground, otherwise how can you have a sense of nation?

Wang Whether we like it or not, not everyone is comfortable with the concept of the nation-state. In Europe it has been taken for granted because it has been there for so long and the borders have not changed much. In East Asia, the idea of a nation-state, with its national boundaries, one language, one culture, one religion and so on, is very alien. In that respect one cannot expect East Asian people to be as clear of their identity as the French or the British are.

Malvezin Most of the countries are only 50 years old at the most. They need time.

Wang People are learning, learning to say I'm a Singaporean, or I'm a Malaysian,[7] but notwithstanding, they keep saying, I'm a Chinese, or a Malay. For them, there is no contradiction between their ethnic identity and their national identity. In Europe the perception is different because people are used to adhering to simply one dominant identity. All other identities must be removed, or were removed. It is the parable of Damascus. A Christian can only be Christian if he or she rejects all other identities. It is all or nothing. Once you are a convert, you must reject all your past. That kind of attitude and language is the Christian way. The problem is that it doesn't apply to China. As you know among the Chinese, people have different religions simultaneously. They go to a Buddhist temple for certain things and a Daoist temple for other things. If you tell them to be a Christian, they are willing to, provided the Christians would allow them to be Buddhist and Daoist at the same time. But you can't. Actually, it is one of the reasons why most of the Chinese do not convert to Christianity, because of its exclusive nature. It goes against the Chinese culture to be exclusively something. The Christian priests find the Chinese who still want to worship their ancestors and still believe in their "fengshui" and superstition are not sincere. But the Chinese could believe in Jesus Christ and remain all that they were before that!

Malvezin Applying your remark to the meaning of diaspora, does it mean, in your view, that a diaspora can only exist in reference to the notion of exclusivity, in which case it is therefore only a figment of the imagination, a matter of perception.

Wang Exactly! A Chinese finds it difficult to understand the bitterness of the relations between different cults, for example, between the Catholics and the Protestants, or even amongst the Protestants themselves, Luther against Calvin, so on and so forth. It is puzzling since it is all about the same religion, so what is the fuss? There is still an enormous gap between the Orthodox Church and the Roman Catholic Church. Why? Because each has an exclusive vision.

Malvezin That's the essence of every monotheist religion.

Wang That is the point, but such an approach and belief in an exclusive vision of the world is completely foreign to the Chinese soul. I am of course not talking of the Muslims living in Asia. I do think in a way that because of this exclusive religious belief, the political culture becomes exclusive as well.

Malvezin So, there is some truth in saying that the Chinese diaspora, whatever that is, remains Chinese in essence, and pragmatic, which, in political terms, means a lot.

Wang Pragmatism? No doubt about that, but there is a difference between being versatile and pragmatic. If and when their interests are not well protected or defended, why should they accept it for ever?

Malvezin Indeed, but I see a paradox there. A diaspora is in a way a minority, and it has to be careful. So what you describe is the right of the minorities not to be abused. They want their identity to be respected. Yet, we live in a world where human mobility and cross-culturalism are increasing, a phenomenon that is a threat to the nation-state as we know it.

Wang Yes, there is a disturbing paradox, which challenges the political leadership of any new nation. A leader could feel that our nation-building task is not yet completed, and already it is challenged from outside. What to do? The fact remains that technology has changed, the way the world economy works. You can't ignore the mobility of the financial capital, the movement of goods, and the speed of information. It is part of the realities that are surrounding you. So, it is not possible to say I'm in the middle of the nation-building process, leave me alone! All these new nations have to cope with conditions that are much more difficult than in Europe when the nation-building process took place. I don't think that Western leaders have any idea of how much more difficult it is for Asia today to follow the same path. The financial crisis has proven, if we needed the proof, that we are terribly vulnerable. Overnight, Asia can see a capital drain taking place, for little reason. In that context it is vain to pretend that the nation-state process taking place in Asia is safe. The Asian leaders have to do a balancing act. While consolidating their country's identity, at the same time they have to open it up so that the local economy can take advantage of a global economy. It's a contradiction. How to do both so that you can still save your country's integrity, sovereignty, and at the same time not lose out in the rat-race for economic survival?

Malvezin Isn't it the case for every economy?

Wang It is, but try to imagine what it means to build up an economy under the existing conditions of globalization. It's not the same as it was before. How did France and Britain build up their economy in the past? They did it with large colonial empires they controlled. They were unchallenged, and so were the United States. So that was a privileged time.

Malvezin In the process, you must admit that the Chinese diaspora does not help. Why did Malaysia have to enforce a bumiputra policy,[8] if not because the Chinese were economically speaking the predominant force, in a country where they were outnumbered?[9]

Wang Malaysia had no idea that it would become a nation. During the British time, it was a mixture of many small states, with a society made of feudal lords, small people and labourers. Then the traders and merchants came in from elsewhere. When the British left, you did not have one society but many. The ingredients were there and it was important to understand them. What you point out is the question of assimilation. How can it be done, and in fact can it be done from where you start? The Indonesian method was a failure because it was denying a reality. The Malaysian Government once it had recognized the reality did not try to change it by force. It can't work. Assimilation is something that ultimately may take a very long time, if it ever succeeds. So the best, in the meantime, and it is the only practicable way, is to respect the ethnic value of each social group. That is what the policy in practice in Malaysia, yesterday and now, did. Dr Mahathir[10] himself will tell you that to assimilate all these minorities is just not workable. You can dream that the sharing of the same experiences for a long period of time will unify the people so they become one nation, one society, with a sense of equity in which everybody feels he or she has a chance, but is it really necessary to achieve such identity to create a country?

Malvezin We don't have many examples of multicultural societies.

Wang In the West, and it is quite puzzling for us. Take for example, the Czechs and the Slovaks. Of course Czechoslovakia was an artificial country in the first place. But how are the two societies different from one another?

Malvezin I'm sure they would say themselves that they have many differences.

Wang For someone in Asia, it is not so obvious. And with the logic behind such insignificant differences, to break up in tiny bits and pieces, what chances are there to build a new nation at all ? If the kind of self-determination that was used as a principle in Central Europe at the break-up of the Austro-Hungarian Empire and then after the cold war were used in Asia, it would be very dangerous and would bring chaos and self-destruction. One wonders how the standard of living of the people can be improved if this kind of fragmentation, based on some narrow ideological principles, is allowed to make the differences permanent. To emphasize such differences takes a lot of energy, and in the meantime, nothing can be achieved. This is really not what Asia wants to learn from Europe, and I hope that Asian people won't buy it.

Malvezin At the heart of your remark is the question of trust. If minorities are starting to be distrustful, or alternatively, if the dominant social group starts to have doubts about the allegiance of a minority group, if, to come back to the concept of the Chinese diaspora, governments start for one reason or another to believe that its allegiance is not towards the place where they live but their homeland, whether it is true or not being there irrelevant, what can be achieved?

Wang To assume that a Chinese is tuned to the mainland implies that he knows their culture, he has connections at all levels and knows what to do, where and when. All these, just because he is ethnically Chinese. In fact, many overseas Chinese don't know anything simply because they have not been brought up in a Chinese environment or in a Chinese way in China. Some of them may not know a single thing about Chinese history. Think of the Chinese Americans, and the other people of Chinese origin anywhere else in the world. I don't believe they have much to share in common. Of course, what remains is that they can speak Chinese and that becomes an advantage if you are dealing with China. But is it really an outstanding advantage? I think people overestimate its usefulness, even if the Mainlanders feel much more comfortable doing business in their own language. In that context everybody who knows their language would be at an advantage over those who don't. But that is not enough because any foreigner fluent in the language would then have to be considered a member of the Chinese diaspora if that is the criteria. So, it is not a valid point.

Malvezin Maybe, but we could look at the phenomena from another angle. It is said that there is an Asian American vote in the United States, which means that somehow as a group, the Chinese Americans are trying to become a pressure group, grouping their votes to support their favourite candidate.[11] There were talks of China trying to influence the Presidential election. Although there is not a shred of evidence, it still bothers the common folk.

Wang I personally believe that all the fuss is merely a matter of local politics. The Asian Americans or the Chinese Americans do not want to be left behind. They want to increase their local participation to defend their minority interests against the people who are prejudiced against them. It is no more than that and they have no impact whatsoever on foreign affairs. To link that to China may look possible, but I really believe that it does not make sense.

Malvezin Why then is the American press making headlines as soon as a Chinese American or an overseas Chinese is making a donation to the Democratic Party or the Republican one, while it does not bother to bring up the matter if it is a European or an Indian, or anybody else, for that matter?

Wang All this has to do with the American political culture and the way minority interests have been able to affect mainstream politics. However, when one is talking about foreign affairs, it is clear to me that the national interests of the country are not affected by minority views. The national interest of a country is always defined by a much broader perspective, especially for the United States, which is a superpower and thus has a tremendous range of objectives and ambitions. And no minority can affect that.

Notes

1 Originally published in *Asian Affairs,* no. 14 (Winter 2000/2001). Reprinted with permission of Taylor & Francis. Unless otherwise indicated, all footnotes are from the original essay. The title is added by the editors.

2 The last twenty years of the Ming dynasty (1368–1644) are seen by Professor Wang Gungwu as the peak of Chinese free-ranging commercial activity in Southeast Asia before modern times. Three conditions were critical in enabling the Chinese to develop their trade activities: a) a greatly weakened central government in Beijing, which allowed the coastal provinces to engage in foreign trade; b) the reduction of Japanese activity in the region in accordance with the Tokugawa policy, which left the Chinese with no other Asian rivals; c) the fierce rivalry between the Dutch and the Spanish, which gave the Chinese privateers room to manoeuvre.

> Can the same three conditions be applied here when we talk about the "China maritime threat"? The first condition in a new form has existed to a large degree since the 1980s. Will it be reversed when centralized power is strengthened? Will the continental mindset be reestablished in Beijing? I think not, certainly not intentionally. . . . The second condition does not exist. Although China does not have another obvious rival in Asia other than Japan, Japan is very much an active protagonist. . . . The third condition of rivalry between major powers on the China coast may be compared to the US–Soviet cold war before 1989. That struggle for power and influence helped the Chinese in Southeast Asia to master the skills of industrial and financial capitalism and build their entrepreneurial networks. In addition, the rivalry also helped China take great strides into the global market economy in the 1980s. This condition too, no longer exists. But could an analogy be found in the economic rivalry between Japan and the United States? This is unlikely to turn into a serious conflict. If it occurs, it could only further stimulate China's future maritime commitments. But the geopolitics of the region are so sensitive, especially in Northeast Asia and in the United States and Russia, that any conflict between major protagonists would do untold damage to every country's economic development. If there

is a new danger to be identified, it lies elsewhere, possibly in a direct confrontation between China and the United States, which many US strategists and journalists seem to look forward to. The ethnic Chinese who have settled in the United States and allied countries need not be a liability. Their growing numbers, especially in North America, will ensure their vested interest in helping to maintain and expand areas of co-operation between their host countries and China. Such a task, of course, requires sensitivity too, and finesse in handling the local political culture. Clumsily done, efforts on China's behalf could backfire and bring back an atmosphere of suspicion and hostility towards the Chinese Overseas.

(Wang Gungwu, *The Chinese Overseas, From Earthbound to the Quest for Autonomy*, Cambridge, MA, Harvard University Press, 2000)

3 I still have some disquiet about the use of the term diaspora, not because in English it has until recently been applied only to the Jews, nor because the word refers to exile (in Hebrew) or dispersion (in Greek), which are rather specific manifestations of the phenomenon of sojourning and migration. Of course it is misleading and politically sensitive for the Chinese to be compared to the Jews in the Muslim world of Southeast Asia, but if the reality makes the comparison appropriate, so be it. My reservations come from the problems the Chinese encountered with the concept of sojourner (*huaqiao*) and the political use both China and hostile governments have made of that term. From China's point of view, "huaqiao" was a powerful name for a single body of overseas Chinese. It was openly used to bring about ethnic if not nationalist or racist binding of all Chinese at home and abroad. In the countries which have large Chinese minorities, that term had become a major source of the suspicion that the Chinese minorities could never feel loyalty towards their host nations. After some thirty years of debate, the term "huaqiao" no longer includes those Chinese with foreign passports, and is being replaced by others like "haiwai", "huaren" and "huayi", which disclaim formal China connections. The question which lingers in my mind is: will the word diaspora be used to revive the idea of a single body of Chinese, reminiscent of the old term, the "huaqiao"? Is this intended by those Chinese who favour its use ? Once the term is widely used, would it be possible to keep it as a technical term in the social sciences, or will it acquire the emotive power that would actually change our views about the nature of the various Chinese communities overseas?

(Wang Gungwu, "A Single Chinese Diaspora?" in *Imagining the Chinese Diaspora*, Canberra, Centre for the Study of the Chinese Southern Diaspora, Research School of Pacific and Asian Studies, ANU, 1999)

4 When Wang Ling-chi and his colleagues decided to stress the idea of the Chinese overseas "growing roots where they land" (*luodi shengen*) as the main theme for the conference held in San Francisco (1997), they were drawing special attention to a phenomenon that has been ignored for many decades by both Chinese and foreign scholars. The motives for this neglect was mixed. The Chinese did not take it seriously because they were convinced of the ultimate loyalty to China of most people of Chinese descent settled abroad, despite the fact that many of them consistently denied any allegiance to the government of China. Foreign scholars tended to focus on the apparent clannishness of most Chinese and concluded that "Once a Chinese, always a Chinese" was not merely a physical

fact and culturally credible, but also included political loyalty towards the Chinese nation. There were other factors which lent support to this conclusion: a passionate nationalism had spread among many Chinese communities abroad in the first half of the century; and the communist victory of 1949 placed all Chinese overseas who did not support the Guomindang in Taiwan on the wrong side of the global Cold War.

(Wang Gungwu, *Preface, The Chinese Diaspora, Selected Essays,* Vol. 1, Singapore: Times Academic Press, 1998)

5 Edmund Terence Gomez, *Chinese Business in Malaysia* (Richmond: Curzon Press, 1999), pp. 6–7.

6 The so-called "new migrants" are mainly professionals and students, and no longer belong to the lower class of the Chinese society. This new elite has settled in new places since the early 1980s, such as the United States, Canada, Australia and Europe. If we take the case of the tertiary level students who have "migrated", even though they theoretically spent a short period of time in their host country, the features show specific situations depending on the destination of study. Since the economic reforms and open-door policy, around 300,000 students and scholars have been studying abroad. Two important decrees have in this regard been incentives for more and more Chinese students (1984, "Guanyu zifei liuxue de zanxing guiding", decree issued by the State Council and in 1992 "Zhichi liuxue, guli huiguo, laiqu ziyou" (supporting overseas studies, encouraging the return of Chinese students, and upholding the freedom of their movement) slogan). Ninety per cent of them chose the United States, Japan, Canada or Australia as their destination (US 160,000; Japan 100,000; Canada 60,000; Australia 60,000; Germany 10,000; UK 8,000).

7 When Sir Stamford Raffles sailed up the Singapore River in 1819, he found only a small settlement of some 150 people along the banks. As the British turned Singapore into a thriving free port, immigrant settlers soon came from China, India, the Malay Peninsula and the Indonesian islands. The first to be attracted by the opportunities in Singapore were the inhabitants (mainly Malays and Chinese) of the older settlement of Malacca, then under Dutch rule. Neither the Dutch authorities' stringent measures to discourage emigration nor the threat of piracy in the Malacca Straits prevented hundreds of Malaccans from finding their way to Singapore. A major group of early immigrants were Indonesians from the neighbouring islands, among them Javanese, Bugis and Balinese (mainly traders and labourers). Racial, religious and cultural affinities with the indigenous Malays facilitated inter-marriages. The Malays and Indonesians contributed substantially to Singapore's early population growth. It was not until 1860 that the first proper census was undertaken, which indicated that the population had grown to 80,792. When Raffles landed, it was reported that there were only some 30 Chinese in Singapore, engaged in pepper and gambier planting. The establishment of British rule and new trade opportunities marked the beginning of a long period of continuous Chinese immigration. The first junk arrived from Xiamen (Amoy) in February 1821. By the mid-nineteenth century, Chinese immigration was well organized. Many immigrants started their new life in debt due to expenses incurred in making the journey. They were often ill-treated and exploited, until the indentured labour system was abolished in 1914. The early Chinese immigrants came without their womenfolk. In a new environment without their families and relatives, they had no choice but to live under the protection of various clan associations and secret society brotherhoods. As the Chinese community in Singapore eventually settled down from the 1870s, increasing

numbers of women came – encouraged by official government policies. Straits-born and many China-born immigrants settled down to permanent family life in Singapore. Several leading Chinese merchants became British subjects under a naturalization law passed in 1852.

In January 1824, the population numbered 10,683, of which 60 per cent were Malays, 31 per cent Chinese and 7 per cent Indians. By 1830, however, the Chinese had become the largest single ethnic component of the population, a demographic pattern which has continued to this day. By 1867, the Chinese community had swelled to 65 per cent of the population, numbering 55,000. The number of Chinese migrant arrivals varied from year to year – for example, 50,000 in 1880, and 250,000 in 1912. Many of them returned to China after a short stay. The Hokkiens, Teochews, Cantonese and Hakkas were the four major dialect groups. From the beginning, Hokkiens dominated Singapore's commercial life, followed closely by Teochews. The Cantonese were generally engaged in agriculture, but some were artisans, carpenters, tailors and goldsmiths.

The Indian connections with modern Singapore dated from the very first day of its foundation as a British trading post in January 1819. In addition to 120 Indian soldiers and several assistants, Naraina Pillay, an Indian trader from Penang, was also in the Raffles entourage. The liberal policies of the administration and the expanding opportunities for employment drew more Indian immigrants to Singapore from Penang, India and Sri Lanka. They sought work in the government as clerks, technicians, teachers and traders. The decision to make Singapore a penal station in 1823 brought in a few hundred Indian convicts, who were put to work on constructing government buildings, bridges and major roads. Among the buildings built by convict labour were the St Andrew's Cathedral, the Sri Mariamman Temple and the Istana. The British also brought in indentured labourers, almost exclusively from southern India, to construct essential public works such as roads, railways, bridges, canals and wharves. Abuses crept into this labour recruitment system until 1872, when the system was controlled by legislation enacted by the Indian Government. A new form of assisted immigration was introduced in 1908. The local government eventually banned the inflow of Indian indentured immigrants in 1910 due to renewed public agitation against the system. Indian immigration, however, continued until immigration controls were strictly enforced in the early 1950s. The most numerous are the southern Indians, who formed about 80 per cent of Singapore's Indian population since the early days. By the end of the nineteenth century, Singapore was one of the most cosmopolitan cities in Asia.

8 A policy of positive discrimination in favour of the indigenous Malays [eds].

9 Malaya obtained its independence in 1957 and in 1963 the Federation of Malaya merged with Singapore, Sarawak, Sabah and Brunei to form a united Malaysia [eds].

10 Dato Sen Mahathir (1935–), Malaysian politician who served as prime minister from 1981 to 2003 [eds].

11 Cf. the 80/20 Initiative:

> a national nonpartisan Political Action Committee dedicated to work for equality and justice for all Asian Americans. The basic idea is to urge Asian Pacific Americans (APAs) to form a swing bloc vote so that we become a vital political force in affecting the Presidential Election.... The name *80–20* was chosen as indicating what proportion of votes is the most effective to gain political clout. We want to unite 80% of APA voters in each Presidential election to support one presidential candidate.
>
> (From the homepage http://www.80–20initiative.net/) [eds]

Part II

REFLECTIONS

Section 1. Cultural concerns

7

CONFUCIUS THE SAGE[1]

Wang Gungwu

The civilization of China is of such extreme antiquity that probably no one is able to understand it fully; and as the philosophy of Confucius is almost as ancient, the possibility of foreigners appreciating this oriental philosophy at its true worth is very faint. Some people claim that Confucius is a prophet and a world teacher, but the spiritual and mental orientations of the Chinese people are so vastly different from those of other races that it is different to estimate the position that Confucius takes as a universal oracle. I shall not attempt to do so, but I will write about the life and teachings of Confucius concisely for the benefit of those who are yet unacquainted with him and his philosophy.

Confucius was born in 551 BC, some two thousand five hundred years ago in the third historic dynasty, the dynasty of Zhou (*c.*1100–256 BC). He was a genius in more ways than one; and his genius combined with hard work and patience made him a great philosopher. Before he was even middle-aged, he had over three thousand disciples, among whom only seventy-two were greatly devoted to their profound studies of the preservation of humanity, as taught by him.

Confucius and his disciples lived in a troubled period – an age of Revolutionary Wars. The weak-minded emperor was utterly powerless. He was indifferent to the government of his own country and left everything in a state of almost complete confusion. He probably locked himself in his palace with women and wine. The dukes and barons of vassal states within the borders of ancient Cathay, claimed to be kings, appointed their own ministers, trained their own armies and fought their own neighbours. Disorder arose like a swelling blood.

War broke out everywhere. Men were killed, cities were burnt to ashes, rivers were dyed red with blood and the mountains and plains were strewn with striking carrion. Massacres were sport and tortures were fun. China became a battlefield, a torture-chamber and a Broadway stage all rolled into one; and in the midst of the fighting and killing, the ambitious enemies who lived on the borders of Cathay watched and planned. China was in a dangerous state.

At last, Confucius decided it was about time that he injected the word "peace" into the martial minds of the people. He never wanted to participate in politics or in government for selfish purposes, but he could no longer bear to sit down and watch the extermination of his beloved fellow-countrymen, when he was sure he could help.

He and some of his disciples left home and travelled across the war-torn nation to the farthest corner and back again. He offered his services wherever he went. He told the dukes of the dangers of further wars; he spoke of the advantages of peace; he gave beautiful visions of the Utopia – the Shangri La that would grow rapidly if the dukes had kindness, rectitude, decorum, wisdom and sincerity as their cardinal virtues. But no, it was no use! The dukes wanted power and liked war, but did not want peace.

Though failure dogged his wandering footsteps, he went on trying; and hoping to be able to convince some duke, he travelled for a good number of years, before he finally gave up and returned home, nursing a mixed feeling of disappointment and disgust, trying dejectedly to console himself with the fact that he had, after all, tried.

What happened to Cathay, after that, is another story.

The teachings of Confucius are solid and wise. A good point in his moral teaching was this golden rule: "What you do not like yourself, do not extend to others." He insisted on duty to parents, respect for elders, rectitude and self-control, courtesy and moderation, loyalty to king and to friends, honesty and kindness, and decorum and sincerity. Thus the whole teaching of Confucius was in opposition to the loose spirit of his times, a protest against the immoral excesses prevalent then. He placed emphasis on democracy and also on the necessity of a true aristocracy to lead and govern the people. He felt that the rulers of the country must be elected by the people, and must rule the land entirely in the interests of the people, to secure the best means of livelihood for everybody, and to promote the happiness and prosperity of the nation, regarding themselves simply as the servants of the people.

Confucius was always careful not to criticize religion, though he was never much impressed by superstitious beliefs. But for him, the foundation of true happiness was always virtue.

Seven days before his death, at the age of seventy-two, Confucius was heard saying this:

> Great mountains must crumble and strong beams must break and the wise man will wither away like a flower. My time has come to die.

He was sustained by no hope of future life, and he betrayed no sign of apprehension. When the people heard of this, they respected him even more.

Confucius was always confident that people would have faith in his ideals. Truly so. For thousands of years the Chinese people have pinned their faith to his grand ideals. Though they have not succeeded in living up to them, the ideals are the ones which the whole world today is striving to realize. In other words, the paradise which Confucius and the people of the world sought after – "the Garden of Eden" – may be established by man himself.

Great art thou. O perfect Sage!

Note

1 Originally appeared in the *Anderson School Publication* (1946), Ipoh, Malaya.

8

LOCAL AND NATIONAL

A dialogue between tradition and modernity[1]

Wang Gungwu

You will be familiar with the idea that, despite all the talk about national politics, all politics is ultimately local. Something analogous but not about politics can be said of the idea of tradition. From the study of the ethnic Chinese in Singapore and Malaysia, I suggest that, while there are modern national traditions, living traditions are ultimately local, especially among peoples of immigrant origins.

Let me begin with a comparison of the people of Chinese descent in the two countries. Today, they both strive to be modern but have different responses towards tradition. Those in Malaysia are community-centred, with a strong sense of locality, because what is national for them does not provide them with equality. Thus, although they are modernizing themselves through outreach to other communities and to the world outside, their local identities have allowed them to keep many of their own older traditions alive. Those in Singapore, however, had the chance to take a different course and have established a clear national identity with reference to a globalizing world. They no longer live with a sense of what is local and have not had to depend on Chinese-based traditions.

The changes to their respective ways of life have created a significant difference between the Chinese in the two countries. This difference raises questions about how the two communities within their different national frameworks will develop and how either will relate to the other. It makes it important for these Chinese to understand the nature of the divergence. It is a divergence that is especially relevant to the theme of tradition and modernity in this conference. However, before I turn to that theme, I should explain what I mean by the two key words here, local and national, and also have them placed in historical context.

The word "local" here has at least two layers of meaning. Historically, it refers to the strong sense of locality, that is, identification with home district, clan and speech group, that the early Chinese immigrants brought with them from China. Today, it also describes the new sense of locality that has developed in various parts of a large country like Malaysia. For example, those who live in Johor have their own sense of locality when compared with those in Selangor and Perak, and there are significant differences among those who settled in Kelantan, or Kedah and Perlis, or Sarawak, or Sabah, or Penang. There is ample evidence to show that Chinese traditions, especially those belonging to the Little Tradition, have always been closely linked to locality, and that the local and the traditional remain connected in that way, whether these traditions are old or new.

The word "national", however, emphasizes the political good of the larger community, and places that ideal high above parochial interests. The nationalist cause, therefore, plays down the needs and traditions of the local, if not replacing them altogether with new symbols of the nation-state. The idea of the national among the overseas Chinese had begun with a new national consciousness in China. The impact of that on the British in Malaya was considerable. After the independence of Singapore and Malaysia, however, the link with the Chinese nation had to be abandoned in favour of their respective nation-building efforts. In the enlarged and complex federation of Malaysia, the hopes for a new multicultural nation turned into anxiety for the Chinese, as they became concerned that they might not have equal rights in it. Until they could identify fully with that nationhood, the many local communities have turned to their own store of tradition. This has influenced the education they have provided for their children in support of their quest for modernity. Singapore, however, is a small nation-state seeking a modern and global security in a large, unstable and variegated region. Its nation-building policy since independence in 1965 has ensured that the local and the national are not distinguishable. In any case, the idea of the national is seen by many as being shaped by the ethnic Chinese majority.

Both what is local and what is national can also be modern. By modern, I refer to those challenges to local traditions that have been brought to the region by industrial capitalism, colonialism, imperial expansion and social revolution. There is no contradiction between this modernity and both the local and the national. Local traditions can be modified to meet modern challenges. What is national, however, being directly related to the nation-state, led to the independence of former colonies and confirmed the sovereignty of such states in a globalized world. Here are multi-dimensional challenges to the nation, and the interests of the national are always expected to take precedence over the local and the traditional.

Being local

I need now to place these concepts in historical context. Early in the nineteenth century, only the word local really mattered. Whether Chinese immigrants passed through Singapore and moved on, or went directly to the Malay states of both West and East Malaysia, or came to Singapore and went no further, they all had a strong sense of the local. For some, that came from their place of origin in China; for others, it was shaped by their own local communities elsewhere in Southeast Asia. They carried with them their village and dialect group identities, and their distinctive variants of the Chinese Little Traditions from Guangdong and Fujian provinces. In time, most of them adapted themselves to local conditions in this part of the Malay world.

The one notable difference among the Chinese was that between the Baba Chinese who had settled in Malacca and its environs earlier on, and those who arrived from China during the nineteenth century. The former were localized in having distinctive traditions of their own that were developed in a Malay environment, while the latter held to the traditions of their home localities in China. The British found this difference convenient. For their purposes, it was advantageous to employ the Baba, the truly local, to help them establish their trading networks while encouraging some of the later arrivals to exercise their entrepreneurial talents, adapt to local conditions and perhaps settle down. With the establishment of the Straits Settlements, all the local-born were qualified to become Straits Chinese. When British rule was extended to the Malay peninsula, more localized Chinese were brought into the fold as protected subjects, the precursors of the Malayan Chinese the British came to recognize during the first half of the twentieth century.

Under these circumstances, being local implied holding on to certain sets of traditions. For all except the Baba, these initially meant traditions originally from China. But, by the end of the nineteenth century, some Chinese had begun to acquire other local characteristics, for example, those who lived all their lives in Kelantan, Penang and Selangor were distinguishable from those of Singapore. They might have had common dialect origins and shared basic customs, but they had to deal with a different mix of Malays and other races in each place, and they had different experiences of the increasingly powerful British authorities. At this point, although all Chinese were still traditional, they could be divided into those who were primarily China-traditional and those who could be called local-traditional. The latter, local-born for at least one generation, and skilled in a range of local ways whether Malay or British, may be considered a new kind of peranakan. They were distinguishable from the Babas by being Chinese-speaking and comfortable in either Malay or English or both. This was a group evolving most notably in Penang and

Singapore early in the twentieth century, and spreading along the West coast of the Malay peninsula. Both kinds of Chinese, whether China-oriented or local-oriented, could draw on distinctive living traditions.

The condition of being local was open to changes brought to the region by European colonial rulers. By the beginning of the twentieth century, these were characterized by the dominance of capitalist economics and the pressures of social revolution that came to be identified with modernity. The impact of such transformations, however alien they first appeared, spared no one. There was, in any case, nothing to prevent the local from seeking to be modern if they wanted to. Depending on where the Chinese were localized in British Malaya (this included Singapore) and northern Borneo, they were becoming modern at different rates. Differences of access to modernizing environments, and the relative remoteness of some localities, separated those who modernized fast from those who did so gradually. Everywhere were those who were looking to modify, update, even upgrade, their respective traditions. For example, traditional organizations based on dialect and descent groups were intertwined with newer social and occupational clubs and societies. As long as they were established for Chinese, they followed recognizably traditional practices. The one growing difference was that between those who were oriented towards changes in China and those led by Chinese-speaking peranakan whose sources of modernity were found locally or derived directly from Britain.

The chance to be national

But nation-building in the two countries, and the new power of the national, brought further changes. There came the chance for people of all races and communities to reach out for what many saw then as the ultimate in modernity, the nation-state. This was the secret of European power, the source of their economic and military success and, therefore, the critical institution for people living in colonies to regain their self-respect. The driving force was the humiliation of having been conquered and ruled by foreigners. As long as the Chinese were sojourners waiting to return to China, this was not a problem for them in their localities abroad. Their awareness of the national was raised only after the opening of the Treaty Ports of coastal China, some of which were close to the very localities from where most of them had come. It was not surprising that these Chinese were moved by the chance to overthrow the weakened empire ruled by the Manchu and replace it with a Chinese nation. Thus, new leaders like Sun Yat-sen were given a hearing. The encounter with the ideas of race and nation as promoted by China's first modern politician was a riveting one for most overseas Chinese. Over the next three decades, Sun Yat-sen and his nationalist followers began to unite the young and the frustrated and overcome their local differences, no matter where they were and what dialect group they belonged to.

It was this force that brought the concept of "Huaqiao" to the region. This was a call for the unity of all Chinese that placed the emphasis on what was national in China. It was a call that began to diminish the differences among the Chinese of various distinctive localities of British Malaya and elsewhere. The growth of the Chinese press that tied it directly to political, economic and cultural advances in Shanghai, and gave a new national perspective to developments in Guangzhou, Xiamen and Shantou, was a powerful factor for rapid change. The introduction of modern Chinese schools in all the territories quickly transplanted the idea of the national into the consciousness of local-born Chinese of all classes. Even some of the Baba who had looked up to the British, and were uneasy at the strong emotions aroused, found this national cause in China difficult to resist.

A similar national ideal awakened the Malays and other communities as well. During the 1930s, at least three competing national appeals were being made by various groups of Malays, Indians and Chinese. Despite the different sources of inspiration, the drive to nationalist mobilization was a serious barrier to local social harmony. Each set of national leaders sought support exclusively from their respective communities. The British wrestled with the implications for local order, and for the future of their authority in Malaya, until the Pacific War swept all their plans away. The Japanese further aggravated the nationalistic differences, and the war ended with three potential "nations" for the British to pacify when they returned.

The outcome is familiar to us. Intricate negotiations had led to the creation of the Federation of Malaya, with the separate colony of Singapore detached. The Malayan Emergency drove a larger wedge between the Chinese and the Malays. This wedge led eventually to the formation of Malaysia and the failure to keep Singapore in the new federation. Outside, what pressed on both Malaysia and Singapore was the ideological hot war in the region and the efforts at an experimental regionalism with ASEAN. Underlying the whole process were the different degrees of success in nation-building among the neighbours. But there was no turning back on the need to modernize by being national through the nation-state.

The most important result for the Chinese who had stayed on in Singapore and Malaysia and did not return to China was the double divide for them on both nationalist and ideological grounds. The rejection of Chinese nationality, with the abandonment of the idea of being "huaqiao" was the first step. The disillusionment with communism following the excesses of the Cultural Revolution in China was the second. Now was the time for the local Chinese in both countries to focus on the development of the national in their respective adopted countries.

Tradition and modernity

I have suggested that the sense of locality can lead people to modernize the traditions that they have inherited, but the pressure to become national presses people to subsume their local traditions to new unifying symbols. Thus, the dialogue between tradition and modernity held in Singapore and Malaysia has bifurcated over the past three decades. Today, the differences deserve to be studied closely. What lies at the heart of the two separate dialogues?

Singapore has provided the Chinese with a majority status that has been played down by the stress on a multicultural nation-state. The country is, in any case, too small to have internal localities with any meaning. State policy has diluted the appeal of most traditional organizations. It has encouraged the minimizing of residual local differences by stressing the nation-state that has been defined by external pressures on a global scale, especially in economic competition. In that context, what is national has been real for the Chinese there. The nation-building process has been one in which they have participated equally, one in which traditions associated with a Chinese national identity are no longer appropriate. Instead, what have taken precedence are measures to meet global technological challenges that entail different attitudes towards the very idea of tradition itself.

Singapore's uniform national education has, in fact, all but eliminated local traditions. The policy of emphasizing English in order to facilitate nation-building, tap available international resources and globalize the economy, has been carried through. For the Chinese, the Speak Mandarin programme has reduced the value of the original mother tongues. The use of simplified characters has been justified for its practical value, but the emotional linking with China has been carefully avoided. The approach towards tradition has been redefined as one that starts afresh to build a new set of national values, of patriotism and loyalty directed primarily to Singapore. Such a tradition might be further enriched by customs and practices from other parts of the world that have been brought in to enhance the nation's chances for survival and sustained prosperity. All these would one day add up to a distinct national tradition, but that is not a priority and not sought for its own sake. To use the language prevalent today, the challenge is to keep up with the shifting demands of a modernity that is global and ever changing, and that calls for the "creative destruction" of all that stands in the way.

In Malaysia, multiple traditions have drawn sustenance from their different community origins, and from the mix of races and cultures in separate localities. They have survived a nation-building process that has been widely seen as discriminatory. Those of Chinese descent seem to have accepted the process as a temporary stage. In the meantime, they have reserved the right to preserve as many as possible of the organizations they had inherited, and also try to cultivate some modernized but distinctive traditions of their own. They have reacted in this way because they see themselves as targets of a nation-building process that is aimed at changing them to conform to something external to their traditions. They also feel that the struggle to contribute equally to a new nationality has been postponed again and again. Also, the prospect of such equality actually appears to have dimmed over time. The promise of becoming modern through what is national has thus been replaced by one that challenges the Chinese to be modern through adapting their local community traditions to the demands and opportunities of the world outside their country.

Thus, the urge to enhance the local has taken various forms. One has been that of a truly local identity through which they could identify with wherever their new homes are actually located. I have mentioned variations among Chinese communities in localities like Johor, Selangor, Kelantan, Sarawak, Sabah and Penang. Some of the local Chinese in each place could, of course, still hope to influence national policy by making a sub-national contribution, but when they turn to political action, their activities could be seen as communal and against national interests. Whether manifested locally or communally, that is the product of an incomplete national experience that allows, if not encourages, the Chinese to hold on to the traditions they already have and seek to modernize them in their own distinctive ways. It also allows them to reach out beyond national borders to other Chinese who feel incompletely national in similar ways, and use modern communications technology to help them build overarching transnational networks. The proliferation of such networks wherever there are such Chinese may be an index of the resilience of tradition in each modernizing local community.

The two dialogues between tradition and modernity thus provide a contrast for the Chinese in both countries to learn from. They raise many important questions that deserve attention. Let me end with three of them:

1 Local community traditions have survived over long periods of time, and have ensured the vitality of the modern Chinese in Malaysia. Is there still a role for these traditions in the lives of the Chinese in Singapore?

2. The division created between the two groups had come about because the Chinese had to choose between different national frameworks. What kind of framework would make it possible for the Chinese in both countries to share their traditions again?

3 The Chinese of the two countries have adapted creatively to a variety of adverse changes largely beyond their control. How can they ensure that future generations will be able and willing to go on doing so?

The history of the Chinese in Singapore and Malaysia suggests that, when what is national is found wanting or inadequate for one reason or another, the answers to these questions may be found in the idea that traditions are ultimately local.

Note

1 Keynote address at the International Conference on "Ethnic Chinese in Singapore and Malaysia: a dialogue between tradition and modernity" (Singapore, 30 June 2001).

9

REFLECTIONS ON NETWORKS AND STRUCTURES IN ASIA[1]

Wang Gungwu

In this chapter I would like to reflect on why, in this era of globalization, we still use the idea of borders – national and regional, even continental – in our approach to scholarly work? Two good answers to this question are possible. One is that nation-states are real, that is that they are bound by their very nature to do their utmost to defend their sovereignty including, wherever possible, the protection of larger entities like the regions they belong to. In order to do this, the idea of borders, and where and when these borders can be crossed, is vital. The other is that this is also an era of *localization*, one in which small communities worry about their identity as globalization proceeds apace. The more fragile and insecure their identity, the more they will need national polities to shelter them from the global forces they cannot hide from. Both are important reasons for borders, although it is the second that has special appeal for me. Given the deep gulf between the global and the local, we need to pay attention to the nations and regions whose borders still shape the lives of people everywhere.

In this chapter I would like to spend some time discussing the process of "Asianizing Asia", with a stress on reflexivity, history and identities, drawing from my experiences and association with the Asian Studies in Asia Programme (ASIA). Those who have studied the period when large parts of Asia were under Western dominance are likely to think that this theme calls for either restoration or renewal. Both are appealing, even though they remind us of the repeated calls being made from time to time to stop or slow down the process of Westernization and return to our roots. To escape from that, a more fashionable word is conservation as used by the environmentalists. Asia's past, its great traditions, also need conserving so that they do not become extinct. Indeed, many scholars have rightly drawn attention to such a danger and I share the concern for the world not to lose the rich heritage that shaped the civilizations of Asia. For me, "Asianizing Asia" is not about the above concerns. What it stands for is the need for a new framework for Asia's future progress, one that would enable the peoples of Asia to meet the challenges of the globalizing world. To help me approach this complex subject, I shall use two metaphors, that of surface networks and that of deep structures, with the surface networks of economic and political relationships resting on deep structures of history and culture.

Let me explain how I came to use these two metaphors. It began with the debate about old and new globalization, the difference between borderless ages in earlier times when humans roamed the earth or traded and conquered across vast distances, and the kind of post-modern, post-nation-state ideas of borderless communications. One strand in the debate emphasized the tensions in the current linkages – that underneath the efforts to develop global outlooks were many anxiety-causing tensions that could threaten peace throughout the world. In that context, I argued that the tensions in globalization today are largely on the surface and that what was of greater interest were the deep structures that characterized earlier periods of globalization. I used the two metaphors to distinguish between current trends that stressed surface tensions and historical manifestations of trade and conquest relations that were dominated by deep structures of civilizational differences.

Let me give some examples of earlier efforts to study the Other in Asia. Strictly speaking, there was no such thing as "Asian Studies" before modern times. Asia is a European construct, and Asians came to think of themselves as "Asians" as opposed to Europeans only during the past century, notably when they rejected the term "Orientals" as being as derogatory as the term "natives". The question is really whether the scholars in each country inside Asia studied neighbouring countries and peoples seriously, and how that was done. There has been little attention to compare such earlier work with the "Asian Studies" we now know. Anthony Reid's recent attempt to make comparisons provides a history of the way various factors influenced Asian scholars in their study of other Asian states and societies.[2] That is a useful backdrop to what I say below, and so I shall not go over the same ground.

For all peoples, the study of the Other, of what was thought to be foreign and alien, has a long pedigree and had humble, as well as arrogant, beginnings. These stemmed mainly from two different modes of thinking. The first, common to powerful countries and empires, assumed a lofty stance of studying the outsiders who travelled in their countries and traded there, and those who might be potential threats. This mode ignored those who were irrelevant to the well-being of their polities. The second, common to small entities, adopted a respectful desire to know their neighbours, either better to defend against them or to be prepared to flatter them through imitation if and when necessary. Neighbours of equal strength, who were genuinely curious about each other without ulterior motives, appear rare. The reasons why different peoples studied one another are varied and may not all be relevant, but some early expressions of wanting to know each other are important for us today.

It has been suggested that, while scholars from each Asian country established close relations with their counterparts in Western universities, relatively few have done the same with fellow scholars in Asia itself. It is surprising how few scholars study their immediate Asian neighbours within the university context. Among the various reasons offered for this neglect were more obvious ones like shortage of money and research facilities and the historical distrust between the governments concerned. It is also true, however, that many societies respected their scholars more if they kept close links with their teachers and colleagues in the West than if they worked with other Asian colleagues, and this was no less important a factor in the weak links among scholars within Asia itself. It was also thought that this gulf was further exacerbated by the fact that, for young scholars in particular, exciting new methodologies seem to have all come from the West. There are now more scholars and students in Asia studying their neighbouring countries and peoples. Most of them are finding that trying to be self-consciously "Asian" is a new experience, especially if they had learnt to do so via the portals of European and American universities in a "Western" way. How are these scholars and students faring in the study of their neighbours as part of their "discovery" of Asia? How do they compare with their predecessors in Asia who were working in more indigenous traditions – that is, those scholars in earlier generations who studied what they considered to have been foreign, or alien, or the Other? How relevant are the methods and attitudes of the past for the scholars today? How should they go about connecting past approaches to what they are doing now? We need to reflect on how traditional scholarly constraints are still relevant.

The question I would like to begin with is: How was it in the past? At the beginning, there were a number of established structures based on cultures or civilizations mostly isolated from one another and only thinly linked across great distances. The best example would be India and China. We know the early Chinese learned writings on Indian Buddhism that included not only efforts to understand and translate religious doctrine, but also descriptions of Indian states. I discuss this further below. Then there were the many records, both official and unofficial, on Southeast Asian trading ports and kingdoms. One could also point to a sort of Chinese "Orientalism" in the surviving accounts about border peoples and tribal kingdoms. These could be found in the earliest Standard Histories (*zhengshi*), and in official reports and travellers' accounts presented to the Chinese court. They may be compared with Korean, Vietnamese and Japanese records of neighbouring peoples and polities, not least their descriptions of imperial China next door, and also the study of those traditions of Confucianism which their respective governments had adopted and modified.

The range of Arab and Persian studies of their trading partners in eastern Asia, especially those ports of India, Southeast Asia and China, was also very impressive. Significantly, unlike in China, these studies were largely by merchants and not by officials. They preceded the travels of the Polos but shared some of the sense of wonder that may be found in Marco Polo's controversial but influential work. Some of them were more accurate than Polo's and made major contributions to our knowledge of maritime conditions and early Southeast Asian history. Later on, the Mongol empire, and their successor empires in various parts of Eurasia during the thirteenth to eighteenth centuries, produced comparable studies of other areas in Asia in various languages. In Southeast Asia, too, several empires from Majapahit to Vietnam to Ayuthaya left records about some of their neighbours and some of these included details about their dependent entities. In these cases, the writings were mainly court records and officially supported annals.

Japan might have been something of an exception. The Japanese had a long history of systematically studying China for over a thousand years by using and honing the skills, which they had first adopted from China. Switching from classical China to the modern developments of the West was a decision that transformed the country. Soon after the Chinese were humiliated by the West, the Japanese took off in a different direction. As early as the middle of the nineteenth century, Japanese scholars began to turn away from Asia and model themselves on the West. Japan is now the only Asian country that has continuously studied the history of the rest of Asia, in most part using the methods and approaches of Western scholars, for more than a hundred years.

Let me now turn to China for some concrete examples of traditional ways of observing its neighbouring peoples and states. These examples were not so much works of scholarship as writings that reflect official concerns with military challenges and tributary trade. They show the limits of any scholarship done under these circumstances. The three areas that attracted serious studies are as follows:

1 Asian neighbours controlled by indigenous rulers who were Buddhists, Muslims and Hindus.
2 Asian neighbours with non-native regimes, for example, those set up by the Portuguese and Spanish, the Dutch, the English and the French.
3 New Asian neighbours after colonialism.

These studies were looking mainly at practical and useful knowledge. These writings may be further distinguished by the following characteristics:

1 A central collective pragmatism and empiricism largely emanating from the court, but which could be represented by the mandarin elites everywhere.
2 A local community pragmatism and empiricism, expressed by local elites in the coastal provinces and overland frontier regions in the northwest along the Silk Route and the borders with Vietnam and Burma.
3. An individual pragmatism and empiricism towards knowledge, especially prevalent among scholars of the richer trading cities, from the Yangtze and the Pearl River deltas.
4 A premodern scientific curiosity, notably in works by Buddhist monks like Fa Xian (424–498) and Xuan Zang (600–664), but which also may be found in private writings, notes and manuscripts.

Indigenous peoples and polities

The main characteristic of Chinese perspectives of non-Confucian peoples and kingdoms in early accounts would be the sense of cultural distance and physical remoteness. From what has survived, there is, apart from the deep and intense desire to understand the rich heritage of Buddhist scriptures, little evidence of sustained curiosity of other cultures beyond the needs of trade and security. For example, Chinese attention to the military prowesses of the peoples along their borders was obvious, and their interest in the specifics about trading goods, the variety and their sources, their quality and their value, can be clearly discerned.

Most books were written by scholar-mandarins for practical use, and these were appreciated by the imperial and local government officials who needed them. The accounts of foreign countries would carefully record notable aspects of rulership, legitimacy and religious and ritual practices, and details pertaining to the size of their capital cities and their ports. The most important points, especially when these had to do with defence needs, were incorporated in official histories, compendia and encyclopaedias. For obvious reasons, security considerations led the scholars to pay far more attention to continental power, to the tribal confederations and their kingdoms and empires to the north and west of China. In comparison, the writings on the countries across the seas to the east and south, with the possible exception of Japan, were less well served.

The most spectacular development in Chinese studies of the Other arose out of the marriage between Confucian and Buddhist political philosophy. This occurred soon after the end of the Han dynasty in the third century AD. It reached a major turning point with efforts to incorporate the first conquest dynasty in North China into the mainstream of Chinese historiography in the middle of the sixth century. I refer in particular to the history of the Toba Turks who established the Wei dynasty (386–557), exemplified by the work of Wei Shou who wrote the dynastic history, the *Wei shu*. This can be compared with the work of his contemporary, Yang Xuanzhi, who wrote the classic study of the Buddhist temples of Luoyang, the *Luoyang qielanji*.

In order to set this "alien" dynasty within the Han imperial framework laid down by the great historians Sima Qian and Ban Gu for the Western Han dynasty (206 BC–24 AD), a leap of imagination accompanied by what may be seen as clever rationalization was made. The Turkic tribal confederation was recognized as legitimate (*zhengtong*) because it displayed the readiness to fuse the Buddhist world-view on to the Chinese amalgam that was represented by Confucianism. The chapter in the *Wei shu* on Buddhism is still one of the major historical sources on the subject and the relevant chapters of the *Luoyang qielanji* are an invaluable record of early Sino-Indian relations.

The way Wei Shou wrote the *Wei Shu* is especially illuminating. It was written to reflect a fusion of two historical outlooks, but it also extended the Chinese imagination towards appreciating how the distant Other could be embedded in one's own culture. Also, it allowed the Other to be portrayed as an integral part of a kind of orthodox order, and this made it possible thereafter to deal with all foreign conquest dynasties in Standard Histories. The work aroused furious controversy when it first appeared. By the beginning of the Tang dynasty (618–907), early in the seventh century, the histories of all the northern and southern dynasties from the fourth to sixth centuries were rewritten. But it accepted as normal that the northern Turkic and other tribal dynasties could remain in tandem with the southern dynasties established by powerful Chinese families who had moved south of the Yangtze. The *Nan shi* (Southern history) and the *Bei shi* (Northern history) by Li Yanshou (612–678), another northerner, treated all the eight dynasties that had divided the empire as legitimate successors of the Han and precursors of the Tang. This was a compromise which did not satisfy the southern Chinese. They continued to speak of the legitimate Six Dynasties (*liu chao*) of Chinese imperial houses which succeeded one another in the south. The resistance continued for centuries, but the survival of much of the *Wei shu*, and its reconstruction and eventual acceptance as one of the Standard Histories after the Song dynasty, made it easier, however reluctantly, to treat future conquest dynasties in similar ways.

In addition, it was also during this period that much attention was paid to the kingdoms and ports of the South China Sea. The materials were compiled towards the end of the sixth century. The final product, the work of Yao Cha and his son Yao Silian early in the seventh century, was the *Liang shu*. Its chapter 54 is one from which much of our understanding of the nature of state and society of maritime Southeast Asia was derived. Thus, the sixth century marked a turning-point in historiography which helped to normalize the treatment of neighbouring peoples, most notably those in the north and west who were culturally distinct but who could be potential masters of China. It was certainly useful to have had the issue thrashed out before the fall of the Tang dynasty in 906 when the northern frontier regions were once again thrown open, and the foreign threat of conquest dominated the history of the next four centuries.

Almost immediately, the three tribal dynasties of Later Tang (923–936), Later Jin (936–947) and Later Han (947–950) during the Five Dynasties period (907–960) had to be accommodated. Given the sixth-century historiographical solution that was fully endorsed by the Tang dynasty during the seventh century, it is not surprising that the three "alien" dynasties were totally enmeshed and domesticated with the other two, the Liang (907–923) and the Later Zhou (950–960), both Chinese dynasties. All five were then incorporated in the official history, the *Wudai shi* (History of the Five Dynasties), compiled soon after the Song dynasty (960–1276) was founded. In short, the success of Wei Shou's work cleared the way for a new composite historiography. After him, there were no insuperable problems in recognizing as Chinese all other dynasties which displayed the same Sino-Buddhist mix in the Confucian state.

The Khitan Liao dynasty (907–1125) based largely in Manchuria harassed the Song Empire for nearly two centuries. The Jurchen Jin (1115–1234), ancestors of the later Manchus, invaded further south and destroyed the Chinese capital and any claim their rulers had to rule over China. Official records of the Song described both dynasties as deadly enemies and would not have allowed them a place in their Standard Histories. All of China came under Mongol rule in 1279. The Mongol Yuan dynasty (1206–1368) followed the Jurchen Jin in building their great capitals at Beijing, and redefined their Otherness by recognizing all three predecessors, the Song, Liao and Jin dynasties, as Chinese. As long as they embraced the main structures of the Confucian or Neo-Confucian state with its Buddhist characteristics, they all belonged together and there need be no Other among them all. This was not exactly an Indian soul in the Chinese body, nor is it evidence of a proper study of India as the Other, but the efforts at amalgamation clearly illustrate how Chinese attitudes had evolved and continued to evolve.

Han Chinese historians remained uncomfortable with these developments, but they admitted that the legitimacy of the Ming emperors needed an endorsement of the alien Mongols as rulers of the Yuan dynasty. Resigned to this, they felt they had no choice and hastily compiled the *Yuan shi* to fill the gap between the Ming and the line of descent from the Han, the Tang to the Song dynasties. In this way, when the Ming dynasty (founded 1368) fell in 1644 to another conquest dynasty which originated in the northeast lands outside the Great Wall, the Manchu Qing dynasty, mandarin historians of this last Confucian state knew what they had to do. They had little hesitation in preparing Qing records with every intention to portray the dynasty as a legitimate bearer of the heritage of Chinese civilization. Hence the readiness to prepare an Official History of the Qing (*Qing shi*) after the fall of the dynasty in 1912 by its former high mandarins, and the efforts by several modern scholars to write histories of the Qing since then.

I have offered this outline of dynastic histories to underline the basis by which attitudes and the "proper" rhetoric were evolved to allow Chinese scholars to project both the Inner and Outer manifestations of a universal empire. That is, the extension of Confucian standards and criteria intermingled with select Buddhist world-views to cover all China's peoples, whatever their cultural and political origins. This would confirm the major breakthrough in the sixth century – a mark of imaginative historiography in the handling of all issues concerning the Other.

Superficially, it would seem that Chinese approaches to the Other gave the impression that all peoples beyond China belonged to an undifferentiated benighted zone of "barbarians". On the other hand, these approaches, which gave close attention to matters touching commerce and security, were inclusive when the alien peoples who were strong enough to threaten and conquer China adopted Chinese ways, especially Chinese principles of governance. The significance of that becomes clear when we compare it with modern attempts by Chinese scholars to deal with Buddhist Mongols and Tibetans without the Confucian state.

The early acceptance of Buddhist ideas enabled the Chinese to develop a deeper relationship with neighbours like Korea, Japan, Vietnam and Nanzhao-Dali (in modern Yunnan, eventually conquered by the Mongols and incorporated into Yuan China), and also to sympathize with the kingdoms of Champa, Cambodia, Thailand and Burma. This kind of familiarity also helped the Chinese accept the Hinduized world further away. They saw that world as never having been in conflict with their own and, therefore, no effort was made to know much about Hindu India itself.

The attitudes towards the Muslim states of Central Asia were not so straightforward. Here were civilized polities which rivalled the Chinese with their cultural integrity, organizational skills, trading wealth and, where religious conviction was concerned, surpassing the Chinese in passion. The only strategy the Chinese could employ to deal with them was to do their utmost to keep them fragmented into small states and not allow large confederations to form on the Chinese northwest border. From Chinese descriptions of them, there was a respect for, if not fear of, their cultural strength and potential to threaten China itself. That mixture of fear and respect was never translated into acceptance. The various Muslim communities and kingdoms have remained very much part of the cultural Other down to the present.

For these premodern manifestations of studying the Other, there is not much to distinguish between Japanese and Chinese approaches. The main difference was that Japan had developed a stronger sense of a homogeneous identity. Japan was no threat to China except for the Wako marauding on the China coasts which was eventually quashed. The Japanese in turn did not consider China, its only large and powerful neighbour, as a real threat to their integrity, although the Mongol Yuan navy's attacks on Kyushu did leave a deep impression. For China, the only other significant neighbour, Korea, was more or less equal to Japan in power because it had the protection of China. The fact that Japan shared both Buddhism and Confucianism with China ensured that both their approaches towards their respective neighbours were similar. It was not until both the Japanese and the Chinese found the Europeans in Southeast Asia as a challenge they had to face, that they began to diverge in the way they regarded the Other. That was not to come until the nineteenth century.

Neighbours with non-native regimes in Southeast Asia

So far, the peoples who represented the Other to the Chinese were located around China and their rulers were recognized by the Chinese as native to the region. This was to change when the Europeans came east. I shall take a leap here into the sixteenth to eighteenth centuries and consider how the Chinese viewed regimes that they knew were established by people outside the region, and then also how this coloured their knowledge of the region for centuries.

First, let me turn to the Portuguese in Malacca. Their capture of what had been a useful port for Chinese officials and traders during the fifteenth century did not trouble the Chinese. Although coastal officers and provincial mandarins were aware that the Portuguese were a different kind of alien, and had come from afar with superior armed vessels, they did their best to describe them in the context of other local conflicts that had involved the Thais and the Malays. In that context, there was no emphasis on the alien origins of the Portuguese. On the contrary, an effort was made to fit them into the Chinese narrative concerning all the kingdoms of the South China Sea. Chinese writings, the clearest of which were the official documents describing their dealings with armed merchant vessels in Macau, carefully noted the trading interests that could be potentially encouraging to piratical activities. But, as long as they were confident that the Portuguese could not threaten the empire, there was no urge to know more than was necessary to keep them in place.

The kings of Portugal in the distant background were not Buddhist like those of Ayuthaya, nor Muslim like those of Bantam, Mataram and Malacca. Interest in them as Christian visitors and in their religion came only after the Jesuits under Ricci had penetrated into the interior and some of the scholar-priests had reached the imperial court in Beijing. The chapters in official writings dealing with these newcomers into the region, notably that in the standard history of the Ming dynasty, the *Ming shi* (not completed until the middle of the eighteenth century), were watchful and confident. They were not unduly curious about the differences in religion, customs and laws from not only the Chinese, but also from the native peoples in Southeast Asia. The historians who compiled the *Ming shi* did not doubt that the accounts fitted well in what was a formal historiographical structure. The structure was well established and could be flexibly adapted to include any new groups of foreigners. For example, the section on Malacca was an account of a neighbouring territory with close relations with China. The fact that Malacca was in alien (Folangji or Frankish/European) hands did not mean that it was not part of the same Asia that the Chinese always thought they already knew.

Similarities can be drawn with the Spanish in the Philippines. They were closer to home than the Portuguese in Malacca, and there was a detailed private account of Spanish activities in Zhang Xie's *Dongxi yang kao* (Studies of the eastern and western oceans). Unlike Malacca, however, there had not been a significant native polity there with close ties to the Ming throne whose defeat could have aroused greater concern. Given the lack of interest in the indigenous peoples of Luzon Island, what the Spanish did in Manila Bay offered no threat to the empire. Even when reports of the massacres of Chinese in Manila in 1603 reached the court, the response was at best perfunctory. This was consistent with the policy discouraging private overseas trade, a policy that certainly would not have stimulated much attention towards such foreigners arriving off Chinese waters.

The Dutch presence in Java and Malacca and its expansion across the Malay Archipelago did cause more worries to Chinese coastal officials, and there were several unfavourable references to the Dutch. But this was not because of what the Dutch did to the native kingdoms. The reports focused on the aggressive methods used by the Dutch against both the Portuguese and Spanish to gain access to Macau and other ports. They did not even show alarm when the Dutch captured parts of southern Taiwan (Formosa) and built their own Fort Zeelandia within a day's sailing of their own garrisons on the Fujian mainland. Nor was there any meaningful response when the Spanish killed large numbers of Chinese in Manila and the Dutch massacred even more Chinese in Batavia and elsewhere in Java.

This remained the approach towards all kingdoms and polities of Southeast Asia, native or European, until the beginning of the eighteenth century. By that time, the Ming had fallen and the Manchu Qing had consolidated their control over all coastal China. When Chen Lunjiong's *Haiguo wenjianlu* (Record of things heard and seen in the maritime countries) was completed in 1730, it was a valuable updating of what had been happening in the region. But again, much of the information was gathered by his father Chen Ang in the tradition of Song, Yuan and Ming writings about foreign kingdoms. As with Zhang Xie, whose work a century earlier caught the advance of the Spanish, Chen's work included more details of the extensive activities of the Dutch. Neither work raised Chinese consciousness about the new significance of maritime power in the control of islands close to China. In the case of the earlier study by Zhang Xie, one could explain that the weakening Ming court and its officials were too engrossed by war in the north to care. But this could not be said of the Manchu Qing when Chen Lunjiong's book appeared. They had been fully aware of the threat from the Zheng family forces in Taiwan and of the potential of the Dutch to cause trouble. Perhaps the fact that the Qing was then at the peak of their power led them to treat these accounts of the Dutch lightly. The Manchu emperor did not react even when it was reported to him that his Chinese subjects were being massacred by the Dutch East India Company officials in Batavia.

The significant point to make here is that, were it not because of Spanish and Dutch activities, there would have been even less recorded of the Muslim native lands which they had attacked and acquired. I think enough has been said not to have to repeat the same point about what reports there were about the later English and French advances towards China. The records were fuller, and tinged occasionally with warning about the motives of these new Europeans, but there was no significant change of approach. The main development, as you may expect, was that there was less and less about the native peoples and territories that had come under European control.

In 1793, the English sent Lord Macartney to China. The key mandarins in the Qing court did pay his entourage more attention. They knew that these people had established themselves in India and that they were great sailors who were moving closer to the China seas. Soon after, the French also appeared and built their first base in southern Vietnam. Yet it was not until they were well entrenched in Cochin-China and were advancing towards the China border to northern Vietnam that the alarm bells began to ring. By that time, the British had already broken through the Macau–Guangzhou front line in the First Opium war and China's fate for the next century had been determined. Chinese officials and scholars like Lin Zexu, Wei Yuan and Xu Jiyu,[3] rushed to study the Europeans beyond Asia. Whether they thought about it or not, they were past knowing about South and Southeast Asians. The uphill task of studying the West was the new challenge and, despite the strategic importance of both trade and defence for China, they had a hard time doing even that. Except for Japan in the second half of the nineteenth century, culminating in the first major study of an Asian country, the *Riben guozhi* by Huang Zunxian (1848–1905) in 1887, Chinese scholarly interest in Asia itself was further diminished during this period.

Studies of the new Asian neighbours of Southeast Asia

I shall leap over the first half of the twentieth century to look at China's fresh start in the study of Southeast Asia immediately after the end of the years of Japanese occupation. The fact that China was divided after 1949 between the Guomindang in Taiwan and the Communist Party on the mainland coincided with the rise of the new nation-states in the region. The dominance of European political ideas was significant and, for decades, there were few signs that earlier approaches to the study of Asian neighbours would be worth referring to. All countries in Asia, on the one hand, had to adapt to a world of independent and notionally equal states. On the other, two sets of overarching ideologies under the flags of capitalism and communism determined not only the conditions of international behaviour but also the parameters of scholarly study.

China was no exception. Despite the fears of colonial powers and their successor states in Asia, that Asia might return to the conditions prior to the arrival of the Europeans, and that the Chinese empire would soon dominate Southeast Asia again, this did not happen. If Chinese scholars considered this a possibility, it did not survive the realities of Cold War politics. Where Southeast Asia was concerned, the changing discourse of scholarship was deeply influenced by the shifts in power configurations.

From 1945 to the mid-1950s, with former colonial powers and the new states still uncertain which way to develop, both major parties in China continued to focus attention on wooing the loyalties of the overseas Chinese. Much of their scholarly work contained themes that highlighted these campaigns. There were a few exceptions among premodern historians, archaeologists and ethnographers, but the bulk of the books and articles by Chinese scholars published during this period on both sides of the Taiwan Straits looked at the region largely in terms of how they would respond to the struggle to be the only legitimate China.

By the late 1950s, there was a distinct shift of interest in the region as a battleground for broader issues of national goals and progressive and reactionary ideals. The strains in the communist world between China and the Soviet Union spilled over into China's relations with Vietnam and the other two states in Indochina. The attempts to create a set of neutral states in Southeast Asia tied to the non-aligned world and free from narrow Cold War issues were enfeebled when the United States was drawn into the Vietnam War. Under these conditions, scholarship increasingly took a back seat while polemical literature was widely distributed. A classic example where China was concerned can be found in the way books, periodicals and newspapers from Vietnam stopped being available to Chinese scholars in 1965 when the two governments turned away from each other. Similarly, just as Indonesia after Sukarno went through an orgy of destroying all documents, books and papers with any Chinese characters in them, all publications coming out of Indonesia were no longer available in China to all but a few trusted scholars. Indeed the Cold War affected scholarship in other ways as well. For example, in British Malaya and also in the successor states of Malaysia and Singapore, the campaign against communism was systematic and all materials pertaining to that ideology were banned. This was such a blanket ban that all books and magazines published in the People's Republic of China were prohibited, even including their editions of the classics and scholarly books about premodern Chinese history, society and culture. In turn, materials from outside China were sieved carefully and, if translated, were normally made available only to a limited circle of scholars. It is little wonder that Chinese studies of their neighbours were severely limited and largely of no scholarly value.

Finally, with the opening of China under Deng Xiaoping and the end of the Cold War, a new phase of scholarship lies before us. Will Chinese scholarship during this new phase be mainly a resumption of the pre-Cold war phase? For example, will it return to a concern for the Chinese communities in the region and will it take up again the aspirations of the new nation-states whose sovereignty will be respected? Or will there be a larger canvas for normalization in which the pre-European relationships and attitudes between Chinese scholars and the peoples of the region will be restored?

Conclusions

The tradition of Chinese scholarship about the Other was based on two major premises. One was an inclusivist approach, accepting into the fold all those who had helped, or could help, to shape the destiny of China. Where they could not do that and were therefore irrelevant to China's needs, attention paid to them was minimal. This was essentially a pragmatic approach. If there was genuine curiosity about the Other, it was not encouraged and had no impact on China's world view.

The other premise followed from the first. There were hierarchies of the Other, those closer and worthy of study and those which were not. This was balanced by a more abstract Ideal world in which China's place should be appreciated by all those outside and therefore it is necessary for China, in rhetorical terms at least, to treat all foreign and alien entities equally, without favouring one over another. The sentiment is captured by the expression, treat with impartiality or *yishi tongren*.

But from the three areas of cross-cultural historiography surveyed in this chapter, I am led back to the traditions of useful and practical knowledge, as seen in:

1 A central collective pragmatism.
2 A local collective pragmatism.

3 Individual empirical studies, where individuals still seek useful and practical knowledge to augment the first two collective efforts.
4 Scientific curiosity was less evident before the nineteenth century, but early examples of private writings have now blossomed into modern scholarship. This had developed steadily in the twentieth century on the mainland before 1949, and evolved further for several decades since in Hong Kong and Taiwan. From the late 1970s, such curiosity has manifested itself strongly on the mainland as well.

In chronological terms, the developments of the twentieth century are marked by the end of the ideology of inclusivism, accompanied by interim experiments with scientific curiosity, but where mainstream scholarship was still dominated by a highly pragmatic approach. After 1949, a new ideological framework was introduced into China that was inclusivist, at least by using the rhetoric of new internationalism. There was, however, also a residual nationalist framework which denied the assumptions of such inclusivism. Alongside these new developments may be seen outbreaks of individual curiosity which received considerable outside encouragement from models of modern scholarship. Given the parallel influences from all three backgrounds, what is the future of cross-cultural historiography in China? How might it change and within what limits? I shall not speculate further here. I simply suggest that we do not neglect past practices, as they will continue to play a role in determining the directions of future change.

Notes

1 This chapter is a revised version of the keynote lecture given by the author at the Asian Studies in Asia (ASIA) Fellows Program, First Annual Conference in Bangkok on 16 May 2001. It was first published in Melissa Curley and Hong Liu, eds, *China and Southeast Asia: Changing Socio-Cultural Interactions* (Hong Kong: Centre of Asian Studies, Hong Kong University, 2002), pp. 13–26.
2 Tony Reid, "Studying 'Asia' in Asia", *Asian Studies Review* (Vol. 23, No. 2, 1999), pp. 141–151.
3 Wei Yuan (1794–1857), historian; Xu Jiyu (1793–1873), scholar and statesman [eds].

10

CHINESE POLITICAL CULTURE AND SCHOLARSHIP ABOUT THE MALAY WORLD[1]

Wang Gungwu

It is often forgotten that China and the Malay world have had relations with each other for close to 2,000 years. For most of that time, relations were mainly commercial, but there have been radical changes in more recent times. If I were to sum up what the central fact is about China and the Malay world, I would say, at least 1,500 years of good if erratic trading relations, followed by a century of distrust, and distance.

Why was this so? How much was it due to the changes in political culture for both China and the Malay world? How was this reflected in Chinese scholarship? My focus here shall be on the Chinese perspective as I try to relate their scholarship about the Malay world to changes in political culture both in China and in the various Malay polities.

I shall be very brief about the first 1,500 years.

Trading relations between China and the Malay world was the dominant development of the relationship for 15 centuries. It began with China and the Malay world feeling their way slowly to expand maritime links, with the ports on both sides enriched steadily by expanding populations, notably those of Guangdong and Java-Sumatra. By the ninth century, those of eastern China up to the Yangzi delta were also being drawn into the trade.[2] The rapid expansion of Fujian ports as major centres of the trade with the Malay world was the chief feature of the history of the next five centuries, from the tenth century to the fourteenth century. By the thirteenth century, the port of Quanzhou, or Marco Polo's Zaiton, had become a major international commercial port.[3]

At the beginning, neither the Chinese nor the Malays were the most active in the regional trade. Very early on, the trade had become intra-continental, as Indian and Persian merchants, who had known of China through the ancient overland silk route, discovered the sea route to China. Similarly, the Chinese and the Malays also responded to this intra-continental trade and looked westwards beyond the Sunda and Malacca straits. The Chinese were also familiar with Persian and Indian goods and now sought them by sea.[4] In addition, the Chinese converted to Buddhism about the same time that similar Hindu-Buddhist ideas and practices reached the Malay world.[5] And this provided another layer in the Sino-Malay relationship. When Perso-Arab traders brought the Islamic faith to China after the seventh century, yet another connection was made. For centuries, between the ninth and the fourteenth centuries, Muslims of Arab, Persian, Indian and Chinese origins contributed to the spread of Islam in the Malay world and provided another layer of relationships between China and the Malay world.[6]

I have so far used the phrase "the Malay world", inclusively and rather anachronistically. The Chinese did not have the phrase "the Malay world". I have taken the modern usage here and use the Malay world to refer to the early archipelago peoples who spoke Austronesian languages related to early Malay. They had come south from the mainland either by land down the Malay peninsula, or by sea to the Malay archipelago, some then crossing to the Indo-China mainland and others to the Malay peninsula, and yet others across the Indian Ocean to Madagascar. The Chinese records, of course, made no distinction among the peoples of the seas between the Pacific and Indian Oceans; for example, they did not distinguish between "Java" peoples and "Malay" peoples until after the end of the Malacca-Johor empires. Here the key was the use of the Melayu language as a lingua franca throughout the archipelago after the Malacca Empire. Thereafter, "Malay" began to be used mainly to refer to speakers of Melayu. For my purposes, I will treat the whole of the Malay Archipelago as being the Malay world.[7]

The first thousand years saw the growth of a regional maritime trade centred on the South China Sea, with traders mainly from South and West Asia, with some Southeast Asian participation, but it is not clear how many of those from the region could be called Malay peoples. The next six centuries, from the fourteenth to the end of the nineteenth century, saw two phases. The first was when the Chinese developed the technology to send large naval expeditions out to the Indian Ocean. But they saw this as so abnormal that they withdrew altogether and never again intervened in maritime affairs beyond the shores of China itself.[8]

The second phase began soon after the Europeans arrived during the sixteenth century. This began in the Malay world with the fall of Malacca. Steadily but surely, the several naval European powers came to dominate all Southeast and East Asian waters. There was a brief and exceptional period, from about 1640s to 1683, when the Zheng family (Koxinga, his father and his son) in Fujian and Taiwan tried to challenge Western efforts to monopolize the trade of the region. As we know, this was brought to an end by the Manchu Qing conquest of Taiwan.[9]

Underlying these changes was a distinctive political culture. It erected a defensive institution often represented through a tributary system that concentrated on keeping the Chinese people inside, and controlling all relations with non-Chinese peoples, including traders.[10] But there was no question of the state assisting Chinese traders against their foreign competitors. As a result, when the more intrepid Chinese traders did venture forth, they had to fend for themselves against the new naval power of the Europeans. They then found that the Malay polities were pushed out of the lucrative trading centres. When their own efforts to compete with, or resist, that European power invariably ended in their being massacred, as happened several times in Manila and, in 1740, in Batavia, the Chinese traders who survived compromised, as they were wont to do, with those who held power.[11] The historical relationship they had with the Malay elites was pushed away from the major centres to the peripheries. Eventually, even that relationship was eroded away altogether as modern state systems replaced the older riverine kingdoms. Encountering a new economic system, Chinese workers were recruited in large numbers in many parts of the Malay world. This meant that the Chinese not only contributed to the weakening of their former Malay trading partners but also competed directly with Malays at other levels for livelihood. By the end of the nineteenth century, both Chinese and Malays found themselves in a new era, one of distrust and distance.

How were all these developments reflected in Chinese scholarship about the Malay world? The surviving examples we have suggest that there had been Chinese curiosity about that world from the third century AD, especially during the Buddhist pilgrims' period from the fifth to the eighth century. It was also a period when the trade in a variety of incense, spices and medicinal drugs was thriving. Indeed, it is through the Chinese records that we have a chronological outline of the early history of the Malay world. The best examples of such writings are the laconic accounts that have been preserved in the Standard Histories of each dynasty, especially the section on "foreign countries". But there have also been accounts by Buddhist pilgrims or biographies of monks who had set forth to India and travelled through the Malay Archipelago. In addition, searching through both the private and public encyclopaedic collections of the Tang and Song dynasties, it is possible to find intriguing fragments of information about flora and fauna, peoples and customs that confirm the interest of many officials who had served in South China. By the standards of the time, they represented scholarship, not so much of deep inquiry as of intellectual curiosity.[12]

New knowledge continued to be added from time to time during the Song and Yuan dynasties (tenth to fourteenth centuries), but only a few well-known works have survived. We do not know how many other writings at a more popular level, for example, handbooks and guides for maritime trade, maps of the South China Sea routes, were produced. We are left with the writings of officials or former officials that were useful for those who had to deal with the coastal trade.[13] The Ming and early Qing dynasties (1368–1644, 1644–1800) were periods of ever-greater pragmatism. Unless the subject was strategically of interest to the mandarin officials, or of practical value to merchants, little real curiosity was encouraged. The only exceptions were the books that came out of the expeditions of Zheng He and two original works about Hokkien merchants in the Malay world. The best of them were the writings of Ma Huan and others about the Zheng He expeditions.[14] I should also mention Zhang Xie's "Study of the Eastern and Western Oceans" (*Dongxi yangkao*) in the seventeenth century, which marks the first glimpse of Chinese awareness of the peoples later called Malay who could be distinguished from the "Jawa" peoples.[15] The other work, written in the eighteenth century, is Chen Lunjiong's "Record of What was Heard and Seen in Maritime Countries" (*Haiguo wenjianlu*) which is the first Chinese work to identify the Melayu speakers that the Chinese encountered all over the archipelago.[16] The latter was followed by the enlightening records kept by Wang Dahai about Java and neighbouring islands and the work of Xie Qinggao who travelled widely throughout the region; they both had their own ideas as to who were Malay and who were not.[17]

The works mentioned have all added to our knowledge of the Malay world in the broadest sense. Strictly speaking, they were not so much works of scholarship as writings renowned for the information they provided for later scholars. Some did stimulate some scholarly writings, but the work of the scholars tended to be very bookish and rarely included any insights into the Malay world itself.[18] The most common failing is the uncritical inclusion of earlier texts taken out of context and often not consistent with other known writings. As one might expect, this often led to confused accounts that tended to be even more misleading when later scholars went on copying them into their writings, usually without much sense of time or context. There are too many such works to list here, as officials collected information about maritime ports and kingdoms that they thought would be relevant for policy makers at the time. One has to conclude that most of the writings before 1900, for all their value as sources of information, showed little real interest or understanding of Malay culture and society. Unlike the attitudes of the practical merchants who mingled freely among the Malay peoples all over the archipelago, much of the writings that were preserved and widely quoted increasingly reflected the values of the haughty political culture of a relatively closed civilization.

Changes in political culture

From about 1900, the age of distrust and distance for Chinese and Malays may be said to have begun. The reasons are indeed complex, and I shall try to sum them up by focusing on the changes in political culture.

First, the arrival of the Europeans brought new challenges to the long-standing political relationships of the Malay world. As Malay and other traders lost control of the maritime trade, the Chinese were forced to adapt to the new powers. The more they were useful to the Europeans, the more they earned the distrust of Malay trading elites. In Chinese writings of this period, there is no evidence that there was any awareness of the potential for this distrust between Chinese traders and their erstwhile Malay elite friends. Between Zhang Xie in the seventeenth century and Chen Lunjiong in the eighteenth century, one could discern a growing acceptance that European power in the Malay world was strong, but it was not yet so dominant that it could not be resisted. Opportunistic alliances with Malay elites wherever and whenever necessary were still viable options. The more scholarly works of mandarins reporting on European activities, and especially on their advances along the China coasts, did not see any significance in the steady weakening of Malay economic and political power. If anything, the eighteenth century was a period of Manchu glory in bringing peace and prosperity to China, and all the writings of that time reflected the complacency of the imperial court. Where the Malay world was concerned, it can only be said that indifference reigned and Qing China saw no shadow on the horizon that could threaten its power. Even if Chinese scholars had evidence of Malay distrust of the Chinese living among them, that would have been a matter of concern to the Chinese ruling classes.[19]

Second, during the nineteenth century, more and more Chinese traders and workers were brought to the Malay world. The more they came, the deeper they penetrated into the economy and the more they affected the rural lives of ordinary Malay people. Although these Chinese made contributions to economic growth, they were often seen or represented as having displaced the Malays from their rights and their opportunities. This was clearly a shift in political relationships touching on the work and livelihood of larger numbers of Chinese and Malays, and, not surprisingly, it was another source of distrust. Chinese writings of this period, including the massive work of Wei Yuan published after the First Anglo-Chinese "Opium" War, the *Haiguo tuzhi*, were understandably not sensitive to the possible consequences of such large movements of Chinese working people. In fact, the really large emigrations came after his work was published in 1850.[20] What was soon noticed, by the mandarins who began to travel to the Malay world, was the fact that so many of the Chinese were doing so well in the European colonies despite the lack of their recognition and protection by China. These mandarins therefore recommended that policies be changed to give the overseas Chinese official status and encourage them to invest their fortunes in China itself. That set the tone of official writings before the rise of modern nationalism, and was reflected in the new emerging scholarship, notably in the writings of Huang Zunxian who was Consul General to the Straits Settlements. In addition, there was the influence of Kang Youwei[21] who stayed in Malaya and travelled in Java.[22] Later, the popular essays of Liang Qichao[23] opened up the question of revising Chinese historical writings to include the heroic activities of the Chinese pioneers in the Malay world, including a revaluation of the achievements of Admiral Zheng He. Liang was a younger contemporary of Sun Yat-sen and echoed Sun's nationalism. Between the two of them, they pointed to a fundamental change in political culture to that of nationalism that was to envelop Chinese everywhere for the next two generations. This inevitably affected new scholarly writings about the Malay world.[24] There were local Chinese, especially among the Peranakan in Java, who wanted no part of this nationalism but wrote in Malay to introduce Chinese stories, and to record thoughts about their own lives among Malay peoples. But their writings were totally unknown in China and have been neglected by the Chinese who were nationalistic. Their writings are better appreciated today in China. Together with the research about these Peranakan writings by Western scholars like Claudine Salmon, the books and articles by scholars of Chinese origin writing in the Malay world itself have become more accessible in China.[25]

The third point to make is that the changes in political culture were profound. In response to European incursions into China and new ideals of the modern nation-state, many Chinese became openly nationalistic, including those sojourning abroad. The Malay world experienced this new Chinese nationalism and, in turn, responded to the West by developing their own nationalism, first in the Philippines, then in the Netherlands East Indies and also in some parts of British Malaya. At the beginning, this was primarily directed against European dominance, but the underlying distrust of the Chinese and their new nationalism led to the growth of discriminatory actions against Chinese merchants and workers alike. To some extent, these were influenced by the European reactions against the overseas Chinese nationalism found in their colonies. These had led to arrests and deportations, and various forms of discrimination that the local nationalists began to emulate, and they continued to do so even after the Europeans had left.[26]

Both the growth of Chinese nationalism and the reactions against the Chinese were reflected in the Chinese scholarship of the time. On the positive side, books and articles were produced to demonstrate the achievements in Chinese commerce. More defensively, writings underlined the loyalty of the Huaqiao to the Chinese motherland, and encouraged the introduction of Chinese education along nationalist lines.[27] Textbooks were published to stop the process of assimilation that many Chinese feared would be the fate of their descendants. These fears were, on the whole, more about becoming stooges of Western penetration into China than about acceptance of local Malay cultures. But, more often indirectly than directly, the textbooks slighted the cultures of the indigenous Malay peoples and did not encourage any understanding of the people among whom most Chinese lived. This was because the nationalist feelings that were fermented at the time were mainly addressed to the salvation of China against both Western and Japanese ambitions. This concern for China's own security against powerful enemies left most of the scholars with little time to consider the interests of indigenous peoples or those of the overseas Chinese themselves. There were a few exceptions among a younger generation of scholars trained in Nanjing, Shanghai and Xiamen who turned their attention to indigenous culture and society in the Malay world, but they did not become influential until after 1945. Men like Zhang Liqian, Yao Nan and Hsu Yun-ts'iao, and later others like Han Zhenhua and Chen Xujing,[28] are representatives of those who grew increasingly curious about the Malay world itself.[29] Under the political conditions of the inter-war years, they could have done little to stem the growing distrust between Chinese and Malays. And, in the revolutionary fervour in China after 1949 and before 1976, their voices were, in any case, rarely heard. Those scholars who returned to China from the Malay world, notably from Indonesia and Malaysia, did their part to educate the Chinese in China but again, political concerns invariably took precedence over what they had to say.[30]

Fourth, events after the Second World War moved very rapidly for new kinds of political culture to dominate developments in both China and the Malay world. What had begun as anti-colonial and anti-imperialist movements by different groups of political elites soon became a struggle between fervent nationalists on the one hand, and various types of socialists and communists on the other. The divisions were sharpened by the Cold War in Asia and this affected both China and the Malay world. The main divisions among the Chinese were those between Guomindang and Communist parties. In the Malay world, the main divide was that between a Sukarno-led Indonesia alienated from Malaysia and Philippines, and a Suharto-led Indonesia that helped in the establishment of anti-Communist regional organization, ASEAN. These divisions heightened the sense of distrust. Chinese were not only trade competitors in the Malay world, perceived to have their own alien nationalist loyalties, but could also be seen as communists or their sympathizers who supported a godless threat to nation-building by the local nationalist elites. They were seen as offering alternative political cultures to the insecure beginnings of Malay political power. Thus it was easy to justify discriminatory policies against the Chinese that sometimes descended into racist acts.[31]

Again, it is not surprising that Chinese scholarship about the Malay world was affected by the rival political cultures of nationalism and communism. The Guomindang scholars continued to woo the Chinese to support its anti-Communist cause and thus tried to keep alive an older Chinese nationalism. The scholars in the People's Republic of China began by trying to counter-woo the same Chinese in the name of a newer and more progressive patriotism. For at least two decades, both sides in their own ways appealed to the Chinese in the Malay world to identify with the cause of China. In this way, a gap developed between scholars in China and Taiwan, and those among the ethnic Chinese citizens of the three major Malay polities (Indonesia, Malaysia and the Philippines). These ethnic Chinese had begun to identify entirely with local developments and write with greater understanding of a wide range of Malay values and sensitivities. Their efforts, however, were often dwarfed in the eyes of the Malay world leaders by the official positions of the People's Republic of China and Taiwan as reflected in the scholarly writings published there. As a result, the local Chinese efforts did not greatly diminish the distrust and discrimination that had become habitual among many of the local politicians and officials.[32]

More seriously, and this is the fifth point I wish to make, the above developments have had a cumulative impact that has gone beyond distrust. Over the years, local political demands in each of the Malay polities, in their different ways, seem to have aggravated the growing distance between the Malay peoples and those Chinese who are now settled in the Malay world. External politics had increased the distance between Chinese and Malays since the end of the Second World War. That distance has now become internalized under conditions of continued distrust and discrimination. This has led to other manifestations of distance. Most notable is the cultural distance that has expanded with different attitudes towards the secularized modernity that is being offered in the new nation-states. The Chinese, on the whole, embraced this secular faith in science and business with enthusiasm. The Malay world is divided between those who face the challenge with confidence and those who fear the consequences of secularism to their traditional way of life, especially that of Islam.[33] This difference in political culture has become particularly marked in recent years. If the efforts today at mutual understanding within the Malay world between Chinese and Malays do not succeed, it may well make future relations between China and the Malay world increasingly difficult. On the other hand, if China and its scholars studying the Malay world today were to show greater understanding of Malay society and culture, it may ease the position of Chinese who have settled in that culture and society.

It is too early to speculate about the future influence of current scholarship by the Chinese in China. As for the work by loyal citizens of Chinese descent, whether from Indonesia, Malaysia, Brunei or the Philippines, many of them have developed a fine sense of the fears and aspirations of their respective countries. There is little doubt that much more effort is needed before scholars in China and those of the Malay world can dispel the distrust and distance that have grown between the peoples. Also, it is not up to them alone. The world of scholarship is more open now and many scholars from both within and outside the region are making their contributions to the underlying relationship. A broader collaboration among more and more scholars, whatever their origins, to throw light on the problems that have arisen could help improve future China-Malay world relations.[34] But, for that to happen, there must be the recognition that scholars who merely reflect current political demands can do little to ease distrust and distance. There must be real efforts to get at the facts beyond the propaganda needs of the time, and genuine efforts to clarify issues and understand the differences in political cultures. The greatest danger here is not discrimination against any group of people, but discrimination against scholars who are at pains to set out the truth as they know it. When enough scholars are allowed to explore the emerging new realities, and to do so honestly and thoroughly, that may help to dispel distrust and narrow the cultural distance.

Let me end by going back to what I have called the central fact about China and the Malay world. I repeat it here: 1,500 years of trading relations followed by a century of distrust and distance. Can we put that last century behind us, and regard it as an aberration? Or, is the distrust and distance a permanent change in the relationship arising from the changes in modern political cultures? The world has changed so much now. Perhaps we can hope that, under new terms and conditions, China and the Malay world will find a fresh start to re-build a lasting and stable relationship.

Notes

[It is not possible to do justice to all the relevant writings in this brief outline of the subject. Notes will be limited to those that illustrate the quality and limits of Chinese scholarship pertaining to the Malay world.]

1 First published in Ding Choo Ming (ed.) *Chinese Scholarship on the Malay World: A Revaluation of a Scholarly Tradition*, Singapore: Eastern Universities Press, forthcoming. Reprinted with permission of Times Publishing Group.

2 Some of the most relevant examples of Chinese scholarship on Southeast Asia have been introduced in Wang Gungwu, “Southeast Asian Huaqiao in Chinese History-writing”, *Journal of Southeast Asian Studies*, vol. 12, no. 1, 1981 (collected in *China and the Chinese Overseas*, Singapore: Times Academic Press, 1991, pp. 22–40); and “Two Perspectives of Southeast Asian Studies: Singapore and China”, in Henk Schulte Nordholt, Remco Rabin and Paul Kratoska, eds, *Discovering Southeast Asia: Genealogies, Concepts, Comparisons, and Prospects*, Amsterdam: Koninklijk Instituut voor Taal-, Land- en Volkenkunde, 2003. Where the Malay world is con-

cerned, an outline of relations before the tenth century is found in Wang Gungwu, *The Nanhai Trade: The Early History of Chinese Trade in the South China Sea*, revised edition, Singapore: Times Academic Press, 1998 (first published in *Journal of the Malayan Branch of the Royal Asiatic Society*, Monograph Issue, June, 1958). This has a bibliographic note on some of the sources about that world before and after the Tang dynasty (618–907). That history was part of a larger story of Chinese trading relations with maritime Southeast Asia, but it was clear very early on that, in the Malay world, the regular ports for foreign shipping trading between Indian, Persia and West Asia and the port cities of China were those in Java-Sumatra, the Malay Peninsula, and parts of northern and western Borneo.

3 Quanzhou international seminar on China and the Maritime silk route organization committee, *China and the Maritime Silk Route: UNESCO Quanzhou International Seminar on China and the Maritime Silk Route* (Volume II), Fuzhou: People's Publishing, 1994; Billy K. L. So, *Prosperity, Region and Institutions in Maritime China: The South Fujian Pattern, 946–1368*, Cambridge, Mass.: Harvard University Asia Centre and Harvard University Press, 2000; and Angela Schottenhammer, ed., *The Emporium of the World: Maritime Quanzhou, 1000–1400*, Leiden: Brill, 2001. These studies discuss the literature on the place of Quanzhou in the evolution of China's relations with maritime Southeast Asia, notably the growing trade with the Muslim Arab world.

4 For comparison purposes, I should mention some early work on comparable ocean-going trade from the Indian Ocean: Hadi Hassan, *Persian Navigation*, London: Methuen, 1928, and R. C. Majumdar, *Hindu Colonies in the Far East*, Calcutta: General printers and publishers limited, 1944 (second revised edition published by Firma K. L. Mukhopadhyaya, 1963). Other pioneering studies that did not just cover maritime links but illustrated the range of trading goods between China and western Asia were those of Berthold Laufer, *Sino-Iranica: Chinese Contributions to the History of Civilization in Ancient Iran*, Chicago: Field Museum of Natural History Anthropological Series, vol. 15, no. 3, 1919 (New York: Kraus reprint edition, 1967), and the research that was eventually synthesized in Georges Coedes, *Les États Hindouise d'Indochine et d'Indonesie, Histoire de Monde*, tome VIII, Paris, 1948. Another valuable introduction to this field was George F. Hourani, *Arab Seafaring in the Indian Ocean in Ancient and Early Medieval Times*, Princeton: Princeton University Press, 1951. A more recent collection by G. R. Tibbetts, *A Study of the Arabic Texts Containing Material on Southeast Asia*, Leiden: Brill, 1979, provides a useful comparison with the Chinese sources available.

5 The larger story has been told in Erik Zurcher, *The Buddhist Conquest of China: The Spread and Adaptation of Buddhism in Early Medieval China*, two volumes, Leiden: E. J. Brill, 1959. Representative Buddhist sources that touch on religious contacts between China and the Malay world are Fa Xian, *Foguo ji: Travels of Fah-Hian and Sung-Yun, Buddhist Pilgrims from China to India (400 AD and 518 AD)*, translated from Chinese by Samuel Beal, London: Trubner and Co., 1869, and Yijing (I Tsing), *A Record of the Buddhist Religion in India and the Malay Archipelago (AD 671–895)*, translated by J. Takakusu, Oxford: The Clarendon Press, 1895. These can be compared with the material examined in Sukumar Sengupta's *Buddhism in South-east Asia, Mainly Based on Epigraphic Sources*, Calcutta: Atisha Memorial Society, 1994.

6 There is still a great deal we do not know about the early history of Sino-Muslim connections in Southeast Asia. A useful start was provided by S. Q. Fatimi in his *Islam Comes to Malaysia*, edited by Shirle Gordon, Singapore: Malaysian Sociological Research Institute, 1963. For Java, the pioneer efforts by H. J. de Graaf and Th. G. Th. Pigeaud to penetrate the mysteries of this subject are now available thanks to Merle C. Ricklefs, see *Chinese Muslims in Java in the*

15th and 16th Centuries: The Malay Annals of Semarang and Cerbon, Melbourne: Monash Papers on Southeast Asia, no. 12, 1984. Another view of this obscure story may be found in Slametmuljana, *A Story of Majapahit*, Singapore: Singapore University Press, 1976, pp. 201–249. These have to be set beside alternative views that stress the Western roots of Islamization and leave out the role of Chinese Muslims. A recent summary of the main debates about Islamization in Southeast Asia may be found in Anthony Reid, *Charting the Shape of Early Modern Southeast Asia*, Singapore: Institute of Southeast Asian Studies, 2000, pp. 15–38.

7 This applies to all Chinese sources before the seventeenth century. I discuss the emergence of the name Melayu in Wang Gungwu, "The Melayu in *Hai-kuo Wen-chien Lu*" (1963), reprinted in *Only Connect: Sino-Malay Encounters*, Singapore: Times Academic Press, 2002, pp. 37–49. Concerning the spread of the maritime "Malay" peoples for the thousand years before that, see Kenneth R. Hall, *Maritime Trade and State Development in Early Southeast Asia*, Honolulu: University of Hawaii Press, 1985. Fuller studies that examine the rise of Malay polities by skilful use of fragmentary Chinese sources are O. W. Wolters, *Early Indonesian Commerce: A Study of the Origins of Srivijaya*, Ithaca, NY: Cornell University Press, 1967, and *The Fall of Srivijaya in Malay History*, Kuala Lumpur: Oxford University Press, 1970.

8 On the Zheng He voyages of 1405–1433, the literature is now vast. The key documents in Chinese pertaining to Zheng He himself are found in Zheng Hesheng and Zheng Yijun, eds, *Zheng He xiaxiyang ziliao huibian*, in three volumes, Jinan: Qilu Shushe, 1980–1983. Good introductions that include notes on the Chinese sources may be found in Denis Twitchett and Frederick W. Mote, eds, *The Cambridge History of China*, Vol. 7, and *The Ming Dynasty, 1368–1644*, parts 1 and 2, Cambridge: Cambridge University Press, 1988 and 1998; see essays in part 1 by Chan Hok-lam, pp. 205–305, 790–796, and Wolfgang Franke, pp. 726–782; and in part 2, Wang Gungwu, "Ming Foreign Relations: Southeast Asia", pp. 301–332, 992–995. Another useful reference is Roderich Ptak, *China and the Asian Seas: Trade, Travel, and Visions of the Others (1400–1750)*, Brookfield, Vt.: Ashgate, 1998, especially the section on "Early Ming Trade and Cheng Ho's Travels". A readable introduction to the subject may be found in Louise Levathes, *When China Ruled the Seas: The Treasure Fleet of the Dragon Throne, 1405–1433*, New York: Simon and Schuster, 1994.

9 Chinese studies of the three generations of the Zheng family tend to concentrate on what they did to either the Ming or the Qing dynastic houses, or to the Dutch in Taiwan, and less on the trading organization that challenged Western maritime power in East Asia and the Malay world. Notable studies in Chinese are the following: Xu Zaiquan and Wang Weiming, *Zheng Chenggong yanjiu* (Research on Zheng Chenggong), Beijing: Chinese Academy of Social Sciences Press, 1999; Xiamen daxue lishixi bian, *Zheng Chenggong yanjiu lunwen xuan* (Selected essays on Zheng Chenggong), Fuzhou: Fujian renmin chubanshe, 1982. Two studies in European languages provide useful background to Koxinga's activities, but deal little with his impact on Southeast Asia: Ralph C. Croizier, *Koxinga and Chinese Nationalism: History, Myth, and the Hero*, Cambridge: East Asian Research Center, Harvard University, distributed by Harvard University Press, 1977; Patrizia Carioti, *Zheng Chenggong* (in Italian), Naples: Department of Asian Studies, The Oriental Institute, 1995.

10 The most useful study of China's tributary system is still John K. Fairbank, ed., *The Chinese World Order*, Cambridge, Mass.: Harvard University Press, 1968. Most of the essays concern the Ming and Qing periods, but the origins of the system are explored in essays by Fairbank, Yang Lien-sheng and Benjamin I. Schwartz,

pp. 1–33; 276–288. For how the system worked in early relations with Southeast Asia, see Wang, *Nanhai Trade*, pp. 116–117.

11 There were several massacres in the Manila area. Chen Ching-ho, *The Chinese Community in 16th Century Philippines*, East Asia Cultural Studies Series no. 12, Tokyo: Center for East Asia Culture Studies, 1968 sets the background clearly. Details are found in several of the essays collected in Alfonso Felix, Jr, ed., *The Chinese in the Philippines*, Vol. 1: 1570–1770, Manila: Solidaridad Publishing House, 1969. The massacre in Batavia took place in 1740, see J. Th. Vermeulen, *De Chineezen te Batavia en de Troebelen van 1740* (The Chinese in Batavia and the troubles of 1740), translated into Chinese by Tan Yeok Seong in *Nanyang xuebao* and reprinted as *Hongxi canan benmo* in Jakarta in 1962.

12 The first twenty-two *zhengshi* (standard histories) have provided key, albeit brief, accounts of various parts of the Malay world for 1,500 years from the Han dynasty to the Ming dynasty. The earliest examples of the curiosity of officials sent to Southeast Asia date back to the third century AD. They do not directly describe the Malay world, but are largely about Funan, a coastal kingdom in southern Vietnam-Cambodia that supported a key trading centre for trade with the Malay Archipelago. I refer to lost works like Zhu Ying's *Funan yiwuzhi* and Kang Tai's *Wushi waiguozhi*. Fragments of both works are preserved in later encyclopaedic collections like the *Yiwenleiju* (seventh century, compiled by Ouyang Xun), Shanghai: Shanghai guji chubanshe, 1982; the *Taiping yulan* (tenth century, compiled by Li Fang and others), Beijing: Zhonghua, 1963; and the *Taiping guangji* (tenth century, compiled by Li Fang and others), Beijing: Zhonghua, 1961. For the Buddhist records, see note 5 above.

13 Of these, three have been greatly appreciated by later scholars and officials. They each contained notes on areas that were clearly part of the Malay world, but there was a common bias towards the Indian Ocean origins of the ocean-going trade. For the Song dynasty, there are brief references in Zhou Qufei, *Lingwai daida*, Shanghai: Far East Publishing, 1996 (study in German by Almut Netolizky published as Munich East Asian Studies, volume 21, by Franz Steiner Verlag in Wiesbaden in 1977), but the richer source was Zhao Rugua, *Zhu fanzhi jiaozhu*, translated by Friedrich Hirth and W. W. Rockhill (published in St Petersburg in 1912). For the Yuan, Wang Dayuan, *Daoyi zhilue*, can be found in a translation by W. W. Rockhill in *T'oung Pao*, vols 15–16 (1914–1915), and discussed in Ptak, *China and the Asian Seas*, parts X and XI: "Glosses on Wang Dayuan's Daoyi zhilue", and "Images of Maritime Asia in Two Yuan Texts: Daoyi zhilue and Yiyu zhi".

14 Ma Huan, *Yingya shenglan*. This has been translated by J. V. G. Mills as *"The Overall Survey of the Ocean's Shores [1433]"*, Cambridge: Cambridge University Press, 1970; and Fei Xin, *Xingcha shenglan jiaozhu*, edited and annotated by Feng Chengjun, Beijing: Zhonghua, 1954; translated by J. V. G. Mills, as *Hsing-ch'a-sheng-lan: The Overall Survey of the Star Raft*, revised, annotated, and edited by Roderich Ptak, Wiesbaden: Harrassowitz, 1996.

15 Zhang Xie, *Dongxi yangkao* (A study of the eastern and western oceans), Zhonghua jiaotong shiji congkan series, Beijing: Zhonghua, 1981; see Leonard Blusse, "The VOC and the Junk Trade to Batavia: A Problem in Administrative Control", in *Strange Company: Chinese Settlers, Mestizo Women and the Dutch in VOC Batavia*, Dordrecht: Foris Publications, 1986, pp. 97–155.

16 Chen Lunjiong, *Haiguo wenjianlu* (Records of maritime countries), Zhongguo shixue congshu xubian, no. 35, Taipei: Hsueh-sheng shu chu, 1984. See Wang Gungwu, "The Melayu", pp. 37–49.

17 Wang Dahai, *Haidao yizhi jiaozhu* (Records of the islands), edited by Yao Nan and Wu Langxuan, Hong Kong: Xuejin books, 1992; Yang Bingnan (for Xie

Qinggao) *Hailu zhu* (Records of the sea), edited by Feng Chengjun, Beijing: Zhonghua, 1955.

18 There were many collections and studies about foreign countries produced by officials and private scholars during the sixteenth to eighteenth centuries, but they were all limited by the lack of opportunities for the authors to travel abroad. A few, however, demonstrated scholarship of a high quality, for example, He Qiaoyuan, *Min shu*, new edition by Xiamen University History Department, Fuzhou: People's Publishing, in five volumes, 1994.

19 This was clearly demonstrated in the classic statement about the self-sufficiency of Qing China by Emperor Qianlong to Lord Macartney when they met in 1793; Sir George Staunton, *An Authentic Account of an Embassy from the King of Great Britain to the Emperor of China*, London: G. Nicol, 1797; Alain Peyrefitte, *The Immobile Empire*, translated from the French by Jon Rothschild, New York: Knopf and Random House, 1992.

20 Wei Yuan, *Haiguo tuzhi* (Illustrated account of the maritime nations), edited and annotated by Chen Hua *et al.*, Changsha: Yuelu Books, 1998 (earlier edition, 1840–1850); Jane Leonard, *China's Rediscovery of the Maritime World*, Cambridge, Mass.: Council on East Asian Studies, Harvard University, distributed by Harvard University Press, 1984.

21 Kang Youwei (1858–1927), reformist Confucian scholar [eds].

22 For Huang Zunxian's work and influence on local Chinese writings during his years in Singapore, Ye Zhongling, *Huang Zunxian yu nanyang wenxue* (Huang Zunxian and literature in the Nanyang), Singapore: Singapore Society of Asian Studies, 2000; also J. D. Schmidt, *Within the Human Realm: The Poetry of Huang Zunxian, 1848–1905*, Cambridge: Cambridge University Press, 1994, especially the two poems on Singapore, pp. 278–282. As for Kang Youwei, his own writings about his years in Malaya are negligible, but others note his influence on Chinese attitudes towards China. Zhang Kehong, *Kang Youwei zai Xinma* (Kang in Singapore and Malaya), Singapore: Department of Chinese Studies, National University of Singapore, 1998; Lo Jung-pang, ed., *K'ang Yu-wei: A Biography and a Symposium*, Tucson: University of Arizona Press, for the Association for Asian Studies, 1967. Biographical notes by Wu Xianzu on Kang's visits to Singapore and Malaya are reprinted in Wang Gungwu, Chinese Reformists and Revolutionaries in the Straits Settlements, 1900–1911, BA Honours thesis, University of Malaya, Singapore, 1953, Appendix.

23 Liang Qichao (1873–1929), student of Kang Youwei [eds].

24 Liang Qichao's two essays, one on eight great Chinese colonists in Southeast Asia and the other on Zheng He, were first published in *Xinmin congbao*, vol. 3, no. 15 and 21, 1904. Sun Yat-sen made seven visits to British Malaya between 1900 and 1911 and lived off and on in Singapore and Penang for altogether about 2 years. He travelled around the Straits Settlements and the Federated Malay States and inspired some of the earliest Chinese newspapers in the Malay world. He spoke mainly about what the Chinese there could do for China, and the editors and journalists thereafter were greatly influenced by the nationalist calls by him and his followers. Yen Ching-hwang, *The Overseas Chinese and the 1911 Revolution, With Special Reference to Singapore and Malaya*, Kuala Lumpur: Oxford University Press, 1976; Wang Gungwu, "Sun Yat-sen and Singapore", *Journal of South Seas Society* (*Nanyang xuebao*), vol. 15, part 2, 1959, pp. 55–68 (reprinted in *Community and Nation: Essays on Southeast Asia and the Chinese*, selected by Anthony Reid, Singapore and Sydney: Heinemann Educational Books and George Allen and Unwin Australia, 1981, pp. 128–141).

25 Claudine Salmon, *Le moment "sino-malais" de la littérature indonésienne*, Paris: Association Archipel, 1992; *Literature in Malay by the Chinese of Indonesia: A Provi-*

sional Annotated Bibliography, Paris: Editions de la Maison des Sciences de l'Homme, 1981; see *Sastra Cina peranakan dalam bahasa Melayu*, diterjemahkan oleh Dede Oetomo, Jakarta: PN Balai Pustaka, 1985; also Leo Suruyadinata, *Sastra peranakan Tionghoa Indonesia*, Jakarta: Gramedia Widiasarana Indonesia, 1996, and *Political Thinking of the Indonesian Chinese, 1900–1995: A Sourcebook*, Singapore: Singapore University Press, 1997.

26 The literature on the rise of nationalism in the Malay world is now vast. The following are useful: Amat Johari Maoin, *Sejarah Nasionalisma Maphilindo: Malaysia-Philippine-Indonesia*, Kuala Lumpur: Utusan Melayu, 1969; Teodoro A. Agoncillo, *Filipino Nationalism, 1872–1970*, Quezon City: R. P. Garcia Pub. Co., 1974; J. Eliseo Rocamora, *Nationalism in Search of Ideology: The Indonesian Nationalist Party, 1946–1965*, Ithaca, NY: Southeast Asia Program, Dept of Asian Studies, Cornell University, 1974; Khoo Kay Kim, The Beginnings of Political Extremism in Malaya, 1915–1935 (PhD), Dept of History, University of Malaya, 1975; and *Majalah dan akhbar Melayu sebagai sumber sejarah. Bersama dengan satu senarai Berkala-berkala Melayu sebelum merdeka dalam pegangan Perpustakaan Universiti Malaya; dan Satu bibliografi mengenai pengkajian berkala Melayu*, Kuala Lumpur: Perpustakaan Universiti Malaya, 1984; also his *Malay Society: Transformation and Democratisation: A Stimulating and Discerning Study on the Evolution of Malay Society Through the Passage of Time*, Petaling Jaya, Selangor: Pelanduk Publications, 1991.

27 Tan, Liok Ee, *The Politics of Chinese Education in Malaya, 1945–1961*, Kuala Lumpur, New York: Oxford University Press, 1996; and *The Rhetoric of Bangsa and Minzu: Community and Nation in Tension, the Malay Peninsula, 1900–1955*, Melbourne: Centre of Southeast Asian Studies, Monash University, 1988. Also Liao Jianyu (Leo Suryadinata), *Yinni huaren wenhua yu shehui* (Indonesian Chinese culture and society), Singapore: Singapore Society for Asian Studies, 1993.

28 Zhang Liqian (1900–1955), born in Shanghai, taught in Malacca and Singapore in the 1930s and helped found the South Seas Society in 1940 in Singapore. He returned to China in 1941 and was a professor at Beijing University. His publications include *A History of Malacca*. Yao Nan (1912–1996), born in Shanghai, lived in Singapore between 1935 and 1940 and helped found the South Seas Society. On returning to China in 1941, he worked at the Institute of Nanyang Studies and Fudan University. Hsu Yun-ts'iao (Xu Yunqiao) (1905–1981), born in Suzhou, taught in Malaya and Thailand, helped found the South Seas Society, and founded the Institute of Southeast Asian Studies in Singapore in 1962. His publications include *A History of Malaya*. Han Zhenhua (1921–1993), born in Xiamen, received an MA from Zhongshan University in 1948. He was Director of the Nanyang Institute at Xiamen University and President of the China Association for Southeast Asian Studies. His publications include *A Study of Historical Relations between China and Southeast Asia*. Chen Xujing (1903–1967), born in Hainan, went to school in Singapore and received a PhD from the University of Illinois in 1928. Thereafter, he was Vice President of Nankai University and Zhongshan University and President of Lingnan University and Jinan University in Guangzhou. His publications on Southeast Asia include *Nanyang and China*.

29 I shall only mention some of the notable writings that touch on the Malay world, especially those written before and soon after the Second World War, for example: Zhang Liqian, *Malaiya lishi gaiyao* (An outline history of Malaya), Changsha: Commercial Press, 1939; *Maliujia shi* (A history of Malacca), Singapore: 1941; Yao Nan and Zhang Liqian, *Binlangyu zhilüe* (Records of Penang), Shanghai: Commercial Press, 1946; Yao Nan, *Malaiya huaqiao jingji gaikuang* (The overseas Chinese economy in Malaya), Nanjing: Nanyang Economic Society, 1946. Xu Yunqiao (Hsu Yun-ts'iao) has written extensively on Southeast Asia. I shall mention only his major contribution to

Chinese understanding of the Malay world, the translation of Malay Annals: *Malai jinian* (Sejarah Melayu), Selangor: Nanyang shangbao, 1954.

Also, Han Zhenhua, *Woguo Nanhai zhudao shiliao huibian* (Documents on the Nanhai islands), Beijing: Eastern Publishers, 1988; *Zhongwai guanxi lishi yanjiu* (Research relations between China and foreign countries), Hong Kong: Centre for Asian Studies, Hong Kong University, 1999; Chen Xujing, *Nanyang yu Zhongguo* (Nanyang and China), Guangzhou: Lingnan University Social and Economic Research Institute, 1948; *Chen Xujing dongnanya gushi yanjiu heji* (Collected essays on the ancient history of Southeast Asia by Chen Xujing), Shenzhen: Haitian Publishers, 1992.

30 Liu Yongzhuo, *Zhongguo dongnanya yanjiu de huigu yu qianzhan* (Southeast Asian Studies in China, retrospect and prospect), Guangzhou: Guangdong People's Publishing, 1994.

31 Li Xuemin and Huang Kunzhang, *Yinni huaqiao shi* (History of the Chinese in Indonesia), Guangzhou: Guangdong gaodeng jiaoyu, 1987; Pramoedya Ananta Toer, *Hoakiau di Indonesia*, Jakarta: Garba Budaya, 1998; Siauw Tiong Djin, *Siauw Giok Tjhan: Riwayat perjuangan seorang patriot membangun nation Indonesia dan masyarakat bhineka tunggal ika*, Jakarta: Hasta Mitra, 1999; Michael R. Godley and Grayson J. Lloyd, eds, *Perspective on the Chinese Indonesians*, Adelaide: Crawford house Publishing, 2001; see my review in *Bulletin of Indonesian Economic Studies*, Vol. 39, 2003, pp. 403–404; Khoo Kay Kim and Adnan Hj. Nawang, *Darurat 1948–1960*, disunting oleh Kuala Lumpur: Muzium Angkatan Tentera, 1984; Cheah Boon Kheng, *The Masked Comrades: A Study of the Communist United Front in Malaya, 1945–48*, Singapore: Times Books International, 1979; Anthony Short, *The Communist Insurrection in Malaya, 1948–1960*, London: Muller, 1975.

32 Wang Gungwu, "Southeast Asian Huaqiao", pp. 30–35. Also Liu Yongzhuo, *Zhongguo dongnanya yanjiu*, pp. 101–112.

33 William R. Roff, *The Origins of Malay Nationalism*, Singapore: University of Malaya Press, 1967; Hussin Mutalib, *Islam in Malaysia: From Revivalism to Islamic State?*, Singapore: Singapore University Press, 1993; Alijah Gordon, ed., *The Propagation of Islam in the Indonesian-Malay Archipelago*, Kuala Lumpur: Malaysian Sociological Research Institute, 2001; Elie Kedourie, *Islam in the Modern World, and Other Studies*, London: Mansell, 1980. On the appeal of the secular to the Chinese, Wang Gungwu, "State and Faith: Secular Values in Asia and the West", in *Critical Views of September 11: Analyses from Around the World*, edited by Eric Hershberg and Kevin W. Moore, New York: The New Press, 2002, pp. 224–242.

34 The writings of modern Chinese scholars are now better known outside China than they used to be, notably the work of Liang Liji, Wu Zongyu and Zhao Yuezhen who attended this conference, and also some of their predecessors, including scholars who had returned to China from Malaysia and Indonesia in the 1940s and 1950s. Many of them taught, or are still teaching and researching, at the Oriental Studies Department of Peking University, the Malay and Indonesian department of the Beijing University of Foreign Studies, the Institute of Nanyang Research at Xiamen University, and comparable institutes in Guangzhou at Sun Yat-sen University and Jinan University. Their renewed contacts with Malaysian and Indonesian scholars during the past two decades have done much to highlight their respective commitment to scholarly research. Malaysian and Indonesian scholars making regular visits to China and attending conferences with the younger Chinese scholars have also enhanced the quality of work being done. Outside the region, I have mentioned the work of Claudine Salmon and her major contributions to Sino-Malay scholarship. Her presence at this Colloquium reminds us how much we owe to her meticulous research.

11

STATE AND FAITH

Secular values in Asia and the West[1]

Wang Gungwu

In the aftermath of 11 September 2001, much has been written about Islamic fundamentalism, including a great deal of speculation about why Muslim states have failed to modernize. One of the reasons given has been that they have failed to become more secular. This chapter will focus on what lies behind the secular values that have been resisted strongly by some and found more readily acceptable by others. It will also consider the broader comparative question of how countries with different religious backgrounds have met the challenges of the modern and the secular.

Through social science literature as well as common usage, the scholarly community by and large accepts that being modern is a condition closely associated with being secular. Two recent views are representative. Bernard Lewis notes the contrast between what made the Islamic world poor and weak and the West rich and strong. He describes "the standards that matter in the modern world" as economic development and job creation, literacy, educational and scientific achievement, political freedom and respect for human rights. In the context of the role of religion, he argues, "a principal cause of Western progress is the separation of Church and State and the creation of a civil society governed by secular laws" (Lewis 2002: 152–157). The point about the secular foundations of modernity is even more forcefully put by Michael Howard when he writes of "the challenge to Islamic culture and values posed by the secular and materialistic culture of the West" and "the profound and intractable confrontation between a theistic, land-based, and traditional culture . . . and the secular material values of the Enlightenment" (Howard 2002: 17).

Both views link the secular directly with modernity as it has blossomed in the West. One places greater emphasis on civil society, the other on materialistic culture. But for both, the secular derives from Church–State separation and the Enlightenment and would thus appear to have been the product of a unique historical experience, what David Martin calls a

"Christian" phenomenon (Martin 1978: 1). This is closely tied to the long and ongoing struggle for secularization in Western Europe. The process may date its beginnings from the Renaissance and Reformation, but it reached its climax during the second half of the nineteenth century, and is still going on, particularly in other parts of Europe, the Americas and Australasia. Outside the Western world, the word secular is used most commonly in reference to the political model of the secular state that was transplanted to most post-colonial countries in Asia and Africa. The best example of this is India, where secularism has been well developed and receives close attention in the context of contemporary rival fundamentalisms that threaten state authority and public order (Madan 1998: 233–234, 260–265).

Further east in Asia, the word secular has not been directly applied to countries like China and Japan, but many descriptions of modern progress in both those countries point to examples where they have successfully transplanted among their peoples "the secular and materialistic culture of the West". It is interesting that "secular" is not used today to describe the values associated with Confucianism, or for social and political systems that have centred on being this-worldly without having a dominant religion. Confucian and Buddho-Confucian elites have considered it their greatest responsibility to bring harmony to the life of Man between Heaven and Earth without reference to God or gods.

The reason why the term secular is not used for these eastern religions originates from a narrow definition that associates the word with the struggle against the Christian Church and, therefore, places it in the context of freedom from a once totalistic religion. Hence the intense interest as to why the Muslims, with an equally totalistic religion, could not do the same. In contrast, there has been far less curiosity about ancient manifestations of secular values. All questions about comparable values in ancient Greece and Rome, as with ancient China, would turn to words like rational or humanist. By using the word secular exclusively in the context of European intellectual liberation history, however, two important issues have been unnecessarily neglected. One is an improved understanding of why modern secular values have fared better in some parts of the world than in others, and also why East Asia has responded to some secular offerings more readily than to others coming from the West. The other is the likelihood that when the people who accept the modern and secular have different roots for what is rational and humanist in their traditions, they place different emphases on the secular values that they are prepared to accept and may eventually produce for themselves different kinds of modernity (Eisenstadt and Schlucter 1998: 1–18; Eisenstadt 2000: 1–30).

Secular and "Asian" values

The question of secular values was very much on my mind immediately after the 11 September attack in the United States. In my address one month later at a conference on "Asian values and Japan's options", I linked the issue of Asian values to the future of secular values. My view about the notion of "Asian values" is that the debates that this has aroused have a long lineage. The current political references to them represent merely new versions of an older dichotomy. Their roots could be found in ideas concerning the Occident and the Orient. The Japanese made an early contribution to this dichotomy by using Toyo (Eastern Ocean) and Seiyo (Western Ocean) and influenced the Chinese to adopt the same terms, Dongyang and Xiyang. Today, the word "Asian" has been adopted as a substitute for the post-Second World War revision of the word "Oriental". In any case, both sets of alternative terms in Japan and China were really derived from European usage.

The recent manifestation of "Asian values" is a reply to American-led pressure on some Asian governments following the end of the Cold War. Before that, a new dichotomy that opposed ("Western" and secular) capitalist values to ("Eastern" and secular) communist values in support of the notion of a "central balance" in world politics, had put the weight on questions about power and wealth that were obviously this-worldly. The forces arrayed against each other were armed to their nuclear teeth, and the struggle was couched in terms of irreconcilable political and economic systems. After that struggle ended in 1990, the post-Cold War pressures for world peace were accompanied by a note of triumphalism, and seemed to conceal a new mission to civilize the world in secular terms. The "Asian" response originated from some of the less free parts of East and Southeast Asia, not directly from the Islamic states (Mahbubani 1998; Sheridan 1999). It recalls the Japanese and Chinese use of ideas about (Eastern) foundation or substance (*ti*) and (Western) application or function (*yong*) prevalent at the end of the nineteenth century (de Bary 1964: 81–87). The original stress on the sanctity of tradition has been modified by recognizing that Western "application" (the acceptance of modern secular values) in some countries in eastern Asia is now predominant and will become the core of a new "foundation".

In the context of the attention given to the gulf between Western and Islamic values, it is understandable why Samuel Huntington's "clash of civilizations" paradigm has provoked fresh interest. When he depicted how the West might face a combined threat from the Islamic and the "Confucian" world, the outline he presented was understandable, though somewhat paranoid. He may well have asked the question, but did not, whether there could also be a conflict between Christian and Islamic civilizations in which the East Asian "Confucians" would have to choose sides.

Huntington is unpersuasive in suggesting some sort of collaboration between Islam and Confucianism aimed at the West. The evidence he presents is at best circumstantial. But he is also misleading in his use of the word "civilization". As a political scientist, he was primarily describing the continuation of Great Power relations in different formations. From now on, he implies, another set of Great Powers might be seeking new unifying symbols in older divisions derived from different religious traditions and value-systems. The struggle that he envisaged, however, would really be driven by secular power where the West was concerned, and this would be governed by the scientific and humanist spirit that underpins modern secularism (Huntington 1996: 183–186, 207–209; Wang 1996: 70).

It is this secular drive that characterizes our age. This is where the image of "civilizations" as power players in global affairs rings false. The major value systems in the world today each have a distinctive relationship with different kinds of secularism, and these distinctions would be better understood if the value systems were recognized as having different sources. We need to ask what the meaning of secular values is, if only to pursue the reasons why so many Muslims have found it difficult to come to terms with secularism. For comparison, we also need to explore the extent to which the peoples of Hindu India and Confucian China have been secular. Further, how are we to relate the ideas about "Asian" values to the future of secular values as such; that is, what constitutes the secular in Asia (Wang in SSRC 2001)? Islam is one of the great religions of Asia. If there are questions about the troubled reception given to secularism in Islam, should there not be similar doubts about the fate of this secularism with other faiths in Asia? If not, why not? Indeed, if there are "Asian" values, would they not reflect the problems that all Asian religions face?

Alternative conceptions of secularism

Prior to 1990, the world that was divided between capitalism and communism could have been portrayed as a civil war between two secular faiths. Nevertheless, the "central balance" of potential war and terror was an important factor in giving the world relative peace for some 40 years. Since then, after the economic reforms leading to the gradual opening of China and then the fall of the Soviet Union, that balance of terror has given way to total victory for the capitalist cause. As a result, there seems to be a new mission to bring one set of secular values to a globalized world.

These modern secular values derive from the achievements of the Enlightenment project in Europe and across the Atlantic. During the past decade, their major focus shifted from anti-communism to issues of democracy, human rights, and a free global market economy as the core of a "truth" that had just been confirmed by victory. Claims have been made for how this truth is to be universalized, but many thinkers in both Asia and the West know that secular capitalism is neither a natural law that the West has discovered, nor a God-given truth that has been bestowed upon the West. It is, rather, the product of centuries of worldly struggle in search of wealth and power, and also of the search for a happier world at all levels of state and society. It is the hard-won result of painful experiments conducted by generations of social, political and business leaders, not least the intellectuals who helped develop the various fields of mathematics, natural sciences and social sciences. In Asia, for most adult Japanese and large numbers of educated Chinese, this road to progress was not itself new. They had observed with keen interest the traumas in the West that had produced the ideals behind its progress. Some had actually sought the same ideals for their respective countries. Even when they failed, many still hoped that their own societies would ultimately progress in a similar direction.

September 11 reminds us that, apart from what the imperatives of international politics could force Asian leaders to agree on, there is nothing substantive about the values given the name of "Asian". What various Asian governments and their elites have in common was drawn from the history of battles to defend traditional values against the alien ones brought into Asia by the West. These battles opened up discussions about why traditional values seemed to clash with modern secular ones, but the debates, ironically, were largely framed by European standards of what was considered progressive and what was not. When couched in that way, the question of Japan's options where values are concerned becomes highly relevant. The choices that Japan makes are clearly relevant for China as well. How do the Japanese and the Chinese understand which values were secular?

The triumphant note of the 1990s reminds us of an ancient Confucian cosmic belief in the Mandate of Heaven. This was based on the simple principle that the victor must be favoured by Heaven and, therefore, was the bearer of the truth. The pragmatic lessons of history run through Chinese and Japanese history: "the victor is king, the defeated is but a bandit." Thus, the secular mission to bring Western progressive modernity to East Asia should not meet resistance, provided it really triumphs. For the Japanese, there was a thorough defeat in 1945, and therefore they, willingly or not, accepted the winning model for a second round of modernization (Kersten 1996: 109–122). For the Chinese, there had been many humiliations by Britain, France, Russia, by the allied forces at the siege of Peking in 1900, and then by the new imperial Japan down to 1945. China's struggles to respond to these defeats led a new generation of Chinese leaders to adopt communism, an alternative but equally alien ideology, as the true path to modernity. This did not free them from external threats. Their desire for independence and sovereignty gained them the enmity of the Soviet Union, and this forced them to turn to the

United States and ultimately to revise their views about capitalism itself (Shambaugh 1991: 294–300). But, with the long backdrop of Chinese history in mind, it could be said that the Chinese had merely lost battles but never the war. They had endured invasions of mind and body but never the comprehensive defeat experienced by the Japanese. Thus they seem to have retained, however imperfectly, some faith in the rational and humanist tradition that was at the heart of their ancient civilization. How do the values represented in this tradition compare with those identified with the modern secularism of the West?

As manifested in the triumphant West, secularism is a product of the end-game in the epic struggle between Church and State. Clearly no other part of the world shared this unique experience of Church–State separation, or the accompanying process of secularization that could only have occurred when a clash between God and Caesar resulted in victory for Caesar. The process may have begun with the Reformation and the French Enlightenment, but it did not really end until the middle of the nineteenth century (Chadwick 1975: 14–18; McLeod 2000: 178–184). Given this unique history, it was understandable for Western Europe to see all of Asia as having never been secularized. Defined in the narrow terms of the Church–State relationship, that judgement is correct. But it ignores the fact that "the secular", more broadly construed, is not confined to the West. It has wider reference points in faiths that are primarily about this world, i.e. about everything that is not sacred. The idea of what is secular was strictly confined in Muslim polities, but it was more tolerable and acceptable in South Asian religions like Hinduism and Buddhism. And, further east, China has had a distinct tradition of this-worldly faiths that wielded considerable influence among its neighbours. Indeed, when set against this broader historical and conceptual framework, the ancient Mediterranean world of Greece and Rome can also be said to have had its own kind of secular faiths, before the rise of Christianity. Although these faiths were eventually crushed and displaced, the ideas behind them were similar to aspects of ancient Hindu and Buddhist thought, and comparable to the values underlying Chinese secular beliefs.

Since 11 September, debates on whether there can be a separation of religion and state in Islamic countries have been revived. The terms of these debates have their roots in conflicts within monotheistic faiths, that is, Judaism, Christianity and Islam. It is interesting to contrast that discussion with the fierce ongoing debates within India today. In India, Hinduism and Islam have had centuries of internal tension, and now occupy apparently irreconcilable positions in a modern nationalist framework. And, although the idea of a secular state in India has gained a surprising depth of meaning, the commitment to secularism, initially accepted by most Hindus, is now being undermined by a growing fundamentalism among the country's Muslims, Sikhs, and increasing numbers of Hindus themselves. This fundamentalism makes clear that secular values in India are different from those elevated in Western Europe and globalized in North America and Australasia. Taken together with what was peculiar to the secular tradition in China, especially those aspects that have survived till the present day, the Indian case helps us identify the kinds of secular values active in Asia today (Thapar 1998: 17–19).

During the last two centuries, the dominant discourse in Asia has been cast in terms of a "hard" secularism, essentially fundamentalist in nature, that denies the spiritual life altogether, as against a "soft" secularism that co-opts the spiritual for an integrated world-view that would satisfy the needs of the largest numbers of people. A third position, in which secular values are completely subordinated to spiritual values, may still attract specific religious communities and some individuals, but among most elite groups in Asia, it is considered to be turning back the clock of progress, and the likelihood of it being fully taken up in any country today is slim. The background for the secular values on offer in Asia remains that of a choice between hard and soft secularism. Nevertheless, the choice must be made within the context of different underlying ideas of the secular.

The major ideas about what constitutes the secular in Asia today come from three distinct sources. The first was the separation of Church and State in the Christian West; the second emerged from the need to establish a modern state in post-colonial countries like India and others in Southeast Asia; and the third originated from the rational and this-worldly attitudes towards religion of the ancient Greeks and Romans, and also the Chinese. To illustrate this more fully, the three sources of the secular could be distinguished as deriving from three kinds of faiths:

1 Monotheistic religions;
2 South Asian religions; and
3 ancient secular faiths.

The first two are presented here only briefly because the modern secular values they stand for or reject are well known and widely debated. The secular faiths in their modern transformations will be given more attention. These have been mainly studied for their roots in ancient history, but their relevance to the contemporary world has not often been recognized. The events since 11 September, coupled with disparate ideas about "Asian" values, and the possible threat of Islam and Confucianism acting in concert against the West, suggest that the process of changing and modernizing ancient secular faiths has lessons for us today.

The monotheistic religions

The monotheistic religions of Judaism, Christianity and Islam sprang from a common source in the Middle East. The latter two derived their spiritual power from the first, and have been its dominant variants for a long time. Their strong missionary urges have provided them with world-conquering strength. Christianity grew steadily into a sacral imperial power and evolved into several major religious communities. Eventually, its various forms have nested in nation-states and some have been supportive of nationalist goals. Islam was more immediately successful and established a chain of military states on three continents. The religion these states espoused had at least two main divisions, the Sunni and Shi'a, but the fractured condition of the Muslim world of the Ummat after the fifteenth century left it with no powerful states to resist the forces of modern secularization coming from Western Europe. What Christianity and Islam do still have in common is the mission to bring the only true God (that is, the only Truth) to the world. This has been the source of the continuous rivalry between them for more than 1,300 years.

In modern times, the major source of conflict has arisen from their very different attitudes towards the rise of secularism, a word that came into use during the nineteenth century. Within Christianity, which initially resisted but eventually accepted the separation of Church and State, secular values first reached mainstream status during the eighteenth century with the French Enlightenment and the American Revolution, and that status was ultimately achieved among all states with Christian backgrounds. Within Islam, individual political leaders, intellectuals and scientists since the nineteenth century have recognized the secular basis for the modern world. The words they used for what was secular were derived from the word for science and that for the world, namely *'ilmaniyah* (from *'ilm*, meaning science), and *'alamaniyah* (from *'alam*, meaning the world). Azzam Tamini suggests that an even more accurate rendering would be *dunyawiyah* which is rooted in another word for this earth and refers to "that which is worldly, mundane or temporal" (Tamini and Esposito 2000: 13).

The successor states of the Ottoman empire, especially those bordering the Mediterranean, notably Egypt and modern Turkey, but also Palestine, Syria, Tunisia and Algeria, were consistent in adapting secular values to their needs. But there remained fierce opposition among the faithful towards the secularizing elites. The failure of the new states to solve problems of poverty and more generally to defend themselves against Western dominance was seen as proof that they had taken the wrong road. The fact that the powerful Muslim Brotherhood began in Egypt, one of the secularizing states, highlights the direct relation between what was seen as imitative actions of the elites and the popular reaction from the faithful. In

Turkey, Mustafa Kemal Atatürk's determination to use the nationalist state to control Islamic extremism has been an exception among modern Muslim leaders. But secularism in Turkey has by no means won the day, and the reaction against it has been increasing, both in Turkey itself and throughout the Islamic world. Since the Iranian revolution in 1978, increasing numbers of Muslims have come to believe that to be secular without losing one's faith is a challenge, if not a hopeless contradiction. The answer for many, especially the clerics, is that protecting Islam is preferable to the material progress associated with secular values.

In sum, the key difference between the Christian and Muslim worlds today lies in different approaches to the process of secularization. Although not always spelt out in national constitutions, the relentless pressures of the scientific and industrial revolutions working in support of national survival or aggrandizement did not allow any European country to avoid that process. Its success, first in Europe and then across the oceans to the rest of the world, confirmed that secular values provided the foundations for material progress. Thus the ideas and institutions presented by a victorious West to the rest of the world have become the dominant model for most other nations to either reject or emulate.

South Asian religions

The South Asian religions, notably Hinduism and Buddhism, experienced a vastly different history. They had no Church from which the people needed to secularize themselves. Among Hindus, the Brahmin priestly castes emphasized values based on concepts of inward purity, but most people in their "small communities, birth groups, and religious sects" were at the same time "secular" (Frykenberg 1993: 237). The Brahmins served the kings of the warrior castes with loyalty and were rewarded with respect and privilege. The many gods or many manifestations of God of the Hindus, however, did not satisfy everybody, and alternate visions led to the rise of Buddhism, Jainism and later Sikhism. In the end, a multiethnic and multilingual Hinduism prevailed despite the violent conquests by the Muslim armies that came out of Central Asia after the twelfth century.

For the Hindus, there was no conflict between the sacred and the profane. The question of becoming secular did not arise until the formation of British India. Out of that experience came two alternative paths to secularism (Madan 1998: 235–247). One was the religious route sought after by Gandhi and his followers, which stressed the equality of all religions in their common search for God as the Infinite Truth. The other was the colonial or nation-state route. It was this latter that prevailed: the secular state model that the Western colonial powers bestowed upon their successors when they departed after the end of the Second World War. India is the best and most challenging example of this experiment in political modernization, and its Hindu leaders have carried on with this model by appealing to both secular nationalist necessity and a Gandhian rhetoric. In spite of the resurgence of Hindu fundamentalism in the face of Muslim and Sikh fundamentalisms, India has remained firm in the defence of secularism (Madan 1998: 138–144, 98–105). Even with regards to Kashmir, official policy has always insisted that the issue on India's part is merely one of sovereignty in a multi-religious society and not, as with Pakistan, a matter of a religious majority.

The many gods and castes in Hinduism have not stood in the way of Indian secularism. One of the major offshoots of Hinduism, Buddhism, did not fare well on its native soil but migrated to take root in Sri Lanka, Southeast Asia and further east in China, Korea and Japan. In rejecting God or gods, this Buddhism may seem to have been somewhat of a heresy, but in essence, it still focused on an inner tranquillity that derives from the same source as Hinduism. Because it transplanted well away from India, and played an important part in shoring up secular values in East Asia, I shall say more about this later. The point to emphasize here about South Asian religions is that, while neither Hinduism nor Buddhism pushed for secular solutions to the world's problems, they have both been able to tolerate and even embrace certain secular values that they see as posing no threat to their core doctrines (Thapar 1989: 209–218).

Ancient secular faiths

The third source of secular, this-worldly values, is the two faiths that were dominant in the ancient Graeco-Roman world and East Asia. Both have undergone transformations during the past two millennia. The modern phase of these faiths is now led by Western Europe and its extensions in the Americas and Australasia, and its offerings are being emulated to a greater or lesser extent in East Asia. But their separate origins are still important enough to create a strong tension between them. Both would claim the universality of the secularism they represent, deriving in one from a scientific and legal spirit embodied in free individuals, and in the other from an emphasis on social morality and harmony.

Graeco-Roman religions

The worldly spirit of the ancient Graeco-Roman religions flourished for centuries until the ascent of the Emperor Constantine in the fourth century. It then disappeared with the fall of the Roman Empire, when Europe was blanketed by the "Dark Ages", and its secular values were replaced by a new Christian fundamentalism. With the rise of Islam, some Greek scientific texts, notably those on logic, mathematics and astronomy, were preserved and studied, and advances made. That these writings were admired by the early Muslim elites has led to some puzzlement as to why this tension between the secular and the sacred did not lead to a creative fusion. Of particular interest has been the retreat from scientific experimentation and astronomical observation that had reached high standards of achievement among Muslim scholars by the thirteenth century (Huff 1993: 169–186).

Christian humanists who began to look to ancient Greece and Rome from the twelfth century onwards fared no better in introducing alternative views into scholarly debates. In contrast to Islam, whose various communities stood by the words in the Koran, in the Christian world a powerful Church stood in the way of any questioning of orthodox "truths". In these circumstances, the secular values expounded by the Greeks were all but lost to the world. They had to wait another three centuries, until the fall of Constantinople and the division of the Church itself, before light was shone on them again. In short, they had to be rediscovered and re-evaluated among new generations of Christian scholars. Thereafter, these values have modified Christian mission values and, in turn, notably after the Reformation, have been modified by both the Catholic and Protestant heritage.

It is here that the contrast with the Islamic response is most stark. Graeco-Roman secular values did not succeed in modifying Islamic mission values despite the fact that the classical texts that represented that spirit were much appreciated by early Muslim scholars. Without doubt, the success of Graeco-Roman values within the Christian world was stimulated by the Church–State separation after the Renaissance. This provided the necessary conditions for intellectual elites to advance the scientific and technological revolution that has shaped the modern world today. But the key point that I wish to underline with respect to the Graeco-Roman experience is that ancient secular values espoused by political and cultural elites could not initially resist the onslaught of a religion, whether Christianity or Islam, that met the spiritual needs of ordinary people.

Chinese religions

The secular values in ancient Chinese thought had different origins and their evolution followed a different trajectory. They had begun not with God or gods but with a faith in the three-part continuum of Heaven, Earth and Man, in which Man and Earth had prominence and Man was given a firm if not exactly equal place (Weber 1951: 228; Tu 2001: 245). This essentially secular position was endorsed by Confucius when he affirmed that he knew only of this life, and therefore had nothing to say about the after-life. As with the Greeks and Romans, for the Chinese the measure of man was man. This rational humanist beginning became the main thrust in the Confucian ideals of morality and social harmony – in this world. Of course, the Chinese concept of the secular, as with the Greeks and Romans, had nothing to do with secularization from a Church-dominated state and society. For the Confucian scholars who came to dominate the Han dynasty from the second century BC, the universal moral values they espoused could only be grasped and practised by the enlightened elites. They were, therefore, entrusted with managing the empire and tutoring the emperors who were worldly manifestations of Heaven's approval (Wang 1979).

The modern Chinese word for "secular" reveals the tortuous history of Confucianism and the travails of later Confucian elites. The word is *shishu*, meaning of this world, but its original meaning referred to the popular and lowly ways of the common people, and the "backward" values that they held. Their customs and practices were variously transmitted by magicians, shamans and spirit-healers with their dubious rituals, and bore no resemblance to the rational and ethical humanism in the minds of the enlightened few. Confucian secularism was, in the end, no less corruptible than the Graeco-Roman version. After dominating the imperial administration for nearly four centuries, it could not prevent the total collapse of the Later Han dynasty during the third century AD. Not only were the overland frontiers threatened by "barbarians" and the ruling house divided by deadly rivalries, there was also a deep cultural gulf between the Confucian elites and the people they governed. That gap had become intolerable to the peasant majority, and several rebellions based on popular religions broke out throughout the empire. It was in this way that Buddhism, brought into China by a handful of dedicated priests from India, took root. It combined with some of the popular faiths of the Chinese through the common language used to translate the Sutras. The ideas about government and the sophisticated philosophical concepts found in the Sutras soon won over a new generation of rulers and their courtiers, especially those of alien origins from the steppes who conquered much of North China. Eventually the Chinese rulers in the south also converted to Buddhism.

In this way, the secularism of Han Confucianism was gradually modified by the tenets of Mahayana Buddhism as well as by other faiths that remained popular among the majority of people. The Confucian–Buddhist cosmology underlying the idea of rule by virtue did not require a dichotomy between God and Caesar, rendering unnecessary a separation between Heaven and Ruler. There was a lack of binary centres, there was no need for secularization, and this differentiated the Chinese value system from that of Europe.

Thus the Confucians survived, much chastened by their failure. For four centuries, until the beginning of the Tang dynasty in the seventh century, they were content to carve a niche for themselves as a specialized group of empire managers, but also waited for opportunities to recover their lost glories. They reformed and sharpened their concerns with moral values, making it clearer that these were, among other things, based on respect for authority, and ideals of order and social harmony. They could seek compromises with an indigenized Buddhism as well as with the popular Daoism that had been inspired by the Buddhists to formally reinvent itself. The secularism represented by early Confucians could not be revived without a recognition that spiritual needs of the people had to be met. Early in the Song dynasty (960–1278), several determined Confucian thinkers, thoroughly versed in Buddhist and Daoist literature, started on the road of reconstruction. For the Chinese, the emergence of a new Confucianism that culminated in the work of Zhu Xi[2] in the twelfth century may be compared to the scientific "enlightenment" for eighteenth-century Europeans. It soon became the political and moral orthodoxy that helped to legitimize the following Chinese dynasties, including those established by Mongols and Manchus, and then reached out to inspire the regimes of the Korean Yi dynasty (1392–1910) and the Tokugawa Shogunate (1603–1867). Its confidence was not seriously shaken until the Western impact following the defeat in the two Opium Wars of the nineteenth century (de Bary 1975: 29–32).

This brief outline of the rise of early secularisms, followed by decline, compromise and rebirth, and then by ripeness and arrogance, underlines the failures of secular elites to bridge the gap in values between themselves and the subject majorities they ruled over. That failure was experienced by the Graeco-Romans and the Confucian Chinese alike. The later Greeks and Romans could not revivify their heritage by themselves. They had to await enlightened Christian scholars and scientists to breathe new life into their profoundly secular ideas. There was a fecund fusion of ideals and institutions that led to a continuous struggle for supremacy between secularization and evangelical revivals. The tension so far has been a creative one, especially in the United States, but at least for the past half-century, the forces of the modern secular state in Europe and in large parts of the de-colonized world of new nation-states have had to fight hard to keep the challenge of fundamentalist religions under control.

The Confucian Chinese, on the other hand, reinterpreted their own classics in the light of popular Buddhist concepts and succeeded in making some of the doctrines of that religion serve their ends. But, with centuries of sustained success and overwhelming secular power through the Ming and Qing dynasties, the Neo-Confucians succumbed to corruption and degeneration. They lost their ability to respond to new foreign invasions and the challenging ideas brought to China. Their successors since the turn of the twentieth century have cast about to find ways of domesticating the modern secular values from the West that they finally decided to accept.

China's modern secular challenge

The Chinese experience since the fall of state Confucianism remains instructive. After the Qing dynasty fell in 1911, there was an open scramble to find a more successful replacement for the traditional secular ideals that had failed. Numerous ideologies were introduced from Europe – from nationalism to liberal and social democracy, from communism to fascism and national socialism. Significantly, there was little interest in the available religions. Both Islam and Buddhism were familiar to the Chinese intellectuals, but neither were a match for the religion of the Christian missions. Christianity was a partner of European wealth and power and should have attracted the pragmatic Chinese. But the religion was tainted not only by association with imperialism and colonialism world-wide, but also specifically with China's own humiliation. The proud young Chinese of the May Fourth Movement after 1919 chose to measure success in materialistic terms. Thus their only model had to be the secular Great Powers. In the "triumphal" tradition where victor is emperor and loser bandit, the First World War was a fateful example in at least two ways. It raised great doubts about Western Europe as a model and by extension the efficacy of Anglo-American liberal democracy. The failure of the French reduced the appeal of the French Revolution but not altogether. That had been superseded by a new and even more thorough social revolution, that of Leninist Soviet Russia.

The story of the fresh secular conversion of large numbers of young Chinese intellectuals during the 1920s and 1930s has often been told. All that needs emphasizing here is the attraction of scientism through the prism of Social Darwinism, Marx and Freud that led readily to radical politics, to "scientific" socialism and ultimately to secular fundamentalism. Certainly, the basic layer of secular values that Chinese intellectuals had inherited from Confucianism eased the acceptance of the powerful modern versions of what were originally Graeco-Roman tendencies to humanistic rationalism. Marx's description of religion as the opium of the people struck a deep chord. It was real, it was the cause of China's downfall both at war and among the paraphernalia of Chinese opium smokers. The cast-out Confucian literati were depicted as representatives of an outdated mode of production, that of feudalism, and the popular religions practised by ordinary Chinese the worst kinds of superstition. Indeed, all religions soon became superstitions and all who believed in God or gods, spirits and ghosts, and the after-life, were lumped together as superstitious.

Thus was born the newest replacement for the Confucianism that had failed. It was science, the basis of knowledge, that provided all criteria for what was true and worthy, and this marked the formation of a new secular faith. Although secular youths dominated in every political party and most social organizations until the 1940s, it was the Chinese Communist Party after 1949 that secured the absolute power of secularism in China. Members of the Party would have to set aside their religion. Those who still believed in religion would not be welcome to join the Party. Until the death of Mao Zedong and the end of the Cultural Revolution, the future of secular values was assured but that of religion was fairly dim.

I suggested above that the 40 years after the end of the Second World War were mainly the years of a secular civil war fought between the capitalist states led by the United States and the communist states led by the Soviet Union. The secular state in the United States, of course, was never absolute in its secular policies. There was always a tension between religion and civil authority that suggested that both sides sought a balance between the sacred and the secular. It was this balance that separated the Americans from their more anti-clerical contemporaries in Europe. But the Cold War, despite the Christian rhetoric the Americans used against godless communism, satanic forces and the "evil empire", was, in reality, a no-holds-barred rivalry between two models of secular power. The leaders of China understood that, and clearly took the side of absolute secularism against the "sugared bullets" of capitalism. And, as long as there were prospects of victory, the Chinese people followed their leaders. In fact, the word faith became more important than the word secular during the Cultural Revolution, when Mao Zedong became something of an earthly god, the *Little Red Book* a set of catechisms, and the shouted slogans nothing more than mantras.

The present leadership is not unaware of the dangers that absolute secularism could breed. About 20 years ago, Hu Qiaomu (1911–1992), the President of the Academy of Social Sciences, warned, "If we only engage in building a socialist civilization and do not work hard to foster a socialist spiritual civilization at the same time, people will be selfish, profit-seeking and lacking in lofty ideals. In that case, how much will our mental outlook differ from that in capitalist societies?" (Hu 1982, quoted in Wang 1991: 145). This was not very flattering to capitalist societies. The point is that, first, he saw both capitalism and socialism as equally secular, and second, he wanted socialism to be more spiritual if only about secular ideals. If he were alive today, he would have to acknowledge that very few of the young in China share the idealism that inspired the first generation communist party leaders. On the other hand, at the popular level, there is evidence that many seek spiritual sustenance that only religion can give, be it within traditional temples, mosques and churches, or in secret cells, or through untried sects and cults. Although it is not clear what Hu Qiaomu meant by "spiritual", he seems to have been worried that the kind of fundamentalism that thrives on materialist and secular values could erode the high moral ground that his generation of revolutionaries had sacrificed so much to attain. A generation earlier, traditional elites had confidently insisted that Western *yong* (application) could be accepted because Chinese *ti* (foundation) was universal and true for all time. But Mao's slogan, *guwei jinyong* (apply the ancient for modern use), had implicitly turned modern secularism into foundation and left the ancient values, selectively and where relevant, for use and application. That this transformation was readily accepted by the educated young reminds us how ancient secular faiths and modern secular values share the same roots.

A secular China going capitalist and a capitalist America taking a secularist view of religious fundamentalism seem to make strange bedfellows, but they may not be that far apart. For example, where democracy is concerned, the ancient Greek ideal is readily accepted in China although there are reservations about the modern version. The Chinese stress as an ideal the democracy of collectives, with or without kinship ties, while the West gives a higher value to democracy by individuals. With a shift in emphasis, the gap is bridgeable. It is a little more difficult where human rights are concerned if only because the ideal comes from a deep Christian faith that has been secularized. As long as the Chinese remain fundamentalist about their secularism, they are likely to resist this. On the other hand, there are spiritual qualities drawn from older Buddhist and Daoist ideals that could narrow the gap, although their versions of what constitutes rights differ markedly from the Christian. There is, however, no reason why the differences should be regarded as absolute, why the West cannot understand the Chinese idea of placing duties above rights, and the Chinese the Western belief that rights must come first and be protected in order for duties to be accepted (Kent 1993: 44–50, 79–84; Wang 1979). Neither is explicit about ways in which their views are a variety of secular faith, and how that set of differences formed the background of a secular civil war that threatens to go on consuming us. If this were admitted, it would put the current talk about "the clash of civilizations" in context and expose the melodrama that surrounds the debate.

Conclusion

September 11 was a reminder to new secular elites everywhere that there can be no sets of values that are purely secular. It challenged the religious to weigh how far fundamentalism might go if their faiths are linked with political agendas. At the same time, it puzzled most Americans, who are religious and secular in turn, how much the global reach of their secular power is resented if not hated, although it may also have convinced some to believe that only through the application of even greater power can threats to that power be removed.

A survey of the history of secular values shows that spiritual needs of many different kinds have to be met, and that secularism has been enriched by at least two religions, Christianity and Buddhism. It is still unclear whether these secular manifestations have risen above the religions that had nourished them. Will they always be divided by their different moral and spiritual roots, origins that cannot be easily ignored? And what about Islam's past and future contributions? Although early Islam had declined to take the secular ideas of the Greeks further and mould them to sustain its own purer truth, it did enrich the realms of knowledge that the Greeks stimulated. Since the nineteenth century, Muslim elites considered the issue afresh. But they are now divided as to how much they should accept and use European secular values to achieve modern progress and regain pride in their culture. With a few exceptions, they sought compromises with secularism that are now strongly resisted by the fundamentalists among them. When their modernizing states proved to be unable to deliver the wealth and power hoped for and avoid being pawns in a global secular civil war, a growing number of new elites no longer believe that modernity has inevitably to follow a known formula, however successful that might have been elsewhere. Many of them are ready to use Islam to shape a different path through Islamic states, or at least to contribute an inner strength that secular values cannot provide.

Against the return to the vigour of a primary faith, secular values in the modern West, considered to be universal by many, have been used for a series of continuous conflicts, especially by Great Powers seeking imperial dominance and fighting their World Wars. Although these Powers, whether in defeat or in victory, claim to be supported by the divine guidance of inherited religious traditions, their secularism has increasingly been identified with narrow nationalist or ethnic interests. As a result, the universal claims of their secular values have been steadily undermined, never more so than among the Muslims who understand only too well the spiritual roots of these claims in monotheist Christianity and Judaism. This close association of secular values with Judaeo-Christian dominance will remain a major obstacle to accepting any modernity that seems to be defined by these values. For the dominant West to dilute that link with their own spiritual history would be both unpalatable and very difficult to do.

That brand of secularism was so dominant that there was no credible alternative to the civil war between the two power groupings in the Cold War. For the religious, whether Christian, Muslim, Hindu, Buddhist or others, they could only wait to see how the secularists would fare. They were asked to believe that history will prove that the side that wins would hold the Truth. In pursuit of that victory, both sides drove themselves to use the maximum destructive capacities of their secular ways. Leaders in the Middle East and South Asia who were less secular were often cynically used by the secular powers to serve self-proclaimed "universal" interests. Those in East Asia who were already secular, or believed that they had to be secular in order to be modern, were impressed by the fact that global capitalism won that civil war. Clearly for them, even greater commitment to secular values is needed for them to attain the elusive modernity they have long wanted.

But not all elites are convinced that this is the end of history. In face of the certainty and arrogance underlying that proclamation, various religions and their revivalist manifestations began to find that their previously muted voices are now being heard. What had been weak resistance for the past 200 years against the advent of the secular, has found new strength in a fundamentalist defence against encroaching secularism. It points now to the callous results of the secular civil war that the world has just been through, notably where rich and poor seem further apart than ever, where selfish national interests have been paramount and where the powerful exercise double standards for their own gains. Large numbers of the Muslim leadership in the Middle East are convinced that the most glaring injustice has fallen on their heads. Thus the scepticism of the very basis of secular power has grown among them, and calls to resist that power through fundamental Islam have been most persistently made.

At present, "the West" and "East Asia" are the two nodes of modern secularism. It appears that the West has every reason to be confident of its own set of secular values. Japan and China are still trying to improve on the alternative versions they have had, Japan by continually adopting specific institutions from Western Europe and the United States, while China is seeking inspiration across a wide spectrum of secularism that spans that of communism, capitalism and its Confucian past. Both countries are redefining what they have accepted of modern secular values as "foundation" (*ti*) by "applying" (*yong*) what they can of their past to minimize the spiritual damage that this modern secularism might do to their peoples. As for those in South Asia, the secularists are fighting off the steady growth of fundamentalism among their Islamic and other religious communities, but they have no alternative but to select carefully the modern values that they can safely adopt into their valued traditions.

Given this new awareness of threat, what is the future of secular values? As in the past, there can be too much secularism. When Graeco-Roman and Confucian values were dominant in their respective regions, they both failed. The former could have been revived by Islam, but this did not happen. Ultimately, Graeco-Roman values were only rejuvenated by a divided Christianity. Similarly, Confucian values were in decline until they were reinterpreted through a unique blend of Buddhist and Daoist ideas and thus regained a dominance that they retained until the twentieth century. These comparisons suggest that secularism by itself cannot satisfy the human psyche.

But what can soften and rescue modern secularism today? When secular values are globalized, their limitations are even more widely exposed. Thus they arouse an opposition that is also global. For the doubters, including those for whom a return to organized religion is not an option, a new dichotomy is needed to highlight the spiritual vacuum that has been revealed. Therefore, whether themselves fervently secular or not, they would focus on the values that contradict the global capitalism now most closely identified with the modern secular. Although we may be sceptical about how strong these efforts to dramatize a growing desperation are gathering strength world-wide, there is little doubt that a credible response is needed to minimize the tensions that have been produced. We have seen that Christianity and the South Asian religions have contributed to a balance of secular and spiritual values, but sections of Islam have been alienated, not least by a perception of a persistent crusading bias against it. The long-standing issue of Muslim–Christian tensions itself is too complex to be dealt with here, but the need to remove that bias must be a precondition for engaging Islam in the wider quest for modernity. For that to begin anew, it is most unhelpful to portray the Confucian East as allying with a Christian West against Islam, or allying with Islam against a Christian West.

September 11 has reminded us that a divided secularism can be challenged. Hence the calls for dialogue between erstwhile protagonists. That among various groups of religious modernizers is not new. They are accustomed to dialogue as they have had to defend themselves against fundamentalists among the secular and the religious alike for many decades. What is new is that the secularists need a deeper dialogue among themselves to face a common danger. Most important of all, many of them have to admit to the errors and weaknesses of their own propensity to be fundamentalist. Wherever secularists are seen as belittling religion and dismissing the spiritual needs of most people, whenever they couch their faiths in terms of absolute nationalist interests, and when they insist that only their claim of universalism is valid and all other claims must conform to their standards, they will meet with organized opposition. The proponents of secularism must re-examine the roots of modern secularism and consider how they can eschew the fundamentalism that has divided them. For them, letting religion back in is not the answer. But, without sufficient attention to spiritual needs, especially of people in the poorer nations of the world, secularism does not deserve the respect it has had so far.

Notes

1 First published in Eric Herschberg and Kevin W. Moore, eds, *Critical Views of September 11: Analyses from Around the World*, New York: The New Press, 2002, pp. 224–242. Reprinted with permission of The Social Science Research Council, New York.

2 Zhu Xi (1130–1200), leading Neo-Confucian philosopher [eds].

References

Chadwick, Owen, *The Secularization of the European Mind in the 19th Century*, Cambridge: Cambridge University Press, 1975.

De Bary, William T., ed., *Sources of Chinese Tradition*, vol. 2, New York: Columbia University Press, 1964.

De Bary, William T., *The Unfolding of Neo-Confucianism*, New York: Columbia University Press, 1975.

De Bary, William T., *Asian Values and Human Rights: a Confucian Communitarian Perspective*, Cambridge, Mass.: Harvard University Press, 1998.

Eisenstadt, Shmuel N., ed., *The Origins and Diversity of Axial Age Civilizations*, Albany, NY: State University of New York Press, 1986.

Eisenstadt, Shmuel N., and Wolfgang Schlucter, "Paths to Early Modernities – A Comparative View", *Daedalus* (Issue on Early Modernities), Summer 1998.

Eisenstadt, Shmuel N., "Multiple Modernities", *Daedalus* (Issue on Multiple Modernities), Winter 2000.

Frykenberg, Robert Eric, "Hindu Fundamentalism and the Structural Stability of India", in Martin E. Marty and R. Scott Appleby, eds, 1993, *Fundamentalisms and the State: Remaking Polities, Economies, and Militance*, Chicago and London: University of Chicago Press, pp. 233–255.

Gilbert, Alan D., *The Making of Post-Christian Britain: A History of the Secularization of Modern Society*, London: Longman, 1980.

Howard, Michael, "Stumbling into Battle", *Harper's*, January 2002.

Hu Qiaomu, "Questions on the Ideological Front" (Speech given on 8 August, 1981), *Beijing Review*, vol. 25, no. 4, 25 January 1982, quoted in Wang Gungwu, *The Chineseness of China: Selected Essays*, Hong Kong: Oxford University Press, 1991.

Huff, Toby E., *The Rise of Early Modern Science: Islam, China and the West*, Cambridge: Cambridge University Press, 1993.

Huntington, Samuel P., *The Clash of Civilizations and the Remaking of World Order*, New York: Simon and Schuster, 1996.

Kent, Ann, *Between Freedom and Subsistence: China and Human Rights*, Hong Kong: Oxford University Press, 1993.

Kersten, Rikki, *Democracy in Post War Japan: Maruyama Masao and the Search for Autonomy*, London: Routledge, 1996.

Lewis, Bernard, *What Went Wrong? Western Impact and Middle Eastern Response*, New York: Oxford University Press, 2002.

McLeod, Hugh, *Secularization in Western Europe, 1948–1914*, Basingstoke: Macmillan, 2000.

Madan, T. N., *Modern Myths, Locked Minds: Secularism and Fundamentalism in India*, Delhi: Oxford University Press, 1998.

Mahbubani, Kishore, *Can Asians Think?* Singapore: Times, 1998.

Martin, David, *A General Theory of Secularization*, Oxford: Basil Blackwell, 1978.

Marty, Martin E., and R. Scott Appleby, eds, *Fundamentalisms and the State: Remaking Polities, Economies, and Militance*, Chicago and London: University of Chicago Press, 1993.

Shambaugh, David L., *Beautiful Imperialist: China Perceives America, 1972–1990*, Princeton: Princeton University Press, 1991.

Sheridan, Greg, *Asian Values Western Dreams: Understanding the New Asia*, St. Leonard's, NSW: Allen and Unwin, 1999.

Tamini, Azzam, and John L. Esposito, eds, *Islam and Secularism in the Middle East*, London: Hurst and Company, 2000.

Thapar, Romila, "Imagined Religious Communities? Ancient History and the Modern Search for a Hindu Identity", *Modern Asian Studies*, 1989, vol. 23, no. 2, pp. 209–231.

Thapar, Romila, "Secularism: The Importance of Democracy", in Hiranmay Karlekar, ed., *Independent India: The First Fifty Years*, Delhi: Oxford University Press, 1998.

Tu Wei-ming, "The Ecological Turn in New Confucian Humanism: Implications for China and the World", *Daedalus: Journal of the American Academy of Arts and Sciences*, vol. 130, no. 4, Fall 2001, pp. 243–264.

Wang Gungwu, "Juxtaposing Past and Present in China Today", *The China Quarterly*, March 1975, pp. 1–24.

Wang Gungwu, *Power, Rights and Duties in Chinese History: The 40th George Ernest Morrison Lecture in Ethnology*, Canberra: Australian National University, 1979.

Wang Gungwu, review of *The Clash of Civilizations* by Samuel P. Huntington, *The National Interest*, no. 46, 1996.

Wang Gungwu, "After September 11 The Future of Secular Values", Social Science Research Council, htp://www.ssrc.org/sept11/essays/wang.htm, 2001.

Wang Gungwu, "The Limits of Secularism", *The Straits Times*, 25 November 2001.

Weber, Max, *The Religion of China: Confucianism and Taoism*, translated by Hans H. Gerth, Glencoe, Il.: Free Press, 1951.

Weber, Max, *The Agrarian Sociology of Ancient Civilizations*, London: New Left Books, 1976.

Wilson, Bryan R., *Religion in Secular Society*, Harmondsworth: Penguin, 1969.

12

SECULAR CHINA[1]

Wang Gungwu

For the topic of this memorial lecture dedicated to Giri Deshingkar (1932–2000) I have chosen to talk about secular China. I started thinking about secularism in our part of the world about two years ago and first spoke about it at a conference on Japan. There had been, for some time, much talk about failed states and failed economies. Japan was a shining example of how quickly a country could be modernized. So was Korea following Japan's success; and also Taiwan and the other little dragons. And then there was China reinventing and transforming itself at an amazing pace. All this had led many scholars to talk about what these countries had in common and also much talk about Confucianism. What caught my attention was the worldliness that all these areas shared and why these countries were never described as secular, even when it was the secular part of the Western success model that appealed most readily to all of them.

My thoughts on this subject came to a head when Bernard Lewis and many others after the 11 September tragedy in New York highlighted the rejection of the secular as one of the main reasons why fundamentalist Islam turned inwards and became hostile towards modernity.[2] At the Japan conference held a few weeks afterwards, I began to ask about the future of secular values. This was accompanied by my curiosity about why the word secular was not used about China even though China has been strongly this-worldly, and could even be described as extremist in its attitudes towards religion and the spiritual life since the early twentieth century.

By using the word secular, I realize I am wandering into very difficult terrain. There are so many ways that word has been used. And it has been a particularly powerful word in India, for the past half century at least. On the origins and ramifications of that word in the context of Indian politics and society, I have been inspired by what T. N. Madan has done in his classic study on secularism and fundamentalism in India, *Modern Myths, Locked Minds*. There is, of course, a vast literature on the subject for India alone. And for good reason. For a country that is home to ancient religions like Hinduism and Buddhism, and one that is home to one of the largest Muslim populations in any single country, secularism is a very special phenomenon. It has needed a lot of explication and re-examination.[3] And till this day outsiders like myself who have tried to follow the development of the ideal of secular India have experienced both enlightenment and concern as to how the concept of secularism can be realized here.

You are all familiar with the origins of the word as derived from European languages and cultures. It had many shifts in meaning and emphases throughout European history, but it has always been associated with the Christian Church, and normally evaluated in terms of relationships with that Church. Beginning with a "secular" as opposed to a "religious" clergy, it had evolved to mean the civil, lay and temporal and then, to heighten the contrast even more, the word was used to stress opposition to the Church and underline the non-religious and non-sacred. Ultimately, it became conceivable to "secularize" a person or an institution, and turn someone or something away from religious or spiritual purposes to material and worldly ones. Not surprisingly, these incremental changes in Western European countries while they modernized themselves after the Enlightenment of the eighteenth century ultimately led to an ideology of secularism.[4]

During the mid-nineteenth century, this ideology began to take shape. The emphasis was placed on taking issues of morality away from its dependence on religious doctrine and redefining a system of values that would be concerned with the well-being of people in this life alone. It can be said that Europe and the Christian West have been steadily secularizing along these lines for the past 500 years. The United States followed that tradition, and has a constitution that clearly separates Church and State on many issues. But, because of its different history where religious freedom was concerned, there remains considerable opposition at the grass-roots level to an ideology of secularism. Nevertheless, throughout the West, there is a general assumption that modernity demands that the most careful attention be paid to affairs of this world and not the next.

As for India, I have been fascinated by the twists and turns on this question during the period under British rule and in the politics of independence under its nationalist leaders, like Gandhi, Jinnah and Nehru, just to name a few. In the years after the country's independence, it has been difficult from the outside to grasp all aspects of the lively debates on Indian secularism. The glimpses I have had of the events of the past decade have only increased my puzzlement as to how that extraordinary story will unfold. To date, the brilliant chapter at the end of Madan's book, "The crisis of Indian secularism", has offered me the clearest picture, even though the events during the 5 years since the book was published have blurred some of the clarity I thought I had in my mind.[5] Clearly, there are many things I do not know about the ancient religion of Hinduism and about the Islam that is practised in India. For my purposes today, when talking about secular China, I have taken Madan's account to mark the limits of my understanding of Indian secularism and hope that you will forgive me for not going any further than that. I shall also not try to analyse all the ways that the word secular has been used in other parts of the world, or the refinements in meaning in various parts of the modern West. Instead, I shall simply introduce the idea of the secular in Chinese history.

As mentioned earlier, the adjective secular is rarely used for China in Western writings. This is largely because the connotations of separation of Church and State obviously did not apply to China. Given that specific usage, the lack of a Church may render the word unusable when we speak of socio-political phenomena in China. In his *Economic Ethics of the World Religions,* Max Weber noted that the Chinese lacked a special kind of religious ethic, and both his translator, Hans H. Gerth, and C. K. Yang who introduced *The Religion of China* did not use "secular" to describe that lack. I found it interesting that the few references to secularism in China have come from recent Catholic writings that point to the way that the present government in Beijing seems to have moved to a position whereby the State is persecuting Christians (and, more specifically, Catholics who look to Rome and are deemed unpatriotic). These writings suggest that what is happening may be compared to the way the Beijing authorities have pulled out all the stops in pursuing the followers of the Falungong.[6]

What I want to emphasize is that the Chinese have been primarily concerned with the worldly and the temporal from ancient times. This means that, unlike the West which had to deal with a powerful Church for centuries, the Chinese had begun with a secular outlook that ensured that no Church could be established to challenge political authority. In short, we may say that, in Europe, the secular evolved from a religious core or, as some might argue, the secular departed from a religious norm, whereas in China, what was worldly was the norm. This worldliness was taken so much for granted as the foundation of Chinese life that the Chinese have not found it necessary to emphasize the words needed to convey the idea of being secular. Indeed, when the European concept of secular was introduced to China, there was some difficulty finding the right word to capture its specific meaning. Religious affairs were never so influential in China that an indigenous concept was needed to determine how to deny or minimize the power of religion. Over the past century, the only idea of European secularism that gained the attention of Chinese leaders and intellectuals was that of "secular education". The Chinese were struck by the strenuous efforts made by many Western states to keep religion out of their public schools. In this context, the Chinese chose the word *shisu* to translate secular as being the closest rendering of the idea of Church–State separation, but that did not alter the fact that the Chinese had no idea what an official Church meant.

The Chinese word for secular consists of two characters: the first is *shi*, meaning a lifetime or generation, or an age or era and, inspired by Buddhist thought, is the time warp of what constitutes the word for "world" (in Chinese, *shijie*, the world). The other character is *su*, and this refers to common customs, the popular and vulgar matters that most people live with, or think that life is all about. Together, *shisu*, the word underlines everything in life that is this-worldly. But *shisu* is not a modern word. It dates back to the beginnings of Chinese written history centuries before the unification of Qin Shihuang (259–210 BC) in the third century BC. When the word was first used, it already represented the normal established expectations of the common people, those ways and customs that were transmitted from generation to generation. There was a strong sense of continuity, but at a lower social level. The task of transmission here was not the higher task of transmitting the Dao or the Way (*chuandao*) or of the classics or sutras (*chuanjing*). This kind of separation between the higher and the lower continuities did not have a European equivalent. Indeed, modern social science (in this case, the anthropologists) had to devise the idea of the Great Tradition in contrast with that of the Little Tradition in order to suggest that this separation was not at all like that between Church and State. In that context, the idea of the secular may seem to imply that the Little Tradition of the common people is worthy of official support.

But there is another twist to this story. The Chinese found that they did not have a word that accurately translated the modern Western concept of tradition. They eventually chose the word *chuantong*, a word that had been occasionally used in the past as a general term to include the higher responsibilities of *chuandao* (transmit the Way) or *chuanjing* (transmit the classics or sutras). But the original sense of *chuantong* was more diffuse and less tangible. Now the Chinese have enlarged the meaning of *chuantong* to emphasize that what was transmitted was a well-structured system of values, backed by great wisdom and authority, a system that combined all that had been transmitted, that is, the sum and essence of the Way, the Classics, or the Great Teachings. This is the nearest the Chinese have reached to capturing the sense of temporal orthodoxy passed down the generations. Originally, the power to define and delimit an orthodoxy rested with the ruler as Son of Heaven, who was the embodiment on earth of the cosmic forces that ruled all our lives. When this was transformed in the twentieth century into actual power passed on to the modern State, the legitimacy of that new State had to be couched in terms of rejecting what was decadent in the past and establishing what was progressive and desirable for the future. Thus, there was no question of transmitting the Great Tradition in its original form. But the idea of supporting the secular as something customary, common and popular was quite acceptable.[7]

It is significant that the Chinese found an ancient word to translate the modern idea of the secular, albeit not precisely, because there had been no history of Church–State separation. The word *shi*, meaning a generation or an age, was close to the original meaning of *saeculum*, "an age", and had been similarly extended to apply to "this world". And the word *su* captures what was lay, non-religious and non-sacred. Of particular importance to our understanding of the long history of a secular China is the fact that the ideograph *shi*, of this world, was one of the most commonly used words in the Chinese language. I could go on for pages to illustrate this by listing the numerous ways this expression of the worldly combines with other characters to convey some of the more materialistic features of Chinese society and culture. But let me briefly outline what this signifies.

The key is found in the fact that the word represents the continuity of lifetimes and generations. This is at the heart of the Chinese family system that Confucius and his disciples so strongly supported as the foundation of human order and harmony on Earth and under Heaven. Heaven and Earth go on forever, and the third leg of the Trinity, Man, had to do its part to match that continuity, and this to be done on this Earth. Here the spirits and ghosts of ancestors could link the present with the past, and what Man did on Earth in his lifetime could contribute to shape the future for his descendants. In that worldly lifetime on Earth, Man could engage in sacral actions through elaborate rituals, and some of the practices might have provided spiritually satisfying experiences to those who engaged in them. Many anthropologists today would say that they were comparable to religious acts, if not their exact equivalents. And this has given rise to the idea of secular religions, and we have evidence that this is prevalent in modern China.[8]

But let me return to the idea of a China that has been secular throughout most of its history. Insofar as the philosophers and generations of officials have emphasized the centrality of worldly matters in all public affairs and the rationality of all their duties, there may not be much room for dispute. But it was, of course, not that simple. During the ancient Shang dynasty (fifteenth to eleventh centuries BC), there had been considerable stress on religious ritual pertaining to the royal ancestors, and elaborate methods of divination were devised to guide public actions. The successor rulers of the Zhou dynasty (eleventh to third centuries BC), in their concern for dynastic maintenance and renewal, turned to more rational uses of the Royal Rites of Heaven-worship, and this tendency was further strengthened during the centuries of division that lasted some 500 years down to the third century BC. When the hundreds of little polities fought one another until only seven major states remained during the period of the Warring States, the secularization of public affairs became the new norm. The emergence of several groups of activist teachers and thinkers who offered their services to the seven contending ruling houses led to a greater emphasis on practical matters like economic surpluses, efficient armies, and tough administration as the basis for political success. In all the major writings preserved from this period that form the backbone of Chinese thought, there has been a uniform acceptance that it was the successful life on this earth, however defined, that really mattered. And this applied to ruler, functionary and commoner alike.

The most successful of the thinkers were Confucius and his disciples, the Legalists and, for a while, Mo Zi and his more plebeian followers. It was probably no accident that the Legalists provided the advice that brought about the unification of China. They were the most ruthless, logical, practical and secular of them all. We all know that Emperor Qin Shihuang, under whom the empire was unified, did not last long and the Qin dynasty was quickly succeeded by the Han. Indeed, the Han emperors invited other groups of activist thinkers to help work out more benign principles of government. But the administrative structure previously erected according to Legalist methods was largely retained. The hundred years of Han imperial peace that followed guaranteed the dynasty's longevity. And in these times of peace, the Confucians surfaced as a group who could offer the most integrated set of ideals that married practical government with moral theory, especially ideals that demonstrated their willingness to be loyal to the emperor as Son of Heaven. It was no wonder that Han Wudi (141–87 BC) invited these Confucians to be his close advisers and tutors to his heirs and, in addition, to help him recruit the best candidates to serve the empire.[9]

Within a generation, Confucian literati and their families came to dominate the key offices of government and make their doctrines the foundation of public life. And, true to Confucius' insistence that people should be concerned with this life and not speculate about the next, all public activity was secular. Rituals to show respect to ancestors were important to the ruling class and the populace, but they served to underline the importance of material advancement and well-being, including wealth making. Family practices were duties that had to be performed but they offered no kind of salvation, and even the public practices of the imperial house headed by the Son of Heaven carried no such message for his subject people.

This strong emphasis on worldly success sidelined the reservations put forth by major thinkers like Lao Zi, Zhuang Zi and their later followers, as well as other alternative visions presented by those who also rejected the new Confucian orthodoxy. The predominance of such this-worldly values eventually led to an arid discourse based on moral exhortations that offered no spiritual solace to most people, whether high or low. There were constructive critics of official Confucianism from the first century BC through the Latter Han dynasty (AD 25–220). One could point to the much respected writings by people like Yang Xiong, Wang Chong and Wang Fu, but none of them could provide imaginative alternatives for those people who wanted a more spiritual life.[10] I believe that this lack of a spiritual alternative cleared the way for the powerful impact of Buddhism when it was first brought to the Han capital of Chang'an by Indian monks during the first and second centuries AD.

The success of Buddhism was indeed a dramatic story that has been well studied and I do not need to dwell on the events that led to the marginalizing and enfeeblement of official Confucianism for nearly 300 years. The point I wish to make is that Han Confucianism had become so secular, so confident in its monopoly of public life, so neglectful of the spiritual vacuum that it had helped to create among the common people, that thousands and eventually millions turned to the Buddhist faith not long after its introduction into China. On this matter, the fourth to sixth centuries during which China was divided into the northern and southern dynasties provide important indicators of the nature of secular China. Whether with the Chinese themselves, or with the various tribal confederations that invaded North China, Buddhism made rapid progress among them as a well-organized religion. That was the first and only time that an alien religion met such a reception in China. It was so successful that indigenous local groups that had earlier found satisfaction in Daoism proceeded to emulate Buddhist institutions and establish their own claims to be an organized religion as well. Within a century after the end of the Confucian monopoly of public affairs, there were two rival organized religions that served the bulk of the population.

These two religions, however, did not succeed in removing the deep-seated secularity that dominated the public domain. Although the emperors of several dynasties during the period of division in both north and south China were deeply Buddhist and employed priests and devoted believers close to the throne, the functions of the state were still largely carried out along the lines established during the Han. After all, these functions had evolved over a period of several hundred years and had proven to have been valuable instruments of imperial power and vital to every dynasty that was ambitious to end divisions and reunify the empire. We could almost speak of the centrality of a secular political culture that had permeated public concerns to such an extent that no religion or religion-based systems could replace that culture. Thus, despite imperial patronage, Buddhist ideals of government did not last and, whenever the emperors faced serious threats to their rule, they turned for help to worldly Confucians who were committed to public service. And again and again, the Confucians showed their resilience, their capacity to ride the religious storms and offer secular havens for most ruling houses to survive longer, if not to achieve the unification that guaranteed a more lasting peace for all.

When I was last with Giri Deshingkar at Sariska, I wrote about the importance of the famous "Record of the Buddhist Monasteries of

Luoyang", the *Luoyang qielanji*, by Yang Xuanzhi (d. 555?), completed in the year 530.[11] For me, that work marked the epitome of the Buddhist conquest of China. Today, I shall mention two other works of the same period of division before the reunification by the Sui emperor in 589 to illustrate the resilience of the secular culture of earlier times. The first is "A New Account of Tales of the World", the *Shishuo xinyu*, sponsored by Li Yiqing (403–444), completed 100 years earlier than the Monasteries of Luoyang, about 430.[12] The second is the "Family Instructions for the Yan Clan", the *Yanshi jiaxun*, by Yan Zhitui (531–591), completed 160 years later.[13] Both works have become classics worthy to be listed with all the great works of ancient China that stand for the Chinese tradition of secularity.

I offer some remarks about them because they were prominent works written during the period of Buddhist ascendance. Both authors were aware of the pervasive influence of religion in the daily lives of most Chinese. The *Tales of the World*, collected under the aegis of a member of the imperial family, consisted mainly of stories concerning the upper classes and were hardly representative of the Chinese people. These stories show how the elites of the third and fourth centuries adjusted to the decline of Confucianism as an official orthodoxy. In doing so, they were able to let their imagination run more freely in ways stimulated by Buddhist and Daoist concepts. Although these elite families and individuals would not deign to follow popular practices in public, they had absorbed ideas that provided them with a sense of the transcendent that Confucianism had never encouraged. In most of the stories, matters of birth, life and death were discussed in a much broader framework and speculation about ghosts and spirits and the next life was pursued. But, at least at their level of society, nothing was changed where the education of their male progeny was concerned. The key social goals in the stories were temporal, totally consistent with the preparation for service to Man and rewards on this earth.[14] And the fact that the collection was one of the most popular for centuries testifies to the persistence of values that enabled future generations of Confucians to return to imperial service both strengthened and enriched.

The second work, the *Family Instructions of the Yan Clan*, showed a deeper understanding of Buddhist philosophy. The century and a half between the two works underlines the extent to which Buddhism had penetrated into the sub-conscious of the literati class. This book was a personal and intimate document whose author wanted to transmit all that he had learnt in life to his descendants. Written after great monasteries had sprung up everywhere and even more were being built across the land, the author was fully aware what richness of ideas and experiences had been successfully transplanted to China by the Buddhists and why. *Family Instructions*, in fact, includes a long chapter entitled "Turn your heart (to Buddhism)" that reads like a paean to the religion, with a strong endorsement of the concept of retribution.[15] Because of this, strict Confucians later on questioned why the book was included as one of the Confucian classics and, during the Qing dynasty, more than 1,000 years later, an attempt was made to remove it from the Confucian canon altogether. But fortunately, that narrow view of Confucianism did not prevail. For his private life, his very moving "Last Will" at the end of the book shows the impact of Buddhist sensibility on his willingness to modify Confucian ritual and practice. He was even prepared to place Buddha ahead of Confucius for having a more profound wisdom. But what really distinguished the work was its highly rational, and ultimately secular, tone. The principles that he underlined for his sons, and the duties he expected them to perform, were undoubtedly of this world. Throughout the book, he consistently reminded them that life's meaning unfolded in this world and it was never too early to prepare oneself for the responsibilities that flowed from that reality.[16]

In short, these two works reflected a deep-rooted Confucian secularism that had become lean and tough while at the same time surprisingly adaptable. That enabled Confucians to survive and make compromises with other elites when they thought there were alternative values and ideas they could use for the service of more worldly causes. This ability was to prove decisive again when Confucian thought regained prominence during the latter half of the Tang dynasty. Two decades after the court turned against the Buddhist monasteries in the ninth century, the Tang empire collapsed, followed by over 60 years of fragmentation. During these years, the desire for a return to a centralized state based on the secular ideals of Confucianism grew stronger. Indeed, the Song emperors after 960, as they began to reunify what they could of the Tang empire, set out deliberately to restore Confucian principles of governance. What was new, however, was that the new generations of Confucian thinkers were not confined to received texts and interpretations, but were people who had absorbed much of the intellectual ferment created by the Buddhist and Daoist challenges. They were sympathetic to the idea that the orthodox version of Confucianism needed an injection of the fresh concepts that had filled the spiritual vacuum among all Chinese for more than six centuries. The scholars, many themselves from commoner families, found inspiration in transmuting new ideas that the common people had found welcome. These included ideas that openly tied moral purpose to religious faith and concerns for the next life. By incorporating some of these into the new Confucianism, and especially by linking them to rituals and family practices within the clan system, more Confucian ideas became comprehensible to ordinary Chinese.[17]

I am obviously over-simplifying here because this lecture is not a history of Confucian thought. What needs to be underlined, however, is the fact that, despite drastic political upheavals at the end of the Han and then at the end of the Tang, there was a strong return to secular Confucian values. What followed during the Song dynasty were even more trials and tribulations for this Neo-Confucianism. The dynasty was militarily weak in spite of educating the most literate administration in Chinese history, and Neo-Confucianism did not have a magic wand to wave away the series of tribal-led invaders that tormented the dynasty until the Mongols finally conquered all of China in 1279. When Khubilai Khan established the Yuan dynasty and brought the ways of the steppelands into the Chinese political system, there was little room for Confucian principles. The bulk of the literati educated for public service were unemployed and the Mongols openly turned to Buddhist and Daoist advisers, and even some Muslim administrators from Central Asia, in order to strengthen their control over the Chinese populace. How the Confucians survived this major onslaught on their public profession was a remarkable story, but perhaps the most remarkable feature of that survival was how their commitment to secular principles remained intact till the opportunity came for them to prove themselves useful again.[18]

An equally dramatic change came about when the Mongols were thrown out in 1368. A former Buddhist monk, possibly supported by rebels with a Manichaean religious background, came to the throne, and he immediately brought all the Confucians he could trust to help him restore Chinese secularist rule. But this was not because he was that fond of Confucian ideals. What impressed him was the dedicated way these Confucians were trained to serve the dynastic house and their willingness to use the examination system to produce more people of the same mould.

Throughout the Ming dynasty (1368–1644), there was a tension between Confucian scholars and various groups of court favourites. The Ming emperors invariably placed the interests of the ruling house above all else, and any of the Confucian scholars who did not conform were treated very harshly indeed. But the secular values that had served the Confucians so well over the centuries continued to protect their role at court.

When the dynasty was overthrown, once again by invaders from the northern borders, this time the Manchus who established the Qing dynasty (1644–1911), the new rulers brought their own amalgam of shamanism mixed with Buddhism. But they too recognized the value of the Confucians. Although literati families all over the empire had vigorously resisted Manchu rule for many years, there were Confucians who were prepared to offer their secular skills to the new regime. Indeed, the Manchus wooed them by reviving the examination system. They insisted on the secular orthodoxy that most Confucians were ready to support, and recruited them to administer the civilian parts of government under close Manchu surveillance. The successful officials were also encouraged to turn to scholarship and give learned support to the orthodox Confucianism that the dynasty favoured.[19]

It is with this background in mind that some scholars have wondered whether a secular China could offer an alternative modernity to that established by Europe. Therefore, would the real questions to ask be the following: how quickly and thoroughly could China update its secular achievements? In what ways could China's secularism mesh in, or converge with, the modern secularism set forth in the European model?

China's defeats by the West in the nineteenth century clearly proved that the Chinese were technologically behind, their legal and administrative systems had obvious weaknesses and their imperial power structure was no match for a coalition of modern nation-states. But, in terms of the eighteenth-century Enlightenment project and the secularist breakthrough that flowered in Europe in the nineteenth century, the great gap in China that a new generation of Chinese intellectuals identified was its lack of science and a scientific spirit. This discovery led the young revolutionaries of the twentieth century not only to destroy the despotic power structure that a Manchu-supported Confucian orthodoxy had reinforced but also to reject everything that did not meet the standards of the new scientific truths that they brought in from the West.

In the excitement, they were convinced that a scientific materialism could replace everything in their traditions, and that everything that was not scientific was superstition. The speed at which some turned to godless communism has attracted much comment, and I need not dwell on that here. The point to emphasize here is that this scientific thrust was supported by China's own worldly materialist traditions. The new thrust simply went much further towards its logical conclusion and acquired fundamentalist characteristics that the earlier secularism had avoided. Once it was decided that the past was all superstition and despotism, it was easy to reach the conviction that science and democracy would solve all China's problems, as Chen Duxiu (1879–1942), the first secretary-general of the Chinese Communist Party, was to pronounce on behalf of the rebellious young some 90 years ago.[20]

What the new leaders of China did this past century was to build on its traditional secularism and turn modern science into a fundamentalist secular creed. As a result, the Chinese state became extremist in its total rejection of religion and in its contempt for any spiritual quest that sought solace in organized faith. In its most extreme form, this secular faith encouraged the destruction of churches, temples, monasteries and mosques during the frenzied years of the Great Proletarian Cultural Revolution. Since 1978, there has been a pulling back. The worst forms of anti-religious acts have been condemned, and official recognition of the four "established" religions (or five if Catholicism is separated from Protestant Christianity) has been restored. On the surface, there has been a return to something comparable to the superior but tolerant attitude that Confucian mandarins had about popular religions in pre-modern China. But a strong residue of secular fundamentalism remains. Unlike the earlier secularism, where the elites empathized, if not fully shared, the religious and spiritual premises that governed all lives in China, today's 60 million members of the Chinese Communist Party are expected to scorn anything that does not have a scientific pedigree.[21] It is not clear how this will evolve in the decades to come. If the fundamentalists prevail, religion will continue to be suspect and only state-approved doctrines and practices will be allowed. Any departure from what may be seen as no more than "secularized state religions" would be put down as acts of rebellion or threats to social order. But, if traditions of governance rooted in Confucian secularism survive and are restored as guides to ruling practices, there are other possibilities. One scenario suggests that a CCP mandarinate will emerge that would tolerate religious believers and even admit some into the Party and allow them to emerge among the ruling elites of the land. Under those circumstances, fundamentalist secularism would gradually be modified to the point when a modern secular state genuinely tolerant of religious pluralism is accepted as the norm.

Because I am speaking in India and in the shadow of Giri Deshingkar's view of China, let me end by sharing a thought about the contrast between secularism in China and India. I shall use two sets of four words that seem to mark out some of the differences. The first four words are taken from the nineteenth-century Indian Muslim poet Mirza Ghalib (1797–1869) when he advised Sayyid Ahmad Khan (1817–1898), the founder of the Aligarh Muslim University in India, not to look so much to the Mughal past. The lines were:

> Open thine eyes, and examine the Englishmen,
> Their style, their manner, their trade and their art.[22]

Of the four that Ghalib wanted Sayyid Ahmad Khan to examine, only "their trade" might have attracted the Chinese merchants on the coast, but that was precisely what the mandarin rulers had set out to limit and control. In no way would they have encouraged Chinese merchants to learn from English trading ways. And that would have been even more true of the English "manner" and the English "style" which, on the whole, the Chinese mandarins actively disliked. The fourth referring to the "art" of the English, some Chinese might have found interesting. They would have paid attention to British design and industrial arts, and also to their inventiveness in the use of materials. But, most of the time, what would have impressed the Chinese most was something that Ghalib did not refer to, "their power", that is, what made the British powerful.

The second set of four words I found in an essay written by Arthur

Waley (1889–1966) in 1942. Waley was a great translator of Chinese classics and literature. He never travelled to China himself but cultivated a fine sensibility about what Chinese civilization stood for. In 1942, he spoke of a new development when European poets, scholars and thinkers began to visit China instead of the usual soldiers, sailors, missionaries, merchants and officials that had been so dominant in the past. He was dubious about these men who had only gone to China in order to (and these were his four words) "convert, trade, rule or fight".[23]

When I look at these four words, I wonder what India's greatest leader Mahatma Gandhi (1867–1948) would have made of them. It seems to me that Gandhi would have rejected all four of them if they had been applied to India. He would have rejected "fight" because he would have thought that there had been too much fighting and killing in India already, and he saw no way of winning his particular war for independence on the battlefield. He would also have rejected the word "convert". What he would have admired was "to discover" and "to awaken", the way parts of Christian belief had helped him revivify his own faith. And clearly, he rejected British "rule". Indeed, his non-violent solutions to political problems remain original and inspiring paths to true independence even today. Lastly, we know that he rejected the kind of trade in mass-produced manufactures that gave the British their dominance in Indian markets and undermined the traditional economy and culture of the Indian peasantry. His way may not be practical in a globalized world, but he deeply wanted a return to a simpler and more spiritual life

In contrast, Chinese political leaders reacted positively on all four counts. The word "fight" certainly captured China's full attention, especially after China's first humiliating defeat by Britain in 1842. As for "trade", that had begun much earlier on the China coast, but its full impact did not come until after all the fighting was done. This the Chinese liked because they thought that they had the measure of the British. "To convert" was something more one-sided. The Chinese themselves paid little attention to converting others, and most Chinese resented attempts to impose an alien religion upon them. If there was any conversion, it was the conversion of the Chinese to modern science, seen by most of them as the key to progress, wealth and power. Finally, the word "rule" was only a partial, if not peripheral, experience for most Chinese. The British only ruled over bits of the Treaty Ports, and some Chinese communities outside China. The response among these Chinese was mixed, although the essential features of modern governance did attract attention from community leaders.

But there was no Chinese leader who even remotely thought like Gandhi, and few could even begin to understand what he really stood for. Among Chinese leaders, those who preached reform and revolution like Kang Youwei (1858–1927) and Sun Yat-sen (1866–1925), and nationalists like Chiang Kai-shek (1887–1975) and the young Mao Zedong (1893–1976), all responded positively to the secular values that the British offered. It was almost as if there was a matching, however imperfect, of secularisms. Taking the long view, the reason why the Chinese could take to these four words so readily was because the words were largely rooted in the secular China shaped over the 2,000 years before. It was not the same as European secularism, nor that of India, but what directed the evolution of that China was certainly secular.

Notes

1 This address was delivered as the Giri Deshingkar Memorial Lecture, Delhi, on 21 February 2003. Educated at SOAS, London, Giri Deshingkar was a distinguished China scholar and strategic thinker. He taught at Delhi University for 15 years before joining the Center for the Studies of Developing Societies, which he directed from 1987 to 1992. He helped found the Institute of Chinese Studies and the journal *China Report*. See "In Memoriam: GD Deshingkar," *China Report: A Journal of East Asian Studies*, vol. 36, no. 4 (Oct.–Dec. 2000), pp. 389–390 [eds].

2 Bernard Lewis, *What Went Wrong? Western Impact and Middle Eastern Response*, New York: Oxford University Press, 2001, pp. 152–157. Another example was Michael Howard, "Stumbling Into Battle", *Harper's*, January 2002, p. 17.

3 T. N. Madan, *Modern Myths, Locked Minds: Secularism and Fundamentalism in India*, New Delhi: Oxford University Press, 1997. Among other writings, I have also benefited from several of the essays collected in part four of *Secularism and its Critics*, edited by Rajeev Bhargava, New Delhi: Oxford University Press, 1998, notably the essay by Stanley J. Tambiah, "The Crisis of Secularism in India", pp. 418–453.

4 Owen Chadwick, *The Secularization of the European Mind in the 19th Century*, Cambridge: Cambridge University Press, 1975; Hugh McLeod, *Secularization in Western Europe, 1848–1914*, Basingstoke: Macmillan, 2000; Alan D. Gilbert, *The Making of Post-Christian Britain: A History of the Secularization of Modern Society*, London: Longman, 1980.

5 Without my knowledge, T. N. Madan was asked to chair this lecture. It was a privilege to have him beside me. He subsequently told me that he has written a new introduction to the fourth impression of his book (2003). This picks up some of the issues that have been debated since 1997. Given that the debate in India is inconclusive, a fresh look at a China variant might be a useful contrast.

6 I do not suggest that China is secular in the sense that there had been any kind of Church–State relationship, only that there is a secular China that has been dominant for most of the past 2,000 years. There are modern references to the secular nature of teachings by philosophers like Confucius, for example, Herbert Fingarette, *Confucius: The Secular as Sacred*, New York: Harper and Row, 1972. Understandably, secular has not been used to describe the mixed and complex nature of China as a whole; C. K. Yang, *Religion in Chinese Society: A Study of Contemporary Social Functions of Religion and Some of Their Historical Factors*, Berkeley, Ca: University of California Press, 1961; Marcel Granet, *The Religion of the Chinese People* [1922], translated by Maurice Freedman, Oxford: Basil Blackwell, 1975; Max Weber, *The Religion of China: Confucianism and Taoism*, translated by Hans H. Gerth [1951], introduction by C. K. Yang, New York: The Macmillan Company, 1964, pp. xiii–xliii.

In recent writings, "secular" has been used for Tibet where the "church" is seen to be in conflict with the "secular state". Similarly, articles by Christians on religion in China do now mention secular China. Two recent essays not published in religious magazines are worth noting: Jason Kindopp, "China's War on 'Cults'", *Current History*, September 2002, pp. 259–266, and Franz Schurmann, *Predictions* #75, 29 August 2000, on the challenge of Falungong to "secular forces" in China (http://www.pacificnews.org. html).

7 There is a long tradition of collecting material on popular customs (*fengsu*) in China that goes back to Ying Shao (*c.*140–*c.*206), *Fengsu tongyi* (Comprehensive meaning of customs). Thereafter, popular customs are often recorded in the Gazetteers of counties and provinces. After the denunciation of "feudal" Confucianism in the 1920s and 1930s, there was a new awakening of interest in folklore studies, notably the work of Gu Jiegang and his colleagues and the Folklore Research Institute at Sun Yat-sen University in Guangzhou. These works stressed the enduring features of these customs, even though some radicals would consider some of them nothing but superstition.

8 The best example for China is the "worship" of the god-like Mao Zedong at the height of the Great Proletarian Cultural Revolution; see Maurice Meisner, *Mao's China and After: A History of the People's Republic*, 3rd edition, New York: The Free Press, pp. 291–350.

9 The writings of Michael Loewe are authoritative on this subject. Three are relevant: *Crisis and Conflict in Han China, 104 BC to AD 9*, London: Allen and Unwin, 1974; *Chinese Ideas of Life and Death: Faith, Myth and Reason in the Han Period*, London: Allen and Unwin, 1982; *Divination, Mythology and Religion in Han China*, Cambridge: Cambridge University Press, 1994.

10 The *Fa yan* (model sayings) of Yang Xiong (53 BC–AD 18) was a major philosophical text in the canon, noted in Michael Nylan and Nathan Sivin, "The First Neo-Confucianism: An Introduction to Yang Hsiung's 'Canon of Supreme Mystery' (T'ai Hsuan ching, *c.*4 BC)", in Charles Le Blanc and Susan Blader, eds, *Chinese Ideas about Nature and Society: Studies in Honour of Derk Bodde*, Hong Kong: Hong Kong University Press, 1987, pp. 41–99. The *Lun heng* (doctrines evaluated) of Wang Chong (27–*c.*97) is better known. It has a full English translation in two volumes by Alfred Forke, published in 1907–1911 and reprinted by New York: Paragon Gallery, 1962. The *Qianfu lun* (discourses of a recluse) of Wang Fu (*c.*76–*c.*157) has also been translated; Margaret J. Pearson, *Wang Fu and the Comments of a Recluse*, Tempe, Ar.: Centre for Asian Studies, Arizona State University, 1989. For an example of a more orthodox Confucian of the same period, see Ch'en Ch'i-yun, *Hsun Yueh (AD 148–209): The Life and Reflections of an Early Medieval Confucian*, Cambridge: Cambridge University Press, 1975; also the chapters by Loewe and Ch'en in *The Cambridge History of China*, Volume I, *The Ch'in and Han Empires, 221 BC–AD 220*, edited by Denis Twitchett and Michael Loewe, Cambridge: Cambridge University Press, 1986, pp. 661–725 and pp. 767–807.

11 *A Record of Buddhist Monasteries in Lo-yang*, translated by Wang Yi-t'ung, Princeton: Princeton University Press, 1984. This has also been translated by W. F. Jenner as *Memories of Loyang: Yang Hsuan-chih and the Lost Capital, 493–535*, Oxford: Clarendon Press, 1981.

12 *Shih-shuo hsin-yu: A New Account of Tales of the World*, translated by Richard B. Mather, Minneapolis: University of Minnesota Press, 1976. A new edition, *New Account of Tales of the World*, has been published in Michigan Monographs in Chinese Studies, University of Michigan Press, 2002.

13 Yen Chih-t'ui (Yan Zhitui), *Family Instructions for the Yen Clan: Yen-shih Chia-hsun*, An annotated translation by Teng Ssu-yu, Leiden: E. J. Brill, 1968. For a broad survey of the decline of Confucian philosophy during the fourth to sixth centuries, see

Paul Demieville's essay, chapter 16 (and Timothy Barrett's Postscript) in *The Cambridge History of China,* Volume I, *The Ch'in and Han Empires,* pp. 826–878.

14 Richard B. Mather also speaks of a growing individualism being encouraged in children during this period, but the criteria of talent and success remained temporal: "Filial Paragons and Spoiled Brats: A Glimpse of Medieval Chinese Children in the *Shishuo xinyu*", in Anne Behnke Kinney, ed., *Chinese Views of Childhood,* Honolulu: University of Hawai'i Press, 1995, pp. 111–126. For a fuller study of this question of individualism, Qian Nanxiu, *Spirit and Self in Medieval China: The Shih-shuo Hsin-yu and its Legacy,* Honolulu: University of Hawai'i Press, 2001.

15 *Family Instructions,* pp. 137–152; for a useful discussion of the powerful presence of Buddhist ideas in Yan Zhitui's lifetime, see Whalen Lai, "Society and the Sacred in the Secular City: Temple Legends of the *Lo-yang Chieh-lan-chi*", in Albert E. Dien, ed., *State and Society in Early Medieval China,* Hong Kong: Hong Kong University Press, 1990, pp. 246–268.

16 *Family Instructions,* pp. 209–211.

17 Peter K. Bols, *"This Culture of Ours": An Intellectual Transition in Tang and Sung China,* Stanford: Stanford University Press, 1992, pp. 148–175.

18 Jennifer W. Jay, *A Change of Dynasties: Loyalism in Thirteenth Century China*, Bellingham, Wa.: Western Washington University Center for East Asian Studies, 1991, pp. 243–264; also John D. Langlois, Jr., ed., *China under Mongol Rule,* Princeton: Princeton University Press, 1981, essay by Langlois, "Political Thought in Chin-hua under the Mongols", pp. 137–185.

19 Philip A Kuhn, *Soulstealers: The Chinese Sorcery Scare of 1768,* Cambridge, Mass.: Harvard University Press, 1990, pp. 187–222, captures the tensions between a Manchu emperor and the bureaucratic system he inherited. Other works show how Han officials dedicated themselves to scholarship: R. Kent Guy, *The Emperor's Four Treasures: Scholars and the State in the Later Ch'ien-lung Era,* Cambridge, Mass.: Council on East Asian Studies, Harvard University Press, 1987; Kai-wing Chow, *The Rise of Confucian Ritualism in Late Imperial China: Ethics, Classics, and Lineage Discourse,* Stanford: Stanford University Press, 1994; Benjamin A. Elman, *Classicism, Politics, and Kinship: The Ch'ang-chou School of New Text Confucianism in Late Imperial China,* Berkeley, Ca.: University of California Press, 1990.

20 Chen Duxiu's famous statement made in 1919, quoted in Wang Gungwu, "May Fourth and the GPCR: The Cultural Revolution Remedy", in *The Chineseness of China,* Hong Kong: Oxford University Press, 1991, p. 241.

21 Jiang Zemin's preface to a popular science series, "Raise high the scientific quality of the whole nation" (23 December 1999), and the hundreds of essays on similar themes collected in the *Zhongguo jingshen wenming jianshe nianjian 2001* (China cultural and ethical progress yearbook), Beijing: Xuexi Publishers, 2002, 1,116 pages. These essays reflect the extraordinary efforts made to transmit a secular spirit among the young in China.

22 Ralph Russell and Khurshidul Islam, *Ghalib, 1797–1869. Life and Letters,* New Delhi: Oxford University Press, 1994 (first published by Harvard University Press, 1969), pp. 90–91. The lines quoted here are found in Rajmohan Gandhi, *Revenge and Reconciliation: Understanding South Asian History,* Delhi and London: Penguin Books India, 1999, p. 136, which quotes from Hafeez Malik, *Sir Sayyid Ahmad Kahn and Muslim Modernisation in India and Pakistan,* New York: Columbia University Press, 1980, p. 58.

23 Hsiao Ch'ien (Xiao Qian, compiler), *A Harp with a Thousand Strings: A Chinese Anthology in Six Parts,* London: Pilot Press, 1944, pp. 381–383. Both the Ghalib and Waley sets of words are discussed in my forthcoming book, *Anglo-Chinese Encounters Since 1800: War, Trade, Science and Governance,* Cambridge: Cambridge University Press, 2003.

13

MIXING MEMORY AND DESIRE

Tracking the migrant cycles[1]

Wang Gungwu

Let me begin by reading the following lines from T. S. Eliot's *The Waste Land*:

> April is the cruelest month, breeding
> Lilacs out of the dead land, mixing
> Memory and desire, stirring
> Dull roots with spring rain.
>
> T. S. Eliot, "The Waste Land" (1922)

The poem was written after the First World War had devastated Europe. I first read these lines in 1947, 2 years after the Japanese had transformed the lives of the Chinese in British Malaya and fatally damaged Nationalist China. "The Waste Land" was introduced to me by a fellow undergraduate at the National Central University in Nanjing in 1947. We were in the middle of a civil war in China. I was 17 years old and had just come from a colonial education in Malaya. My friend had come back from the interior of China. He knew the Chinese classics, especially literature, both prose and poetry, but he also read many of the best writings of Western literature.[2] In addition, he was following British poets like W. H. Auden and Stephen Spender. He found our classes in Chinese and Western literature less interesting than going to the British Council Library to read the latest poetry in English. There I saw him copying by hand the whole of the *Four Quartets* by T. S. Eliot.[3] I was impressed and intrigued by my friend who, in the middle of student demonstrations against American imperialism and the Guomindang government, saw English literature as an enrichment of his own heritage. I had a strong desire to emulate him. Till this day, the memory of seeing him treat Eliot with such reverence still fills me with wonder.

It is not yet April,[4] and we do not live in the dead land, but there are stirrings of spring in research and documentation on the Chinese overseas. So it may not be inappropriate to quote from Eliot's poem here. The words I want to stress are memory and desire. The words capture my own mood, wishing to recall what has been done for the Chinese who had left home, and to understand the kinds of desires, dreams, hopes, longings these sojourners had, especially those for security, wealth and adventure, once they were away from China. The wide range of their desires is of the greatest interest. How does one begin to understand the nature of these desires if they are not documented in some way? This has made me curious about the memories that these Chinese have shared at different stages of migration, and in the many different places they went to. How much of their desires are consciously or unconsciously reflected in what they remember? Historians are concerned with what are found in recorded documents and hesitate to deal with what is unknown. This leads me to look at the way we might try to document what is unknown, and how we might find new ways to augment the documents we have.

A few words about documents, and then I shall come back to memory and desire. It seems to me there are three large groups of documents that I shall call the formal, the practical and the expressive. For each of these, there were public and private faces and they varied greatly in time and place. In places where the Chinese had the numbers to be seen as a community (however small), we can take the many periods and occasions when sojourners abroad organized themselves the best they could, and distinguish them from the times when migrations were institutionalized either by the host country or by the sending authorities. At various levels of these people movements, we get glimpses of the conditions under which individual migrants remembered their pasts and articulated their hopes for their future. To track some of the migrant cycles that the Chinese experienced, I shall first describe what I mean by formal, practical and expressive documents.

The formal is the most obvious. They are found in the official archives that provide the backbone of all documentary collections for historians. These archives range from basic administrative records registering arrivals and locating where the immigrants live and work, to the speeches and the acrimonious debates about what to do about migration policy, how to deal with those already settled and those planning to come. The reports may be found in dusty files, printed collections, political tracts, or recorded and quoted in magazine articles and newspaper accounts. Modern well-managed countries preserve these more or less systematically, but they are vulnerable to loss and decay when there is any breakdown of order. Outside archives and libraries, such formal documents would include buildings and monuments, and the memoirs of all those public figures who were involved in the management of migration matters, and also all the scholarly writings that have tried to immortalize the migrant sagas. Here the desire to keep records and the duty to remember have, on the whole, interacted effectively, especially in areas where there has been a strong bureaucratic and healthy historical tradition. But often the criteria as to what should or should not be retained have been inconsistent if not discriminatory, and actions to preserve the documents for the public to use have been slow and desultory, if not often come too late.

The practical is much more varied. When written down, it would include everything noted down by private persons or organizations because there was a need to remember, even if it were merely for immediate use. They would include appointment records, accounts and receipts, legal briefs, business notes, correspondence of all kinds, the meeting minutes of social and cultural organizations, and the daily newspapers that people depended on for local and useful information. Also included are family papers like genealogies and biographies and other clan records. But it is not limited to literate evidence that may or may not find their way into archives and libraries. The practical would also include the household goods in the migrant homes, the essential tools and instruments in their work-places, and the vehicles they used in a foreign land. It would include not only what they brought with them but also what they devised locally to enable them to adapt to different living conditions. Some of the most practical that would help support the community's solidarity would be public festivals, temple operas, and social events like weddings and funerals. Certainly, the places where the men could eat and drink and meet their women, the temples that bound them in hope and solace, the medical shops and centres that kept them healthy and alive, the societies that linked them to their homes in China, and the cemeteries for their dead, all belong to this category of the practical.

These documents were not always recognized and consciously preserved, but modern museums have changed that. We are better served by new generations of professionals who have often gone out of their way to identify what needs to be saved. Here memory has not been systematic, and actions to rescue the past for posterity have been erratic, even accidental, when they happen at all. In growing urban areas, the pressures of rapid development often threaten these documents as companies come and go, and migrant people are more mobile, and also when the settled among them are liable to forget what is no longer useful. Outside of towns, it is even easier to neglect what was once valued as land and labour that are now put to new uses. Old plantations and mining towns, and the temples and cemeteries that served their working populations, have often given way to roads and factories or returned to the jungle. There is now new desire by some communities, their heritage professionals, and local politicians and teachers to have some of these practical documents preserved. But, in many cases, the costs are prohibitive and only the determined and dedicated have succeeded in having the documents restored and protected.

As for the expressive documents, these are the most closely linked to desires and have not always been as easy to recognize as the other two kinds. They go beyond the recording of facts and data that are usually found in formal and practical documents, although the expressive bits may also be located in the formal and practical documents if you are clear in your own mind what you are looking for. For example, in an official document, one may find accounts relaying specific examples of heroism or cowardice, greed or generosity, ingenuity or criminality brought about by strong desires. Some administrative and court records included stories that revealed the rich variety of experiences of migrant peoples, many of which confirmed how truth was often stranger and more unforgettable than fiction. This is even truer of the practical documents, notably in newspapers after they became popular and inclusive towards the end of the nineteenth century. Many, and especially those that had magazine sections, narrated or discussed the unexpected and remarkable, the pains of failure and the delights of achievement, the joys and agonies of meeting and parting and, above all, gave opportunities to the literate to put their feelings down as prose or poetry. Other examples, and again these came later when more migrants were literate, were the letters written home. Although most of these were conventional and practical, conveying family news and answering inquiries, some occasionally included anecdotes of unusual people whom the migrants had met, or incidents of exceptional kindness or cruelty, or descriptions of strange sights and sounds and places of exceptional beauty or ugliness.

Expressive documents are more often found when the Chinese stopped sojourning. Some of these Chinese returned to China to record their experiences; others chose to settle down abroad and set out to explain what they achieved by so doing. Most often, these are the most consciously produced by the second generation or the third, especially those born to families of some means who were given new educational opportunities. This was particularly true of those who went to Southeast Asia where the families needed time and opportunity to progress from rags to riches. Thus, although Chinese traders have been going to the Nanyang for centuries, expressive documents were late in appearing and became noticeable only in the nineteenth century. In comparison, more literate sojourners headed for the goldfields of California in the US, British Columbia in Canada and Victoria in Australia and, especially in the US, where they were joined by students sent by the Chinese government and those sent by Christian missions working in various parts of China.[5] The literate could express themselves almost immediately and also knew how their documents might be preserved. But for most other areas where migrant Chinese went, it was not until the twentieth century that expressive documents began regularly to surface, especially in the most difficult area of literature, i.e. short stories, novels and poetry.

Returning to memory and desire, I would like to focus on these expressive documents. I believe that such documents capture a valuable dimension of the transnational networks that is the theme of this conference. For the rest of this chapter, I shall relate some of my experiences with the kinds of desire that enliven migrant societies. Inevitably much of what follows is a personal document and I seek your indulgence for letting me share that with you this morning.

I came across two contrasting sets of desires when I was still a boy living in Ipoh, a small mining town in the state of Perak in northern Malaya. The first was when a schoolmate of mine went back to Penang where his parents came from to attend the wedding of his eldest sister. He brought back photographs of the wedding ceremony, with the bride dressed in a traditional Chinese wedding dress together with her mother dressed in the *sarong kebaya* that Straits (called "Baba" by some) Chinese had adapted from what Malay women wore. He showed them to us with great pride and told us that he would one day want to marry in the same way. He said that he was hurt by the way newly arrived Chinese scorned his local family customs, and that his family was more truly Chinese than some of the Chinese who loudly claimed to be patriotic Chinese. He felt strongly that what generations of his family had loyally maintained should be respected and preserved.[6]

About the same time, relatives of family friends arrived as refugees from the Japanese invasion of China. They had come from Shanghai where they were all born. I found them very different from the rest of us and their memories very fresh and exciting. Through the eldest of them, I met a strong longing for the home he had left. Together, we learnt patriotic songs about the war in China, went to tearful Chinese films, read lively Shanghai magazines. But what struck me most was his admiration for an aunt who stayed on in Shanghai. I was shown photographs of her wedding to his uncle. She was radiant in a beautiful wedding gown that would have drawn sighs from brides-to-be in London or Paris. I learnt that she was born of Cantonese parents in Sydney and had grown up with English as her first language. Her father founded a department store in Sydney and the success of that venture led him to establish similar stores in Hong Kong and Shanghai.[7] These stores grew to be part of an international chain that has pride of place in the business history of modern China. Following the success, the aunt moved to Shanghai and made that her home. To my friend, she was the epitome of all that was modern and progressive, and symbolized the China that he wanted to see flourish. In today's terms, she was transnational before the word was invented.

The two sets of desires stayed in my memory as I followed some of the later documents, both formal and practical, that recorded what happened to the Baba or Peranakan Chinese on the one hand and the people and society of Shanghai on the other. Today, there are innumerable books that seek to capture both these subjects. On the Baba, there have been many memoirs, biographies, family histories, numerous scholarly studies of people, artifacts, rituals and commemorations and a wide range of affectionate accounts, much of which has enriched the book by Khoo Joo Ee entitled *The Straits Chinese: A Cultural History* (1996).[8] But I have not found anything that quite captures the strong desires my school friend had about keeping his family traditions alive against the unjustified scorn expressed by Chinese who had just come from China.

Similarly, the mountain of books and articles about old and new Shanghai is now overwhelming. I now know the city in ways that my young refugee friend could not have known. Certainly, he was not able in 1940 to communicate all that he felt for the city. His aunt's story has now been told. This was done through her letters, memorabilia and oral accounts, in a book compiled by a Shanghai journalist 2 years ago. I read it with keen interest, especially when I realized that she was the aunt of my childhood friend. I was particularly moved when I read about how his aunt felt about the death of her husband in the hands of fanatical Communist youth, and why she stayed on in Shanghai to dedicate herself to teaching English to another generation. She continued to do so into her eighties, until a few years before she died. Every page of the book added to my understanding of how this daughter of Sydney, despite all that happened to her and her family, came to love Shanghai.[9] I think I also began to feel something for the sense of awe that my childhood friend had expressed at his aunt's return to China, but I am not sure that anything can help me describe his fervent desire at the time that Shanghai be the hope of modern China. This has certainly been made more multi-layered by the fact that, for the very practical reason of being a success in his adopted country, he eventually chose not to return.

These two of my memories marked the beginnings of my awareness of what constitutes people's desires that are so difficult to preserve. There are millions of such desires that contain insights concerning the wandering Chinese which are forever lost because we lacked the ways to have them documented. But let me not give way to sentimentality here. When feelings are strong, and the opportunity arises, I am confident that people do have the ability and the determination to get their story recorded whether in prose or verse or in a non-literary form.

The ideal medium to express these desires would be, to give a few examples, creative writings, compositions, paintings, sculptures, buildings, food and clothing and various kinds of design. The choice of medium varies with the social, economic and political environment the Chinese have to face. In areas where literacy in any language is low, expressions are more likely to occur in music and dance, and paintings and sculptures. Where aesthetic preferences are in the visual arts, there would be good examples in the world of design in addition to that of painting and architecture. Elsewhere, there may be room for creativity with food and clothing. And where literacy and a strong literary tradition already exist, the quality of fiction, drama and poetry could be expected to be high. Personally I am most attracted to literary expression. The Chinese themselves have a rich writing tradition, so much so that, where they do not have a large readership in the Chinese language, they could adapt to using foreign languages to bring forth what they have to say. The measure of their success in writing works of quality may be determined by the literary traditions of the people they have settled among, and how receptive the host peoples are to writings by new immigrants.

I do not need to go far in Southeast Asia to find expressive works in the fine arts. Chinese contributions to painting, architecture and design have been around for generations and may be found throughout the region. With literature, however, we know how much has been done in the nineteenth century in languages like Vietnamese, Thai and Bahasa Melayu Tionghua.[10] But, with some exceptions, the emphasis then has been more on transmission and entertainment than on creativity. This was particularly true with the retelling of stories drawn from the great romances of China. How much of these can be said to be expressive, however indirectly, of the desires that the settled Chinese community felt about their new homes has yet to be established. It was not until the twentieth century when a sizeable audience literate in Chinese emerged, especially in the cities and towns of British Malaya, that creative writings in Chinese inspired by the *baihua* movement in China came into its own.[11] This literature was, for a while, largely dominated by themes drawn from China, and the desires that are found in them reflect those of the recent immigrants and rarely capture a local perspective. Certainly the settled Straits Chinese could not express themselves in this way and, from the point of view of quality, their writings in English could not match those in Chinese by the sojourners for at least another generation.[12]

The more recent writings by settled Chinese in languages like Thai, Bahasa Indonesia and English are gaining recognition, but few have gained the wide transnational audiences that those writing in English in the West have attained. Clearly, the Chinese living in the West have a marked advantage in their literary contributions. Of course, they are also represented in painting and other fine arts and even in areas like design, fashion and the culinary arts. But, given the powerful literary traditions in migrant nations like the United States, Canada and Australia, literature has attracted the largest numbers of practitioners, and increasingly we are seeing major contributions being made to mainstream literature in those countries. When we see how much their work has succeeded in expressing their manifold desires for a wider public, it suggests that we have indeed lost much in documenting the desires of those Chinese who had sojourned or settled outside the English language realms.[13]

I am partial to literate expressions of desires because they are more direct and far easier to understand. Today, these are not limited to the printed word but can be powerfully transmitted through films and the electronic media, where they, of course, draw on many of the other skills in expression that I have mentioned above. But there is a paradox here. Creative expressions, especially those of high quality, quickly rise above nationality or ethnicity or even the language medium chosen. At that point, we go past the point when we talk about what is Chinese and what is not. It is no longer a question of the desires of diasporic or displaced Chinese, but the literary genius of transnationals whose best work may be compared with other writers whether of migrant origins or not. Such achievements that belong to humankind deserve our admiration but, in the context of our concern here with documents about the Chinese overseas, it may not necessarily add to our store of the expressive documents that our libraries and archives are short of.

This brings me now to the migrant cycles in the title of this lecture that I hope memory and desire can help me track. My two stories of undocumented desires marked two ends of the Chinese sojourner spectrum. At one end, with my Straits Chinese schoolmate, the desire to firm up the roots that his ancestors had already sunk into their adopted homes, in this case, the Malaya of the Straits Chinese who had settled there four or more generations ago. How long should their desires and memories be considered as recognizably Chinese? Should they not be seen as something quite distinctively new? At the other end, with my friend from Shanghai, the longing for a home just abandoned, and his affection for an uncle's family, determined that my friend should stop sojourning and go home as soon as he could. How should we distinguish these desires and memories from those of Chinese in China? As long as they come from those who are self-consciously sojourners who are awaiting a chance to return to China, are they not merely variants of homesick longings found in China itself? The gap between the two sets of desires is wider than I understood when I first heard them. The more I know now, the more it appears that the spectrum of desires in between are fluid and transitional. What these responses in between can offer to our collection of expressive documents concerning the Chinese overseas may turn out to be more elusive than illuminating. Let me explore this further.

I did not follow the stories of my two young friends further, having my own confused desires to deal with. The Japanese occupied Malaya from 1941 to 1945, I went to study in Nanjing where I met the friend who loved T. S. Eliot, the communist victory there drove me back to Malaya to face a hopeful nation-building future, and I subsequently made a fateful decision to pursue an academic career in Chinese history. Step by step, I found myself narrowing the spread of my desires in order to help me find my professional niche.

Even as I did that, something led me back to China's relations with our region, a field still poorly researched. Thus, I began my apprenticeship with work on Kang Youwei and Sun Yat-sen in the Straits Settlements and then, going far back into the ancient past, the search for the Nanhai trade between China and Southeast Asia.[14] This brought me in touch with two pioneers who guided me in my early work: Chen Yusong (Tan Yeok Seong) and Xu Yunqiao (Hsu Yun-ts'iao). There was here also a clear contrast between the two. Tan Yeok Seong was a Hokkien descended from generations who were committed to the Nanyang and who called Malaya his home. He was closer in spirit to my Straits Chinese friend, with the important difference that he had studied in Xiamen University and knew Chinese well.[15] Hsu Yun-ts'iao, on the other hand, was a newcomer to Southeast Asia. He came from Suzhou on the south bank of the Yangzi river in Jiangsu province. He brought a sojourner's sensibility to his studies, but he saw China and the Nanyang as historically and economically inseparable.[16] As a result, the more I did my readings in their personal libraries and with their guidance, the more I felt the need to know China better. Thus I turned totally towards Sinology and the history of China. This gave prominence to one of my desires, to be the Chinese scholar that my parents would be proud of.

But it was not so simple. I remained outside of China and lived among a variety of peoples in Singapore and Kuala Lumpur, including a great variety of people of Chinese descent. I married Margaret who, although born in Shanghai, learnt to love the Malaya that later became the Federation of Malaysia and the Republic of Singapore. Soon my desires intermingled with all those who chose to make their homes there. China became a vocation and a memory while I tamed my earlier desires so that I could accept my role as a local university man. My academic colleagues remained curious why I did not follow up my Nanhai trade story beyond the tenth century. Friends outside the campus also asked me to talk about the Nanyang Chinese both past and present. Furthermore, among the questions regularly asked of me were the story of Admiral Zheng He's visits to Malacca between 1405 and 1433, and the reasons why those expeditions were stopped. Above all, the anti-communist and nation-building politics of the time ensured that someone keenly interested in Chinese history would be under suspicion. To make matters worse, I was not allowed to read any books and journals published in China without the approval of the Malayan security authorities.[17]

This was how my various desires converged, leading me to place China's maritime troubles in history side by side with what sojourner and settled Chinese were doing in various parts of Southeast Asia. By adjusting my interests to a longer perspective of Chinese ventures overseas, I was introduced to what the early sojourners desired and how little they remembered. From China's point of view, there were cycles of care and neglect. As the Chinese were seen in the eyes of indigenous rulers and other Asian traders from India and West Asia, there were different cycles of useful service and competitive threat. More recently, when the Europeans arrived in force, there were even more distinctive cycles of collaborationist merchants and effective but unruly labour that needed to be carefully managed. And, at the same time, from the perspective of the Chinese overseas themselves, there were recurring and sometimes contradictory cycles of longing for a strong China that could protect them coupled with a preference for weak officials serving the coastal provinces of China who would leave them and their families in China alone.

What I did not expect was to have my desires shrink to a deepening concern for immediate challenges to the Chinese communities among whom I lived. I was drawn forward to twentieth-century problems, to the period I had started with in 1952, to the reformers and revolutionaries who transformed the politics of China. This was in some ways advantageous for me. The documents both formal and practical were more plentiful and accessible, and the protagonists were alive and around. Also, nation-building in our region, including in China itself, was pressing and seemingly urgent. Above all, the struggle for Malaysia that led to the independence of Singapore in 1965 highlighted the vital question of voting numbers where the ethnic Chinese were concerned.[18] It was simply not possible for the desire to remain Chinese in one way or another to be untouched by the growing pressures for change at all levels. Here the variety of Chinese responses to the new pressures showed how tangled their desires had become. They also revealed the coming together and crisscrossing of various cycles of attention and neglect, threat and usefulness, fears and hopes that had from time to time troubled Chinese lives in Southeast Asia. This was particularly true of those who wanted to remain culturally Chinese in countries ruled by indigenous Southeast Asians.

The mid and late 1960s became a turning point for most Chinese overseas. The Cold War could not save the Malayan Communist Party and those Chinese who had supported similar parties around the region. The Vietnam War was the climax of the Cold War in Asia and this saw the destruction (perhaps temporary) of the Chinese communities in Vietnam and Cambodia. This was followed by the Great Proletarian Cultural Revolution in Mao Zedong's China, accompanied by the ill-treatment of returned overseas Chinese and all those with overseas connections. Then there was the abortive coup in Indonesia, the so-called Gestapu of September 1965, during which all documents in Chinese were openly and officially destroyed. After that, the spirit of Bandung on which so many Chinese overseas had pinned their hopes also came to an end. Also, largely because of fears about the dangers of ethnic conflict, the new nations of the region adopted tightly controlled policies about their people's right of self-expression. About the same time, countries like the

United States and Canada, followed by Australia, began to revise their immigration policies. This made it possible for more Chinese to move there. With all these changes, there could no longer be a simple one-dimensional spectrum of desires. In Southeast Asia, in particular, choices had to be made from a complex web of possibilities.

At least, this would seem to be so on the surface and there is little doubt that the formal and practical documents we have would reflect this development. But precisely because desires have rarely been articulated and are, in any case, difficult to chart, there will be big gaps in the expressive documents. And, without that, our picture of continuous challenge and change is surely incomplete. In any case, the desires of the large Chinese populations of the region have changed beyond recognition during these years, and the speed of change has left most of them bewildered and fearful. Under these circumstances, how could their memories be reliably recorded either by themselves or by others? Memories are notoriously faulty and selective but now, even what may be truly remembered is likely to have been fragmented by the pressures of events beyond their control.

It is in this context that we observe that a new overarching migrant cycle, or perhaps more than one, is developing. The main thrust of the cycle derives from a China that has changed tack close to 180 degrees within the last couple of decades. The prospect of a strong and prosperous China would be unfamiliar to those who know little history or could only dimly remember the past 150 years of China's disunity and decline. The signs are that great changes lie ahead and all Chinese everywhere are gearing themselves up for them. Beneath the overhanging arch are at least three lesser cycles. The first of these is experienced by former sojourners who have long settled down or now wish to settle down in new national homes. Another cycle would impinge on those who have moved on as re-migrants to other foreign lands and are seeking a new rhythm to a renewed stage of sojourning. And, not any less important, the third cycle is being carried by fresh immigrants out of China, those who are eagerly bringing their Chinese desires to the nations still willing to take them.

To go back to Eliot's "The Waste Land", is there now a new stirring of dull roots with spring rains? We know how pragmatic most Chinese are. The official bodies are there to collect the formal and practical documents, and most of those should survive for future stories to be told from. Given so many rapid changes in a lifetime, what more can the migrants expect? What if earlier desires and memories are not documented? Does that really matter? In their eyes, probably all that is needed is courage and luck and the willingness to take risks whenever necessary. There will be fresh lots of desires that the previous sets, even if remembered, could do little to explicate. As fresh migrants and re-migrants, they will need all their wits about them to deal with the perilous and the unforeseen. An imperfect record should be good enough, it is still better than having none. If their predecessors had coped without roadmaps, so can they. The world is simply too demanding for them to have the luxury of learning from the past.

I recognize the note of helplessness behind the Chinese traditional optimism here and offer my sympathies. But my heart belongs with the documenters, and not for professional reasons. We all need to know. The fact that the Chinese overseas knew so imperfectly about their past is no reason why we should continue to do so. Indeed, what little we do know can, in many cases, provide insights to what will happen. I recall writing about 10 years ago, in a Foreword for the book edited by Ronald Skeldon entitled *Reluctant Exiles? Migration from Hong Kong and the New Overseas Chinese*, the following words: "What is remarkable is that this is the first time that any Chinese population has been studied as an emigrant group while in the throes of migrating."[19] I still think that this is a remarkable project and look forward to the invaluable documents that it will provide for future historians. But, when I wrote those words, I was only focused on formal and practical documents. If I were to write the foreword again, I would have included an appeal for the memories and expressive desires to be sought out as documents. This gathering of librarians, archivists and scholars, I hope, will join me in this appeal. Too many migrant desires have been left without the memories needed to leave an impact, or at the least, some clear impressions. But, with the new processes now open to scrutiny and the current sources available for a fuller record, this is no waste land. Perhaps all we need is more spring rain.

Notes

1 This is a revised version of the keynote address delivered at the Second International Conference of Institutes and Libraries for Overseas Chinese Studies (Hong Kong, 13–15 March 2003).

2 My friend could recite Chinese poetry of most dynasties and was deeply immersed in the prose fiction of the Ming and Qing dynasties. When I first met him, he had read all the poems of his favourite American poet, Walt Whitman, especially his *Leaves of Grass*. He also recommended that I read the youthful poems of W. H. Auden and Stephen Spender. He stayed on in China and eventually became one of the most respected professors of German Literature in Beijing.

3 The first copy of *Four Quartets* to arrive in China, I was told by the British Council Librarian.

4 This lecture was given on 13 March 2003.

5 The literature on the mining and trading sojourners in North America and Australasia has grown by leaps and bounds during the past two decades; see the bibliographies in Lynn Pan, ed., *The Encyclopedia of the Chinese Overseas*, Singapore: Archipelago Press and Landmark Books, and Cambridge, Mass.: Harvard University Press, 1998, pp. 375–387; Chan Sucheng, *This Bitter-Sweet Soil: The Chinese in California Agriculture, 1860–1910*, Berkeley: University of California

Press, 1986, pp. 453–481; and Adam McKeown, *Chinese Migrant Networks and Cultural Change: Peru, Chicago, Hawaii, 1900–1936*, Chicago: University of Chicago Press, 2001, pp. 315–340. The students sent by the Chinese government have received much attention from scholars in China, but we still have a lot to learn about those who went to the United States with the help of the Christian missions.

6 He was the first person to draw my attention to how much the Baba or Peranakan Straits Chinese were hurt when newly arrived Chinese from China looked down on their efforts to preserve old Chinese customs, especially on their inability to speak Chinese. In turn, as Chinese-educated Chinese grew more nationalistic and anti-colonial, they were hurt and angry when local-born English-educated scoffed at their traditional customs and their lack of English language skills. The parallel streams of English and Chinese schools were an important source of intra-community tension from the 1920s to the 1960s.

7 Most historians of Chinese business would recognize that my friend's aunt was a member of the famous Kwok family that founded the Sincere and Wing On companies; Wellington K. K. Chan, "Organization and Strategy of China's Two Premier Department Stores: The Wing On and Sincere Companies, 1900–1941". In *South China: State, Culture and Social Change During the 20th Century*, Leo Douw and Peter Post, eds, Amsterdam, New York: North-Holland, 1996; and "Personal Styles, Cultural Values, and Management: The Sincere and Wing On Companies in Shanghai and Hong Kong, 1900–1941", in *Asian Department Stores*, edited by Kerrie L. MacPherson, Honolulu and Richmond: University of Hawaii Press and Curzon, 1998.

8 Published by Pepin Press, Amsterdam. There is an excellent bibliography in Khoo Joo Ee's book.

9 Chen Danyan, *Shanghai di jinzhi yuye* (Gold branch and jade leaf in Shanghai; English title: Shanghai Princess), Beijing: Zuojia Publishers, 2nd edition, 2000. The book was first published in September 1999, and a second edition was produced in June 2000. By the time I bought my copy, the book had been through eight printings.

10 The pioneering studies by Claudine Salmon have opened this rich field of documentation. Her most important works pertaining to the writings of the Chinese in Southeast Asia are *Literature in Malay by the Chinese of Indonesia : A Provisional Annotated Bibliography*, Paris: Editions de la Maison des sciences de l'homme, 1981, and the excellent set of essays that she edited, *Literary Migrations: Traditional Chinese Fiction in Asia (17–20th Centuries)*, Beijing: International Culture Publishing, 1987.

11 The writings of Malayan Chinese of the pre-war period are collected in Fang Xiu, ed., *Ma Hua xin wenxue daxi, 1919–1942* (Malayan Chinese new literature), in ten volumes, Singapore: World Book Company, 1972. Fang Xiu had first written a three-volume history, *Ma Hua xin wenxue shigao* (Draft history of Malayan Chinese new literature), Singapore: World Book Company, 1965. An abbreviated version was translated by Angus W. McDonald as *Notes on the History of Malayan Chinese New Literature, 1920–1942*, Tokyo: Centre for East Asian Cultural Studies, 1977. Also, see Wang Gungwu, "A Short Introduction to Chinese Writing in Malaya", in *Bunga Emas, An Anthology of Contemporary Malaysian Literature*, edited by T. Wignesan, London: Anthony Blond and Kuala Lumpur: Rayirath (Raybooks) Publications, 1964, pp. 249–256.

12 Lim Boon Keng (1869–1957), the best-known Southeast Asian Chinese of his generation writing in English, wrote many articles for *The Straits Chinese Magazine* (1897–1907) and several volumes of essays in English about China and Chinese viewpoints. His mastery of English was excellent, but his literary skills

and understanding of things Chinese could not match that of his contemporary Qiu Shuyuan (Khoo Seok Wan, 1874–1941), who not only wrote on current affairs but also composed impeccable classical poetry (*Qiu Shuyuan jushi shiji*, 1949). It is anachronistic to do so, but were Lim's more literary work, *Tragedies of Eastern Life: An Introduction to the Problems of Social Psychology*, Shanghai: Commercial Press, 1927, to be compared with works published after 1960, the difference is stark. A sample of the writings by Lee Kok Liang (1927–1992) (*The Mutes in the Sun and Other Stories*, 1964 and *Flowers in the Sky*, 1981), Ee Tiang Hong (1933–1990) (*I of the Many Faces*, 1960, and *Myths for a Wilderness*, 1976), and Goh Poh Seng (b. 1936) (*If We Dream Too Long*, 1972) would illustrate the marked changes in English writing since Lim Boon Keng's pioneering efforts.

13 We have ample evidence to show how some Chinese had become keen on literature by the beginning of the twentieth century. I have noted the writings in Chinese collected by Fang Xiu (note 11). Claudine Salmon has drawn attention to those written in Malay (note 10), but these have been out of print. Efforts to reprint those written in Indonesia have now begun. I have only seen volumes 2–5 in the series *Kesastraan melayu tionghoa dan kebangsaan Indonesia* (Sino-Malay literature and Indonesian nationhood), edited by Marcus, A. S., and Pax Benedanto, Jakarta: Kepustakaan Popular Gramedia, 2001–2002, but they promise to demonstrate the variety of talents already developed before the Second World War.

14 The academic exercise for the Bachelor's degree was Chinese Reformists and Revolutionaries in the Straits Settlements, 1900–1911, Department of History, University of Malaya, 1953 (partly published as "Sun Yat-sen and Singapore", *Nanyang Hsueh-pao* [Journal of the South Sea Society], vol. 15, no. 2, 1959, pp. 55–68); the dissertation for the Master's degree was *The Nanhai Trade: A Study of the Early Chinese Trade in the South China Sea* (1954). This was published as a monograph issue of the *Journal of the Malayan Branch of the Royal Asiatic Society* in 1959 (new edition, Singapore: Times Academic Press, 1998, republished by Eastern Universities Press, 2003).

15 Tan Yeok Seong (1900–1984) first made his name as a scholar of Nanyang history in 1934. His many works have been collected in *Yeyin guan wencun* (Collected writings from the Coconut Shade Studio), Singapore: Nanyang xuehui, in three volumes, 1983.

16 Hsu Yun-ts'iao (1905–1981) was a prolific writer who had over 40 books to his name. He was an educationalist and journalist before he became the first editor of the *Nanyang xuebao* in 1940 and continued as editor until 1957. He also taught a new generation of young scholars at Nanyang University from 1953 to 1961. Among his many writings, his best-known work was on the early history of the maritime world of Southeast Asia, notably Thailand and the Malay peninsula. He has also translated from Malay, Thai, Dutch and English.

17 Thousands of people like me were affected from the 1950s to the 1970s, first in British Malaya and the independent Federation of Malaya and the Colony of Singapore, and then in the Federation of Malaysia and the Republic of Singapore. Thailand and the Philippines had equally tight controls over writings from China. The strongest prohibitions were imposed on the Chinese in Indonesia after 1965 until very recently. Those who were driven back to China from every country in Southeast Asia have related some of their experiences, and anecdotes abound of how badly Chinese sojourners were treated. The attitudes of the younger generations have undergone radical changes and writing about these experiences today may not attract a wide audience.

18 The separation of Singapore from Malaysia is a story that has yet to be fully told. Two recent accounts are illuminating: Lee Kuan Yew, *The Singapore Story*, Singapore: Times Editions, 1998, and Albert Lau, *A Moment of Anguish: Singapore in Malaysia and the Politics of Disengagement,* Singapore: Times Academic Press, 1998.

19 *Reluctant Exiles?* was published by M. E. Sharpe in New York and London in 1994. The foreword is on pp. xi–xiii.

Part III

REFLECTIONS

Section 2. Chinese overseas in historical and comparative perspective

14

A SINGLE CHINESE DIASPORA?[1]

Wang Gungwu

I wish to begin by thanking Professor Reid and his colleagues for their efforts in establishing this new Centre for the study of the Chinese overseas. It had started modestly as a series of lectures to remember Jennifer Cushman, a friend whom we all miss dearly. That series led to the volume entitled *Sojourners and Settlers* which Tony Reid published a couple of years ago.[2] Not content with that, he set out to plan this Chinese Southern Diaspora Centre. He and his colleagues are convinced that the subject of the Chinese who migrated and settled southwards is deserving of serious study, and that the Australian National University (ANU) is the right place to locate such a centre. I agree. Australia does need to encourage teaching and research in this field and the ANU has excellent conditions to get this job done well. It is most gratifying to see it take off now. I am delighted that Tony invited me to give the Centre's inaugural lecture. I need hardly say that this is a Centre I want to be associated with. What I have to say this evening is but a small measure of congratulations to the team that made this Centre possible.

You are probably so used to the phrase Chinese Southern Diaspora by now that you may be surprised that I should want to reflect on the use of the term diaspora here. After all, I recently called the two volumes of essays which Wang Ling-chi and I edited, *The Chinese Diaspora.*[3] I had to do some heart-searching about that. I have long advocated that the Chinese overseas be studied in the context of their respective national environments, and taken out of a dominant China reference point. It is necessary that each Chinese community overseas be open to comparative study, both among themselves and together with other migrant communities. Our two volumes stressed settlement, as in the phrase *luodi shenggen*,[4] meaning growing roots where you land; and also differentiation among the communities in six continents. The thirty-five essays emphasize the great variety among Chinese who have found new homes in different parts of the world.

I still have some disquiet about the use of the term diaspora, not because, in English, it has until recently applied only to the Jews (see

Oxford English Dictionary), nor because the word refers to exile (in Hebrew) or dispersion (in Greek), which are rather specific manifestations of the phenomenon of sojourning and migration.[5] Of course, it is misleading and politically sensitive for the Chinese to be compared to the Jews in the Muslim world of Southeast Asia, but if the reality makes the comparison appropriate, so be it.

My reservations come from the problems the Chinese encountered with the concept of sojourner (*huaqiao*) and the political use both China and hostile governments have made of that term. From China's point of view, *huaqiao* was a powerful name for a single body of overseas Chinese. It was openly used to bring about ethnic if not nationalist or racist binding of all Chinese at home and abroad. In the countries which have large Chinese minorities, that term had become a major source of the suspicion that the Chinese minorities could never feel loyalty towards their host nations. After some 30 years of debate, the term *huaqiao* now no longer includes those Chinese with foreign passports, and is being replaced by others like (*haiwai*) *huaren* and *huayi*, which disclaim formal China connections. The question which lingers in my mind is: will the word diaspora be used to revive the idea of a single body of Chinese, reminiscent of the old term, the *huaqiao*? Is this intended by those Chinese who favour its use? Once the term is widely used, would it be possible to keep it as a technical term in the social sciences, or will it acquire the emotive power that would actually change our views about the nature of the various Chinese communities overseas?

Tony Reid knows my reservations and has encouraged me to look back and reflect on how the Chinese abroad have been studied so far and how the approaches in the past have contributed to the present stage of evolution. This would also give me a chance to examine some of my own premises. My early interest in overseas Chinese history came from three major strands of scholarship. The first was that of the Chinese and Japanese scholars who gave the overseas Chinese a single identity as *huaqiao*, Chinese sojourners. This began with Chinese mandarins at the end of the nineteenth century, then came the reformers and revolutionaries and their Japanese supporters of the early twentieth.[6] Finally the subject was taken up by scholars like Li Changfu, Liu Shimu, Wen Xiongfei[7] and the team in Jinan University in Shanghai who founded, in the 1920s, the first major centre for the study of the *huaqiao*. They were followed by Chen Da,[8] Zhang Liqian, Xu Yunqiao (Hsu Yun-ts'iao), and Yao Nan, the latter three helping to found the Nanyang Xuehui (The South Seas Society) in Singapore in 1940.[9]

The second strand was that of the colonial officials and the scholars they encouraged and commissioned to study the Chinese in the different territories of Southeast Asia. This was developed from their early trading experiences with the various kinds of Chinese which the Portuguese,

Spanish, Dutch and English dealt with as they expanded their trading interests in Southeast Asia and the China coasts. Later, the Dutch, British and French administrators studied their respective Chinese groups with particular care.[10] They saw the Chinese both as potential allies and as possible threats to their regimes. In the twentieth century, Victor Purcell began writing seriously about them in the 1930s and, when he produced his comprehensive study for Southeast Asia in 1951, he emerged as the best example of this group's work.[11] The British Colonial Office after the war funded excellent scholars like Maurice Freedman and Tian Jukang, and their field research set new standards of anthropological enquiry.[12]

The third strand was the work of more recent field scholars, including sociologists and anthropologists who had wanted to study China but were forced to turn to the overseas Chinese when the communist victory in 1949 made it impossible for them to work in China itself. The leading figure in this strand was the American scholar Bill Skinner who worked on the Chinese in Thailand, while others worked on the distinct communities in Indonesia, Malaya, the Philippines and also Cambodia.[13] The China orientation of the scholars in the latter two strands was obvious when Freedman and Skinner led them to come together to launch the very productive and significant London–Cornell project that studied Hong Kong and Taiwan as the only Chinese societies that were accessible to non-Chinese scholars. The second and third strands inspired a new generation of scholars, including Southeast Asians of Chinese descent.[14]

It is significant that none of them used the term diaspora, and all of them treated the term *huaqiao* that emphasized the oneness of the overseas Chinese identity with reservations. Maurice Freedman, who was editor of the *Jewish Journal of Sociology*, and knew the Jewish connotations of diaspora best, did not consider the term appropriate for the Chinese. Instead, non-Chinese scholars favoured two distinct approaches: first, the study of varieties of *huaqiao* in different environments and the Chinese characteristics each of them retained and second, the study of the conditions under which the Chinese might assimilate and accept their place as citizens of the new nation-states of Southeast Asia.[15]

We all know that, early this century, the Chinese were compared with the Jews in Europe.[16] After Nazi persecution and the Holocaust, more recent scholars have been hesitant to use the comparison directly. The first person to raise the issue with me was not a student of the overseas Chinese, but of Indonesia. This was the late Harry Benda. His family were victims of the Holocaust in Czechoslovakia, he lived for many years in Dutch East Indies and he returned to study the new nation of Indonesia.[17] He suggested to me when we met in 1959 that the fate of the Chinese there could be similar to that of the Jews in Germany and I disagreed with him. In fact, as far as I know, he refrained from using the term diaspora in his writings. This was perhaps because he did see each Chinese community as seeking to develop its own distinctive identity away from the one that nationalist Chinese scholars and officials, and some local community leaders, had tried to impose on them. He knew that new political conditions in Southeast Asia during the 1950s were forcing the Chinese to re-consider what nationalism meant for them outside China.

I did not set out to study the Chinese overseas. My interest was always in Chinese history. This is partly because I started life as a Chinese sojourner, a *huaqiao*, someone temporarily resident abroad. If circumstances permitted it, such a person would look foremost to China. I was no exception. My father had come to the region to teach in high schools in Singapore, Kuala Lumpur and Malacca before becoming a principal of the first Chinese high school in Surabaya, where I was born. After he left Surabaya, he became assistant inspector of Chinese schools in Ipoh, in the state of Perak. This was a town with a Chinese majority, with the Malays in nearby suburban kampongs and most Indians housed by European-owned companies or government agencies. Among the Chinese, the tin miners in the Kinta valley were mostly Hakka, and the shopkeepers in the town mostly Cantonese. There was also a mixture of Hokkien, Teochiu and Hainanese, and smaller numbers who spoke other dialects. In short, it was a multicommunal town under Anglo-Malay administration, fairly typical of those in the four Federated Malay States of Malaya.

I was made aware very early that many of the sojourner families I grew up with thought in terms of returning to China one day. Others were ambivalent. They were happy to be out of China, to have a relatively secure living, and seemed content with a local polity that did not interfere much with their lives. Among the Chinese friends I made in the English school that I attended, however, I found many for whom China meant little. Their families had adapted fully to local living and typically spoke, read and wrote Malay and English better than they could any kind of Chinese. To them and to most of the teachers, my concern for the condition of China and for things Chinese was not readily comprehensible.

The events that highlighted the question of Chinese identity for me were the Japanese incursions into China that reached a climax in 1937 with a full-scale invasion. By that time, most Chinese were well accustomed to the rise of Chinese nationalist sentiment among the Chinese resident abroad. China politics had been brought to overseas Chinese sojourners at the turn of the century.[18] It attracted their interest because of the anti-Chinese discriminatory acts around the world, the most virulent occurring in the migrant states of the Americas, Australasia and South Africa.[19] Such acts in Southeast Asia were less hurtful, on the whole, because the colonial powers, unlike the working classes of the European migrant states, found the Chinese useful to their trading and industrial enterprises.

Chinese nationalism spread quickly through the schools and newspapers that mushroomed in the 1910s and 1920s. In this atmosphere, *huaqiao* studies received overt political support in China. I became aware of this literature through my father and his teacher and journalist friends, but thought little of it. What was real was the propaganda conducted to arouse overseas Chinese to save China from the Japanese. After 1937, teams of people travelled around to raise funds for the war in China, to exhort all Chinese to buy Chinese manufactured goods and boycott everything Japanese.[20] A concerted effort was made to persuade overseas Chinese to think in terms of a single Chinese nation, something like what a single and united Chinese diaspora might imply. Success included collecting large donations sent to help the war effort and recruiting young Chinese workers and students to return to China to serve in the armed forces.[21]

During the Japanese occupation period, the sense of Chinese identity grew among everyone of Chinese descent. It was forced upon them, since they were seen as potential enemies. It did not matter if they cared for China, or were more loyal to local or colonial regimes. This background explains why many saw themselves simply as Chinese. It was natural that they should study the Chinese language and live as Chinese and, if they had the chance to do so, return to serve China. For myself, I prepared myself to return to China one day, and studied Chinese with my father with increasing interest and commitment.[22]

This did not cut me off from a rich variety of friendships. In study, in play and in the neighbourhood around my home, especially after the end of the war, I spent far more time with my Malay, Indian, Eurasian and non-Chinese-speaking Chinese neighbours and schoolmates than with Chinese who thought like I did. The growing sense of being Malayan was something I understood and sympathized with, as it became clear that a new country would someday emerge from the colony-protectorate that the British had put together. That empire was coming to an end. The feeling of a local nationalism was growing among my friends.[23] I would like to have shared it with them, but I had a prior duty, and in 1947 I entered my father's old university in Nanjing.[24]

Dramatic political changes in China changed my life. The civil war was about to reach Nanjing, the university closed down, and this led me to rejoin my parents in Ipoh at the end of 1948.[25] When China became communist the next year, I was enrolled at the University of Malaya in Singapore and back among the kinds of friends I had made in school. Most of them were English-educated Chinese who had grown up in cities and towns with Chinese majorities.[26] It was easy for me to identify with them as Chinese, although it was clear that most of them had never been *huaqiao* sojourners like me. For them, they were home, and the projected nation of an independent Malaya was full of promise. For me, the turbulent Chinese nation had become increasingly an abstract entity dedicated to an ideology that seemed alien to the region. Through the prevailing anti-colonialism in Malaya and an Anglo-socialist perspective, I became reconciled to acquiring a new national identity. It was the first step to moving away from being a sojourner towards a conscious decision to settle outside China. What I would become eventually was still uncertain, but learning to be a citizen of the Federation of Malaya was a beginning. Nevertheless, the commitment to know China remained: that is, to finish what I had started to do, to understand what could have gone wrong with that ancient civilization, and what future it still had. Between sojourning and settling down in one place, I discovered that being Chinese was not a handicap but an anchor. Turning thus to the study of Chinese history seemed to be the most natural thing to do.

Thus, I set my mind to be a Chinese historian. Despite the pull of the politics of new nationhood in Malaya, I held to this course. But nation-building was a delicate matter, and new approaches towards history were required. I joined my colleagues to stimulate research on Malayan history, especially so that we might train a new generation of national historians among our students. For myself, I would contribute by studying the Malayan Chinese as they evolved from sojourners to citizens, as they learnt what it meant to be Malayans. I had given a series of radio talks in 1958 which were published as *A Short History of the Nanyang Chinese*.[27] My work on Chinese history had enabled me to relate the story from the beginning of Chinese relations with the region – the Nanhai trade, to the Zheng He naval expeditions and the defensive tributary system, and then to the coolie trade, the Nanyang merchant networks and the patriotic *huaqiao*. I read the local writings, the historical documents, and also the new scholarship on the changing Chinese communities with greater attention, notably the work of Western social scientists of the 1950s. At the same time, the most dramatic developments in the country included the steps taken in the years 1961 to 1965 to form a new Malaysian federation by joining together several former British territories with large Chinese communities.[28] This provided me with a focal point to embark on a comparative study of various Chinese communities trying to adapt to new political realities.

The Malaysia merger was accompanied by Indonesian Confrontation and ended as a failed experiment that threatened good relations between Chinese and Malays. 1965–1966 became a pivotal year for my research. The ejection of Singapore from Malaysia was a bitter blow. In the region, the Vietnam War had begun in earnest and the Sukarno regime ended with a terrifying bloodletting.[29] It was a turning-point for Southeast Asian development. Even more dramatic was the unchaining of Mao Zedong and his effort to consolidate the revolution in China with a Proletarian Cultural Revolution. No one expected that this would eventually lead to the unravelling of Mao's vision in the midst of extensive anarchic conditions.

My interest in Chinese history was revived by the incredible stories reported about China. Was there method in Mao's madness? Was it necessary so that the revolution could escape from the deep-rooted Chinese past? Also, my work on Chinese history had gained attention, and I had to make a difficult choice. Should I stay and continue studying the Chinese in the region at a crucial point of change, or return to my first love, the history of China as it was being re-examined and reinterpreted to meet the transformations on the mainland? In the end, it seemed to me that, at the ANU, I could hope to do both, to study China itself while remaining in the larger Southeast Asian neighbourhood. In Australia, I would never be far from at least the many groups of overseas Chinese close by.

I came to Canberra in 1968 and proceeded to indulge myself in all the books, pamphlets, journals, magazines, newspapers and miscellaneous documents that came out of the Cultural Revolution that had intensified in deadly earnest since 1966. This material was not available in Malaysia during the many years I worked in Kuala Lumpur. It took years before I felt I had caught up on Chinese affairs. Nevertheless, the first two articles I wrote at the ANU were "Chinese Politics in Malaya" and "Malaysia: Contending Elites".[30] I could now study both China and the Chinese communities outside. And because of that, the interplay between China's view of those communities and the view of themselves by the Chinese outside was never far from my mind. This interplay has guided my main writings till this day.

By seeking to connect both perspectives, I have not accepted China's view that China alone has the capacity to give the overseas Chinese what they need in order to remain Chinese. Chinese officials have always underestimated the resources the Chinese overseas have been able to muster to cultivate new kinds of Chineseness among themselves.[31] On the other hand, there has also been a sense of cultural inferiority that has often dogged those outside China. It seems to me that this has made them too modest about their achievements, whether in business, in education, or in technical skills. Their self-estimation has never been stable or well judged, and they were wont to move from cultural cringe one moment to naive boastfulness the next.[32] There are many levels and dimensions in the subtle and uncertain relationships between China and its wandering peoples.

As for scholarly approach, I never tried to do what Maurice Freedman and Bill Skinner did systematically, which was to use what they learnt from the Chinese overseas to explain Chinese society itself.[33] Nor did I focus on the many past and present patterns of Chinese assimilation, nor agree with the studies that looked only at the new norms in Chinese responses to Southeast Asian nationalism. Instead, my work has tended to move between two wishful but ambiguous positions. One was China's wish to see all Chinese abroad as ultimately sojourners, as members of one extended

Chinese family whose loyalty and patriotism they could hope to count on when really needed. The other was the desire among Chinese emigrants and settlers that their children would remain culturally Chinese to some degree and ensure the lines of descent for at least a few generations.[34]

Immersing myself in Chinese history has helped me understand how much China has been both repelled and fascinated by the large numbers of Chinese who have done well by living abroad, by the reasons why so many no longer wanted to return, and by what has made them replace Chinese culture with alien ways. At the same time, keeping up with the latest research on localized Chinese in each respective country around the world has also enabled me to see these communities in many lights. On the one hand, it is obvious that many Chinese have always hoped for renewed and closer links with China. On the other hand, many others, especially in North America, are ambivalent about new Chinese immigrants from Taiwan and Hong Kong. They are concerned that these new migrants seem too eager to live outside China, acquire foreign passports and still play their China cards. The range of responses to external stimuli and internal opportunities has grown so varied that, instead of becoming simpler as many had expected, the subject has become rich with contradiction and changeability.

I spoke of the pivotal year of 1965–1966 which led me to decide to move to Australia to continue with my research. This reminds me that, during the mid-1960s and the 1970s, there was a significant drop in the number of research projects on the Chinese communities in Southeast Asia. The London–Cornell project had turned its main attention to Hong Kong and Taiwan. New research funding on Chinese matters from the 1960s onwards had focused on the PRC itself. The Vietnam War did attract attention to the region, but there was little appeal to students of Chinese communities. Only in Australia, where concern for Indonesia and Malaysia was so intense and students from the region included so many of Chinese descent, was scholarly interest sustained. Scholars like Yen Ching-hwang, C. F. Yong, Jamie Mackie and Charles Coppel stoked the fires when elsewhere there were only embers.[35] Within the region itself, only the indefatigable Leo Suryadinata in Singapore was prepared to brave official disapproval in Indonesia to keep us informed.[36]

The more fundamental reasons for the shift away from research on Chinese minorities as cultural and political communities were two. The first was that, for reasons of security or of deep distrust, the new nation-building governments did not welcome studies about Chinese minorities that had not yet fully integrated into what was considered mainstream society. It was not only foreign scholars who were discouraged from doing so but also their own national scholars. The second was that China after 1966 was in turmoil. The Cultural Revolution turned against everyone and everything associated with the Chinese living abroad. The negative perceptions of them included their capitalist tendencies and bourgeois ways, their seeming lack of principle, and their willingness to compromise to the point of fraternizing with foreigners hostile to China. The revolutionaries distrusted even the patriotic returned overseas Chinese, and abandoned their earlier policy, which Stephen FitzGerald had so carefully analysed, of wooing them back.[37] As a consequence, there was no research on this subject within China for some 15 years. As for the Chinese outside the PRC, reactions were so negative about the consequences of the Cultural Revolution that the question of being Chinese became a painful one. Most chose to avert their eyes from the damage the revolution had done.

Once again, the Chinese overseas were thrown on their own resources. They proved that, as always, they were dynamic and well organized enough to maximize their skills and talents. Their business activities attracted fresh attention. This, after all, was what they had always done best throughout their history outside China.[38] What was new was the re-emergence of Japan as an economic power in the late 1960s. This reminded us that too much had been written about politics and culture and not enough about what so many Chinese overseas were doing every day. Their core activity, after all, has always been trading and dealing, taking risks and squeezing profits in interesting times, and plotting with ingenuity and courage when political odds were at their worst. During the 1960s, they adjusted quickly to the newly independent nations of Southeast Asia and built fresh sets of business networks for themselves. The venturesome among them also learnt to serve the global commercial and industrial cities, both in the region and beyond. Some of the more forward-looking among them had educated their children in the West, and prepared them to provide local agency services for the future borderless world.

In short, when the Suharto coup in Indonesia, the isolation of China, the large-scale naturalization of the Chinese in the region, and the exodus of Chinese from the Indochinese states, seemed to end the *huaqiao* story once and for all, new forces had begun to create different conditions for the ethnic Chinese everywhere. With the international links they fostered, Hong Kong and Singapore provided the centres for this transformation. The Four Tigers, which had responded successfully to the Japan model, opened up approaches to Chinese economic performance. A new generation of social scientists were drawn into the field and they guided research into this extraordinary phenomenon. Of those who were early to record how the Chinese were responding to opportunity, Linda Lim, Richard Robison and Yoshihara Kunio come to mind.[39] They joined the scholars who had identified Japan, South Korea and Taiwan as the new engines of growth and stimulated fresh interest in the Chinese role in Southeast Asia.

It is not surprising that this approach would link up with borderless globalization and eventually point to the diasporic features of Chinese economic activity. But the climax was yet to come. The return of Deng Xiaoping after the death of Mao Zedong was like the moment when the red-faced hero is victorious in Chinese opera. Opening up China again after 30 years of isolation led to an economic surge that surprised the world. It is enough to say that the stages of opening the front gate, then the windows and finally the front door into China determined new patterns of behaviour for Hong Kong and Taiwan Chinese, for those of Chinese descent in the region, and for those further away in the Asia-Pacific. The ramifications are so great and incalculable for the region's Chinese that scholarship has yet to catch up with the changes. Instead, they have spawned many sensational writings, ranging from chauvinistic calls for a Chinese economic commonwealth to fearful projections of a new wave of the "yellow peril".[40]

A striking part of the changes was the number of mainland Chinese who followed Taiwan and Hong Kong Chinese to North America and Australasia and chose not to return. By the middle of the 1980s, there was renewed scholarly work in China on the new *huaqiao*. It sought to connect with the work by scholars in the respective countries to which this new breed of sojourners had gone. The scale of this new activity had not been seen since the 1930s and 1940s. The enthusiasm was closely related to the fervent efforts to invite overseas Chinese investment into the country. To the extent that economic opportunity was open to ethnic Chinese everywhere, a new *huaqiao* syndrome was emerging.[41] Unlike the earlier focus on political identification in an anti-imperialist environment, this syndrome was linked primarily to economic activity, to the communities of Chinese acting like a trade diaspora, that is, to use Abner Cohen's much quoted words, "a *nation* of socially interdependent, but spatially dispersed communities".[42]

The flood of writings explaining China's spectacular success is now overwhelming. Most of them mention the role of the overseas Chinese in the most inclusive way, the very opposite of earlier political and sociological studies that had tended to stress the special attributes of each local community. The new writings are wont to lump Hong Kong and Taiwan Chinese together with all the others spread out over a hundred countries and territories.[43] The advances in market technologies, and the nature of credit and finance services today, have blurred earlier distinctions. Political identities are also treated as increasingly irrelevant, and old terminologies are being challenged. It should not surprise us that many social scientists are now ready to use a term like diaspora to highlight the new dimensions of the Chinese phenomenon. What is intriguing is whether this will encourage Chinese governments to affirm the idea of a single Chinese diaspora again, along the lines of the earlier concept of *huaqiao*-sojourner for all Chinese overseas? Will the use of diaspora lead even those who write outside China, notably those who write in Chinese, also to revive the more familiar term, *huaqiao*, the term that Southeast Asian governments and the Chinese there had spent so much time and trouble trying to discard for the past 40 years?

Several related developments have contributed to a potential revisionism. The three that are recognized by recent scholarship as significant are rooted in economic group behaviour, and display features of other diasporas:

1 The perception that, without official endorsement and support, the Chinese overseas have been evolving multiple levels and kinds of "informal empires" over the centuries, and that their ability to adapt modern communications technology to their use has made them a formidable power in the global economy. Behind the image of "pariah entrepreneurs" and "essential outsiders", they had established what has been called "ungrounded empires" that are both flexible and resilient.[44] Their readiness to innovate from a strong traditional trading base has given them a body of practice and theory to compete with the West, something Gordon Redding and his colleagues have elevated to what they call "Chinese capitalism". [45] This clearly supports the idea of a single Chinese diaspora.
2 The success of the First World Entrepreneurs Convention hosted by the Singapore Chinese Chamber of Commerce and Industry in 1991 has confirmed that Chinese businesses world-wide are keen to build global networks that are not less active and unified than those of the Jews and other successful migrant minorities. Three meetings of the Convention have been held since 1991, in Hong Kong, Bangkok and Vancouver. The Vancouver meeting was held at the beginning of the Asian financial crisis in 1997. In 1999, the fifth Convention in Melbourne will face its first real test.[46] There will be scholarly interest in what this represents if this scale of networking shows great vitality and produces proof of durability.
3 The third is a mutually reinforcing set of institutions going beyond business that has been reinvigorated. Examples of these are the international gatherings of surname or clan associations, the native-place societies and varieties of cultural (for example, music, performing arts, literary and scholarly) organizations that now meet regularly and are trying to strengthen Chinese social and cultural bonds.[47] These have taken modern shapes and skilfully employ modern instruments of communication. They have cellular characteristics but are often amorphous and changeable, quick to form and disperse. There is nothing essentialist about the Chinese identity they affirm, and their members negotiate interminably as to what they want. Yet there is little doubt that they encapsulate a Chinese way to achieve an end which each group wants from time to time.

Underlying all three phenomena is the shadow of China and an unspoken assumption that China's place in the world matters to Chinese and non-Chinese alike. The growing literature on the revived links between China and the Chinese overseas needs to be taken into account, especially about those operating cross-national networks involving Chinese trading groups. From this literature, it is clear that the current salience of the term diaspora is less because of trade than because of the radical changes in global migration patterns and the impact of these changes on policies of integration and assimilation.

Of great relevance here are the tentative steps towards multiculturalism that started in the migrant states of North America and Australasia. Its origins did not have anything to do with the Chinese. The tensions between settlers and migrants since the end of World War II had forced changes to racist and nationalist visions about assimilation. Those ideals had insisted that immigrants should assimilate towards the national majority culture as quickly as possible. But the shaming of the anti-Semites after the Holocaust, the reversal of verdicts in the Black–White civil rights actions in the United States, and the affirmation of liberal human rights values in the West, together led to a multiculturalism that was to substitute for the old "melting-pot" principle of nation-building which all nations thought they had to emulate. It is this shift in policy that cleared the way for the term diaspora to come into general use and be applied to any group that wanted it. Where the Chinese are concerned, there is a growing number in North America who admire the solidarity of the Jewish diaspora and the success of the Jewish lobby in working for the state of Israel.[48] While recognizing the differences between them and the Jews, they want to follow that model where appropriate. For them, this means leaning towards the concept of a single Chinese diaspora.

We have moved away from the narrow usage of the *Oxford English Dictionary* to spread the term so widely that no past connotations need trouble us. The wider its application, the more diluted and less clearly defined the term will be. In addition to the Greek and Armenian, there are now the Irish diaspora, the Afro-American, the Indian and Pakistani, the Italian, Arab, Iranian, and so on. Even the English can no longer be exempt in the former colonies where they have been the "mainstream" majority, especially if the term diaspora can now also be applied to Singaporean Chinese.[49] This could mean that Chinese diaspora has much in common with them all, but it could also mean that the word is flexible and elastic, as so many other social science and historical terms are. It is then up to the scholars to sort out the complicated ways each diaspora determines what it can be. The current acceptance of the term for "dispersed Chinese communities" suggests that scholars of the Chinese overseas have certainly created much new work for themselves for many years to come. The more I think about it, the unhappier I am that the term has come to be applied to the Chinese. I have used the term with great reluctance and regret, and I still believe that it carries the wrong connotation and that, unless it is used carefully to avoid projecting the image of a single Chinese diaspora, it will eventually bring tragedy to the Chinese overseas.

Let me end with two observations. When the news of the rapes of ethnic Chinese women last May was sent around the world, human rights groups protested strongly. In addition, efforts were made to build global networks calling on all Chinese to support a political protest, and seek punishment for the perpetrators of inhuman acts.[50] Equally strong exhortations were made in Hong Kong and Taiwan, some directed against what was seen as feeble responses from the Beijing government. Eventually, Chinese people on the mainland learnt of the tragic events and many responded with understandable anger. The PRC authorities then decided to comment on the matter publicly but mildly to the Indonesian government. Within Southeast Asia, among governments more familiar with unstable Indonesian politics, there was no official response. When a few Chinese community groups around the world hold protest meetings about this tragic event, could that be a forerunner of a potential diasporic solidarity? Or does it remind us how multifarious Chinese communities have become and, therefore, how hard it will be for anyone, including Chinese governments in Beijing and Taipei, to organize a diasporic response?

My other observation follows from that question. From past experience, China received patriotic overseas Chinese support when the country was weak and under foreign attack, and when the majority outside China were recent migrants with no other loyalty. Now the differentiation among the Chinese overseas is much greater. A diaspora today would include many kinds of Chinese for whom there are specific names, or who are accustomed to distinctive identities.[51] After a century of evolution, the Chinese overseas cannot return to their relationships with the old China of the Qing empire or the Guomindang or even the PRC of Mao Zedong. The changes have been deep. Also, China itself is deeply divided between the PRC and Taiwan, and each is able to keep its overseas supporters separate and distrustful of one another. It is not even certain that the idea of a single united China is as sacrosanct as it had been thought to be. If the past is anything to go by, it is doubtful if there will ever be a single Chinese diaspora. Much more likely is that the single word, Chinese, will be less and less able to convey a reality that continues to become more pluralistic. We need more words, each with the necessary adjectives to qualify and identify who exactly we are describing. We need them all to capture the richness and variety of the hundreds of Chinese communities that can now be found.

I began by referring to my acceptance of the word diaspora in the latest collection of essays which Wang Ling-chi and I edited. My own books have preferred "Chinese overseas", to get away from *huaqiao*, always translated as overseas Chinese, and so has ISSCO, the International Society for the Study of the Chinese Overseas which was founded after the San Francisco conference in 1992, and also the new *Encyclopaedia of the Chinese Overseas* edited by Lynn Pan.[52] However, depending on context, I still believe that the terms *huaqiao* (*haiwai*), *huaren* and *huayi*, which I have frequently used, are valid and useful. At the conference in Manila last November which some of you attended, Teresita Ang See used the term ethnic Chinese, and I accepted that when I gave the keynote lecture.[53]

Have I and others been inconsistent? Will we confuse our readers? I expect there will be confusion if we do not specify more exactly why we use a certain term and what is meant by it. But, after 40 years living with the problem, I no longer believe that there must be a single term for such a complex phenomenon. As an historian, I recognize that conditions change, and more names have to be found to mark the more striking changes. What we need is to be alert and open, ready to ascertain the range of meaning of each of the terms we use, and to anticipate the ramifications of using each one for a particular purpose. If we admit that there are many kinds of Chinese, and there are occasions when "Chinese overseas" may be preferred over "ethnic Chinese", or when *huayi* and *huaren* may be more accurate than *huaqiao*, then we should have no difficulty with the idea that there are times when diaspora should supersede other terms in comparative studies. After all, there are already many kinds of diasporas – an immediate example is the name of your centre of the Chinese Southern diaspora! – and we need appropriate adjectives to pinpoint the particular kind we mean. Having moved so decisively from a rather exclusive use of the term to describe one kind of people to a promiscuous application to just about everybody, it may not be so difficult to say that there is no single Chinese diaspora but many different Chinese diasporas.

Notes

1 Inaugural address at the Centre for the Study of the Chinese Southern Diaspora, Australian National University (Canberra, February 1999).

2 Anthony Reid, with the assistance of Kristine Alilunas Rodgers, ed., *Sojourners and Settlers: Histories of Southeast Asia and the Chinese, in Honour of Jennifer Cushman*, St Leonard's, NSW: Allen and Unwin and Asian Studies Association of Australia, 1998.

3 Wang Ling-chi and Wang Gungwu, eds, *The Chinese Diaspora: Selected Essays*, two volumes, Singapore: Times Academic Press, 1998.

4 "*Luodi shenggen*" (literally, fall to the ground, grow roots) was the title of the conference organized in San Francisco in 1991 by Wang Ling-chi and his colleagues of the University of California, Berkeley.

5 Cf. various editions of the *Oxford English Dictionary* before and after the 1970s with the many editions of others like *Webster's Dictionary*.

6 Wang Gungwu, "A Note on the Origins of *Hua-ch'iao*", in *Community and Nation:*

Essays on Southeast Asia and the Chinese, selected by Anthony Reid, Singapore and North Sydney: Heinemann Educational Books and George Allen and Unwin for Asian Studies Association of Australia, 1981. First published in 1977 in *Masalah-Masalah International Masakini*, edited by Lie Tek Tjeng, vol. 7, Jakarta, Lembaga Research Kebudayaan Nasional, L.I.P.I., pp. 71–78.

7 Li Changfu (1899–1966), a scholar of Southeast Asia and the Chinese in the region; Liu Shimu (1889–1952), a scholar of Southeast Asia; Wen Xiongfei (1885–1974), a scholar of Sino-Southeast Asian historical relations (eds).

8 Chen Da (1892–1975), who received his PhD in sociology from Columbia, worked on the Southeast Asian Chinese and their connections with Guangdong and Fujian.

9 The numerous publications of the scholars at Jinan University in the 1920s and 1930s are listed in Xu Yunqiao's (Hsu Yun-ts'iao) useful bibliography, *Nanyang wenxian xulu changbian*, Singapore: Dongnanya yanjiu so, 1959. Chen Da's renowned work on *qiaoxiang* (sojourner villages), *Emigrant Communities in South China*, was published in 1940, the year the Nanyang Xuehui (South Seas Society) was established.

10 Some early examples were works by J. D. Vaughan, *The Manners and Customs of the Chinese of the Straits Settlements*, Singapore, 1879; and Gustav Schlegel, *Thian Ti Hwi, The Hung League or Heaven and Earth League*, Batavia, 1866. The French scholars like Paul Pelliot and Henri Maspero paid more attention to Chinese history and culture than to the Chinese overseas, but their work did illuminate important aspects of China's relations with the Indo-China states.

11 Victor Purcell, *The Chinese in Southeast Asia*, London: Oxford University Press, 1951 (2nd edition 1965). His more detailed study of *The Chinese in Malaya*, first published in 1948, was also authoritative for decades.

12 Maurice Freedman, *Chinese Family and Marriage in Singapore* (1953), was first presented as a report to the Colonial Social Science Research Council and the Government of the Colony of Singapore. Tien Ju Kang's *The Chinese of Sarawak: A Study of Social Structure* (1953) was also an offshoot of the scholarly work supported by the British government at the London School of Economics. Both were students of Raymond Firth, who had reported on social science research in Malaya in 1948 and prepared the ground for their field research. Other notable scholars were Alan J. A. Elliott, who reported on Chinese spirit-medium cults in Singapore (1955), and Marjorie Topley, whose research was on the social organization of women's *chai-t'ang* in Singapore (1958).

13 G. William Skinner, *Chinese Society in Thailand: An Analytical History* (1957) and *Leadership and Power in the Chinese Community of Thailand* (1958), Ithaca: Cornell University Press; Donald E. Willmott, *The Chinese of Semarang: A Changing Minority Community in Indonesia*, Ithaca: Cornell University Press, 1960. For Malaya, notable studies were by Lucian W. Pye, *Guerrilla Communism in Malaya: Its Social and Political Meaning*, Princeton: Princeton University Press, 1956, and William H. Newell, *Treacherous River: A Study of Rural Chinese of North Malaya*, Kuala Lumpur: University of Malaya Press, 1962.

The two PhDs, by George H. Weightman (Cornell) on the Philippine Chinese and of Jacques Amyot (Chicago) on Chinese familism in Manila, were both completed in 1960. Also, the excellent historical study by Edgar Wickberg, *The Chinese in Philippine Life, 1850–1898*, New Haven: Yale University Press, 1965. For Cambodia, the work of William E. Willmott was done for the London School of Economics, *The Chinese in Cambodia*, Vancouver: The University of British Columbia Publications Centre, 1967; and *The Political Structure of the Chinese Community in Cambodia*, London: The Athlone Press, 1970.

14 For example, Tan Giok Lan, Mely, *The Chinese of Sukabumi: A Study in Social and*

Cultural Accommodation, Ithaca, NY: Southeast Asia Program, Cornell University, 1961; Anthony S. Tan, *The Chinese in the Philippines: A Study of Their National Awakening*, Quezon City: R. P. Garcia, 1972. The first of Leo Suryadinata's many writings dates from his Master's thesis in 1969 at Monash University, The Three Major Streams of Peranakan Politics in Java, 1914–1942 (published in 1976). Tan Chee Beng's Cornell PhD thesis was completed in 1979, later published as *The Baba of Melaka: Culture and Identity of a Chinese Peranakan Community in Malaysia*, Petaling Jaya: Pelanduk Publications, 1988.

15 Freedman's reports, Skinner's early books and the work of the Willmott brothers and Weightman are good examples of the first, and Purcell and the later Skinner of the second.

16 The first comparison was attributed to prince Vajirawudh of Thailand. He was inspired by nationalist movements in Europe and sought to develop Thai nationalism. From his observations of the Chinese in Thailand, he drew analogies with the Jews in Europe and embarked on educational policies that would enable the Chinese to assimilate; Walter F. Vella, *Chaiyo! King Vajiravudh and the Development of Thai Nationalism*, Honolulu: University Press of Hawaii, 1978.

17 Harry Benda had a sharp eye for Indonesian politics, especially the potential power of the indigenous Muslim traders who considered the Chinese as their rivals; *The Crescent and the Rising Sun: Indonesia Islam under the Japanese Occupation, 1942–1945*, The Hague: Van Hoeve, 1958. Although he did not write about Chinese communities, he was keenly interested in them in Indonesia and Malaya (and then in West Malaysia and Singapore). We spoke several times on the subject prior to his taking the post of the first director of the Institute of Southeast Asian Studies in Singapore in 1969.

18 Some historians date this from the appointment of the first imperial Qing Consuls in Singapore from 1877; others would say that China politics began when the followers of Kang Youwei and those of Sun Yat-sen sought financial support from the overseas Chinese in Japan, Southeast Asia and North America. In terms of modern political activity involving large numbers of the *huaqiao*, I favour the latter view. For the former, see Wen Chung-chi, The Nineteenth Century Imperial Chinese Consulate in the Straits Settlements, MA Thesis, University of Singapore, 1964. For the latter, see Wang Gungwu, "Sun Yat-sen and Singapore", *Journal of the South Seas Society* (*Nanyang Hsueh-pao*), 1959, vol. 15, no. 2; Yen Ching-hwang, *The Overseas Chinese and the 1911 Revolution, With Special Reference to Singapore and Malaya*, Kuala Lumpur: Oxford University Press, 1976.

19 Tsai Shih-shan, Henry, *China and the Overseas Chinese in the United States, 1868–1911*, Fayetteville: University of Arkansas Press, 1983; Edgar Wickberg, ed., *From China to Canada: A History of the Chinese Communities in Canada*, Toronto: McClelland and Stewart, 1982; Charles A. Price, *The Great White Walls are Built: Restrictive Immigration to North America and Australia, 1836–1888*, Canberra: Australian National University Press, 1974; Andrew Markus, *Fear and Hatred: Purifying Australia and California, 1850–1901*, Sydney: Hale and Iremonger, 1979; Malanie Yap and Dianne Leong Man, *Colour, Confusion and Concessions: The History of the Chinese in South Africa*, Hong Kong: Hong Kong University Press, 1996.

20 Yoji Akashi, *The Nanyang Chinese National Salvation Movement, 1937–1941*, Lawrence: Center for East Asian Studies, University of Kansas, 1970; Stephen Leong Mun Yoon, Sources, Agencies, Manifestations of Overseas Chinese Nationalism in Malaya, 1937–1941, PhD thesis, University of California Los Angeles, 1976.

21 Yoji (1970), pp. 113–158. At the Workshop on the History of the Malayan

Emergency held at the Australian National University in February 1999, Chin Peng, not yet 16 years old in 1939, spoke candidly of his wanting to return to China to fight the Japanese during the early years of the Sino-Japanese War.

22 It was not entirely voluntary. For my benefit, my father offered to teach classical Chinese to the sons of his friends, and regularly challenged me to do better than the boys who had studied in Chinese schools and were older than me by 3 to 4 years. I managed to hold my own and, as my Chinese improved, became absorbed in more difficult literary texts.

23 This became acute during my last months back at Anderson School, Ipoh, from September 1945 to December 1946. The person who most impressed me with his growing national consciousness was the person I shared my desk with, the late Aminuddin Baki. He was, at his untimely death in 1968, the Director of Education of the Federation of Malaya.

24 My father graduated from the Southeastern University (Dongnan Daxue) in Nanjing in 1925, and had always hoped that I would go to his alma mater, renamed National Central University (Zhongyang Daxue) in 1928. He brought me to Nanjing in the summer of 1947 to sit for the entrance examinations; the results were published in the *Zhongyang Daily News* on 6 September 1947. I was admitted to the Department of Foreign Languages.

25 I was at National Central University from October 1947 to December 1948. After the Nationalist armies were defeated at the great battle of Huaihai (Northern Jiangsu) in December 1948, I decided to return to Malaya to rejoin my parents.

26 The University of Malaya, comprising the King Edward VII Medical College and Raffles College (Arts and Science), had its Foundation Day on 8 October 1949. It was the only university in British Malaya (Singapore and the newly established Federation of Malaya) and two-thirds of its students were from the Federation. Almost all its students were products of the English schools of the two territories. A clear majority was Chinese, with significant numbers of Ceylonese, Indians and Eurasians. The Malays were greatly under represented in the early years of the university's history.

27 Singapore: Donald Moore, 1959; reprinted in my essay collection in 1992, *Community and Nation: China, Southeast Asia and Australia*, St. Leonards, NSW: Allen and Unwin, pp. 11–39.

28 I was inspired by the enthusiasm of my colleagues to edit *Malaysia: A Survey* in response to this development. This was published by Praeger in New York and Pall Mall in London in 1964.

29 Reliable accounts of the events of 1965–1966 in Indonesia are still hard to come by. Benedict R. O'G. Anderson and Ruth T. McVey, *A Preliminary Analysis of the October 1, 1965 Coup in Indonesia*, Ithaca, NY: Modern Indonesia Project, Cornell University, 1971; Robert Cribb, ed., *The Indonesian Killings of 1965–1966: Studies from Java and Bali*, Clayton, Vic.: Centre of Southeast Asian Studies, Monash University, 1990.

In contrast, books on the Vietnam War abound. Robert D. Schulzinger's *A Time for War: The United States and Vietnam, 1941–1975*, New York: Oxford University Press, 1997, provides a concise summary of the main features of the war.

30 "Chinese Politics in Malaya", *The China Quarterly*, London, no. 43, pp. 1–30; "Malaysia: Contending Elites", *Current Affairs Bulletin*, Sydney, vol. 47, no. 3, December, pp. 1–12, both published in 1970. In addition, I also commented on the May 1969 riots in West Malaysia, "Political Change in Malaysia", *Pacific Community*, Tokyo, 1970, vol. 1, no. 4, pp. 687–696.

31 The different estimates stem from the quality of Chineseness expected. Those in China measure this in terms of how much the Chinese outside are still like

those in China and remain loyal to what China stands for. Those who have settled abroad are normally content if they speak the language, observe certain customs, and are able to employ Chinese ways and connections effectively. It is, however, important that their Chinese origins be respected and there is no discrimination against them as Chinese.

32 I have only anecdotal evidence, but enough to recognize among Chinese overseas the cringe that colonials have about their countries of origin. Like former colonials from Britain in Australia, there are also expressions of a similar exasperation about those who come from the "home country". In some cases with the Chinese, this is followed by self-congratulation about how well they have done outside China without China's help. These extreme attitudes may be found everywhere, not least in Southeast Asia.

33 The two best examples of Freedman's work would be *Lineage Organisation in Southeastern China* (1958) and *Chinese Lineage and Society: Fukien and Kwangtung* (1966). Other major essays have been collected in *The Study of Chinese Society*, edited by G. William Skinner (1979). Skinner also has a similarly enviable record of contributing profoundly to Chinese sociology: *Marketing and Social Structure in Rural China* (1964) and the reference work *Modern Chinese Society: An Analytical Bibliography* (1973).

34 Wang Gungwu (1991), "Among Non-Chinese", *Daedalus, Journal of the American Academy of Arts and Sciences*, Spring, pp. 135–157; reprinted in *The Living Tree: The Changing Meaning of Being Chinese Today*, edited by Tu Wei-ming, Stanford, CA: Stanford University Press, 1994, pp. 127–146.

35 During these years, Yen Ching-hwang published his *The Overseas Chinese and the 1911 Revolution* (1976, see note 18); a series of essays which were later collected in 1995 in two volumes, *Community and Politics: The Chinese in Colonial Singapore and Malaysia*, and *Studies in Modern Overseas Chinese History;* and *Coolies and Mandarins* (1985) and *A Social History of the Chinese in Singapore and Malaya, 1800–1911* (1986). C. F. Yong also published steadily and his essays were collected in *Chinese Leadership and Power in Colonial Singapore* (1992). His major work of this period was *Tan Kah-Kee: The Making of an Overseas Legend* (1987).

Jamie Mackie produced *The Chinese in Indonesia: Five Essays* in 1976, with an important contribution by Charles Coppel; and Coppel published his authoritative study, *Indonesian Chinese in Crisis*, in 1983. Both published several relevant essays on the subject during the 1970s and 1980s.

36 Among Leo Suryadinata's writings of this period are the following: *Indigenous Indonesians, the Chinese Minority and China: A Study of Perceptions and Policies* (1975); *Peranakan Chinese Politics in Java, 1917–1942* (1976); *The Chinese Minority in Indonesia: Seven Papers* (1978); *Eminent Indonesian Chinese: Biographical Sketches* (1978); *Political Thinking of the Indonesian Chinese, 1900–1977* (1979) and *China and the ASEAN States: the Ethnic Chinese Dimension* (1985). Several of these have been updated since first publication. He also published a series of essays which have been collected in *Chinese Adaptation and Diversity: Essays on Society and Literature in Indonesia, Malaysia and Singapore* (1993), and *The Culture of the Chinese Minority in Indonesia* (1997).

37 Stephen FitzGerald, *China and the Overseas Chinese: A Study of Peking's Changing Policy, 1949–1970*, Cambridge: Cambridge University Press, 1972.

38 Trade was what induced commoner Chinese to travel to East and Southeast Asia, firstly in small numbers before the Song dynasty (960–1276): Wang Gungwu (1958; 1998), *The Nanhai Trade: The Early History of Chinese Trade in the South China Sea*; and then in large enough numbers thereafter to be grouped as a class of *huashang* (Chinese merchants); Wang Gungwu (1990a), "Patterns of Chinese Migration in Historical Perspective", in *Observing Change in Asia –*

Essays in Honour of J. A. C. Mackie, edited by R. J. May and W. J. O'Malley, Bathurst, Crawford House Press, pp. 33–48 (first published in Guangzhou, in Chinese, 1985); and (1990b), "Merchants Without Empire: The Hokkien Sojourning Communities", in *The Rise of Merchant Empires: Long-Distance Trade in the Early Modern World, 1350–1750*, edited by James D. Tracy, Cambridge University Press, pp. 400–421.

39 Linda Y. C. Lim and L. A. Peter Gosling, eds, *The Chinese in Southeast Asia*, Vol. One, *Ethnicity and Economic Activity*, Singapore: Maruzen Asia, 1983; Richard Robison, *Indonesia: The Rise of Capital*, North Sydney, NSW: Allen and Unwin, 1986; Yoshihara Kunio, *The Rise of Ersatz Capitalism in Southeast Asia*, Singapore: Oxford University Press, 1988. More recently, the influential collection of essays edited by Ruth T. McVey, *Southeast Asian Capitalists*, Ithaca, NY: Southeast Asia Program, Cornell University, 1992.

40 Whether it is the Chinese economic commonwealth, Chinese Common Market, Chinese Community, or Greater China, etc., some writers envisage a coming together of all Chinese. The implication is that of a single Chinese diaspora closely linked with the Chinese mainland; David Shambaugh, "The Emergence of 'Greater China'"; Harry Harding, "The Concept of 'Greater China': Themes, Variations and Reservations" and Wang Gungwu, "Greater China and the Chinese Overseas", *The China Quarterly*, no. 136, December 1993, pp. 653–659, 660–686, 926–948.

As for fearful projections, these vary from several recent books on the overseas Chinese (*kakyo*, or *huaqiao*) by Japanese writers, to those by Sterling Seagrave, *Lords of the Rim: The Invisible Empire of the Overseas Chinese*, New York: Putnam's, 1995, to books on security threats, like that by Richard Bernstein and Ross H. Munro, *The Coming Conflict with China*, New York: A. A. Knopf, 1997.

41 This is being shaped by the sheer numbers of people involved. Also, the volume of published work on the Chinese overseas (*huaqiao-huaren*) has grown quickly, now not only in the southern provinces, but also throughout China where any connection with a local person who has migrated or settled abroad is systematically cultivated. The value of such people to the officials of the Overseas Chinese departments has been recognized, and tracing Chinese relatives living abroad is now both a profitable as well as a humanitarian act. Research centres and units have been established by universities and societies, and serious and extensive scholarship is being done at both national and local levels. Numerous books, including volumes of collected essays, as well as dozens of specialist journals, magazines and newsletters provide increasingly well-informed studies about the Chinese world-wide. The impact this has had on China's development and on the fortunes of the Chinese overseas is yet to be accurately assessed, but a sense of intense and effective activity is unavoidable.

42 I first read this in Philip Curtin, *Cross-Cultural Trade in World History*, Cambridge: Cambridge University Press, 1984. Here I cite from Anthony Reid, "Entrepreneurial Minorities, Nationalism, and the State", in *Essential Outsiders: Chinese and Jews in the Modern Transformation of Southeast Asia and Central Europe*, edited by Daniel Chirot and Anthony Reid, Seattle: University of Washington Press, 1997, pp. 33–71.

43 This is particularly true among journalists, especially after *The Economist* gave this inclusive usage its approval, 21 November 1992. Once Hong Kong and Taiwan Chinese are so grouped, it is easy for the role of the Chinese overseas, most of them settled minorities in foreign lands who are distinguished by their ability to flourish under non-Chinese regimes, to be misunderstood and misrepresented. A clear example of this is Constance Lever-Tracy, David Ip and

Noel Tracy, *The Chinese Diaspora and Mainland China: An Emerging Economic Synergy*, New York: St Martin's Press, 1996, where the "Chinese diaspora" consist mainly of the Chinese of Hong Kong and Taiwan.

44 I first came to note the application of the concept of "pariah entrepreneur" to the Chinese in Southeast Asia when Joseph P. Jiang and I attended a conference sponsored by UNESCO in Singapore in December 1963. He had just completed a thesis at Indiana University on the subject. His essay was subsequently published in the volume of the conference, *Leadership and Authority, A Symposium*, Singapore: University of Malaya Press, 1968, pp. 147–162. Most recently, the idea has been refined as "essential outsider" (see note 42). The important point is that the identification is not a static and unchanging one, and those so called have room to negotiate how they wish to be identified from time to time. *Ungrounded Empires* is the striking title of the book of essays edited by Aihwa Ong and Donald Nonini, with the subtitle *The Cultural Politics of Modern Chinese Transnationalism*, New York and London: Routledge, 1997. I explore the theme of identity in "The Study of Chinese Identities in Southeast Asia", in *Changing Identities of the Southeast Asian Chinese since World War II*, edited by Jennifer Cushman and Wang Gungwu, Hong Kong University Press, Hong Kong, 1988, pp. 1–21.

45 *The Spirit of Chinese Capitalism*, Berlin: Walter de Gruyter, 1990. To what extent that capitalism could be characterized as "Chinese" is disputable, but the label has inspired many Chinese entrepreneurs to become more self-conscious and to induce later scholars to go looking for what made them uniquely "Chinese".

46 It was decided in 1998 that the secretariat of the World Chinese Entrepreneurs Convention be located at the Singapore Chinese Chamber of Commerce and Industry for a period. The choice was between Hong Kong and Singapore. So far, the Convention has been meeting outside the Mainland and Taiwan, but both Beijing and Taibei organizations have been keen to bring the Convention to their respective cities. When it finally meets in those two cities, the unity of the "diaspora" with the homeland would be complete. Where then is the exile or the dispersal?

47 Hong Liu, "Old Linkages, New Networks: The Globalization of Overseas Chinese Voluntary Associations and its Implications", *The China Quarterly*, no. 155, September 1998, pp. 582–609.

48 Public debates on this subject are rare, but comparisons of "global" Chinese and Jews and their manifold activities are often made in private and at community group meetings. Unlike in Southeast Asia, the Chinese in North America are more aware of Jewish activism: Chirot and Reid's *Essential Outsiders* (note 42) is better appreciated there than anywhere else.

49 I have never seen "English diaspora" being used and always thought this was because the English know their own language best and are clear about the specificity of the word "diaspora". Now that the word has been loosened from its moorings to the extent it has, how long will it be before we speak of the English diaspora even in Canada, the United States, Australia and other parts of their own former empire?

50 The media were actively supportive in Hong Kong and Taiwan, but the most striking were those made through the Internet. Some websites encouraged vengeful expressions, but some were positive and sought "reconciliation". For example, the World Huaren Federation whose manifesto begins with a forceful statement about the Chinese diaspora. The following quote (from http://www.huaren.org/) captures the spirit of this cyberspace organization:

"Chinese are estimated to be living in over 136 different countries, making it perhaps the most widespread ethnic group in the world. Such diversity is indeed awe-inspiring. Yet, it is the same diversity which creates gulfs among peoples. We often encounter Chinese-Americans or Chinese-Canadians who know or care little of their counterparts elsewhere. Such ignorance and indifference should be corrected. Our task of bringing reconciliation among Chinese-Chinese subgroups and between Chinese and non-Chinese is no doubt ladened with challenges".

51 The word Chinese does not come from any word in the language which carries the meaning of the people of the country now called China. The people have always had many names for themselves, depending on time and place, on tribal, ethnic or cultural origins, on whom they were addressing and on what occasions. The Chinese overseas around the world are the same, but even more so. "Us" has numerous sub-groups and only has a common name when faced with "Them", especially when they feel bullied or discriminated against. For example: hyphenated Chinese (Chinese-American, etc.), those distinguished by speech group and place-name (Hakka and Shanghainese), and by their foreign nationality (peranakan, or Thai, but of Chinese descent or ancestry), and so on.

52 Published in Singapore by Archipelago Press and Landscape Books, 1998; in Richmond by Curzon Press; and in the United States by Harvard University Press. The Chinese edition was published simultaneously by Joint Publications, Ltd. in Hong Kong.

53 The Manila meeting, in November 1998, was the Third ISSCO conference (after San Francisco and Hong Kong). The theme was Intercultural Relations and Cultural Transformation of Ethnic Chinese. My lecture was entitled, "Ethnic Chinese: The Past in Their Future" (see this volume, Chapter 15).

15

ETHNIC CHINESE

The past in their future[1]

Wang Gungwu

I have had the privilege of attending many conferences on the Chinese overseas. This is my saddest. Since we last met in Hong Kong at the end of 1994, there has been a turnaround in the economic fortunes of much of the region. Most of those affected have become understandably more subdued. But nothing prepared us for the tragedy that befell those of Chinese descent in Indonesia in May 1998. Perhaps we should not have been so surprised. By the end of 1997, there were signs that the Indonesian economy was coming apart. Early in 1998, many Indonesians were talking about a return to the anarchic conditions of 1965. The fall in value of the rupiah had become most alarming. Fears of hyperinflation were matched by growing shortages in food and medicines. Hundreds of thousands in the urban centres had lost their livelihoods. There was widespread feeling that the country was on the eve of major change. Then came May 1998, and in three days, with four students killed and the demonstrators on the streets of Jakarta, Solo, Medan, Surabaya, Palembang and others, a complete breakdown of order followed. This led to the burning, looting, killing and rapes of largely those citizens of Chinese descent.

There will be a special session during the conference on this subject, so I shall not dwell on the Indonesian tragedy.[2] Suffice it to say that many Chinese Indonesians found themselves reliving the past, with the fires, the bodies on the streets, and their trading goods being carted away. There were, however, at least two main differences from past occurrences of this kind. This time, all the Chinese victims were citizens of Indonesia. This time, some of their wives and daughters were raped. This last was the worst kind of violence that could happen to any people and it is something that has not happened to Chinese on this scale since the Rape of Nanjing.[3] And we all know how bitter the memory of that event has been for all Chinese. So Chinese Indonesians were forced to relive the past from a different basic position and, as the families of traders, an exceptional class of victims. This has led me to think about all the times that the ethnic Chinese in the region, and perhaps no less in other parts of the world as well, have had to ask the question: which parts of human history are they identifying their present with? Whose past should they choose if it is not one that they can determine for themselves? Is it possible for them to reject history and start afresh to create their own past?

One should begin by asking, what does it mean to identify one's present with history? It is interesting that the famous Indonesian novelist, Pramoedya Ananta Toer, had a similar thought when he spoke in October 1998 on this subject. He did so in the context of the relaunch of his book *Hoakiau di Indonesia* (The Chinese in Indonesia), a collection of articles he wrote in 1959–1960 to tell the story of the evolution of anti-Chinese policies during the long period of Dutch rule. He had written this in response to the anti-Chinese legislation introduced under President Sukarno that year, that is, in 1959, the Government Regulation No. 10/1959, which Pramoedya called "the formal policy of racism". The book he published was then banned. Although his speech in October was brief, he ended with a call for us to end such "crimes against humanity", referring to the deadly riots in May, by turning to history. His article was called "Drawing on History for Harmony".[4]

I have great sympathy with that. My study of the history of the Chinese overseas has led me to believe that confronting one's past is a necessary part of the community's growth and survival. It had begun more simply when the Chinese were mostly merchants and sojourners. It became more complicated when they became *huaqiao* and were asked to become patriotic Chinese, that is, patriotic to the new republican nation of China that emerged after the fall of the imperial Qing dynasty in 1911.[5] Since then, the voices speaking to the Chinese are much more confusing voices. Some demand that, as ethnic minorities in newly established nations, they choose between being loyal and submissive nationals of non-Chinese states (always living under conditions of trial and suspicion), or assert their Chineseness in one way or another. How they are to assert themselves is not clear. Should they concentrate on making money and not make waves? Or simply on studying hard to become scholars and scientists? Should they look to Chinese history, or forget it altogether and admire only the history of their adopted nation?

Let me go back to the question I asked, what does it mean for the Chinese – and here I do not mean only those of Indonesia, but all ethnic Chinese living outside Chinese territories – what does it mean to identify one's future with history? If there is to be a past in their future, what kind of past should it be? The Chinese overseas have so far been limited largely to two choices, that of admiration for Chinese history and that of acceptance of the national histories of the countries in which they have settled and made their home. I shall outline the key features of the two choices and examine the tensions that these have created because the two have been presented on an exclusive, either/or, basis.

The dominant ways of linking the past with one's future are:

1 That the ethnic Chinese acknowledge the given or known history of their own community as long as possible by reproducing what is approved and considered desirable. This can take many forms, but most notably by looking back at various aspects of Chinese history, and identifying with selected parts of that history.
2 That they seek a new history together with their fellow citizens, mostly of different cultural and historical backgrounds, who are themselves also defining their own national pasts. This is particularly true of some countries in Southeast Asia, more so than in others. Most commonly, this is couched in terms of helping the efforts to re-write their national histories.

Apart from these, however, there are two, more inclusive, ways of seeing the past, downplaying both race and nation-state, that have become more feasible in modern times. The two are:

3 That the ethnic Chinese reach out beyond all national borders to embrace a common human history, as befitting an era of globalization.
4 That they weave their own personal pasts in an inclusive way. This is something that modern education and technology have begun to make possible.

Let me take each of these choices mentioned and consider how ethnic Chinese may use the past to better understand their present and their future. I believe what I have to say is applicable to many parts of the world where the Chinese have settled and found new homes for themselves. I shall concentrate here on those ethnic Chinese who chose to live in Southeast Asia, in terms of:

a Those who draw on the past to plan their future; and
b Those whose future has already been determined by the pasts they have identified with.

The community's own past (a given or known past)

The first two choices are made by the community, that is, the majority of ethnic Chinese living in a foreign country. It does not matter how large or small the size of the community, either in terms of numbers or percentages. Whether it is 75 per cent as in Singapore, or less than 1 per cent as in many countries outside of Asia and North America,[6] the question is how the community uses the past to express its aspirations and identity, both among themselves and towards non-Chinese fellow-citizens and the national authorities. In short, the stress is on each group's ability to get the majority of its members to identify more with the community and/or with the nation-state.

The most obvious is something which the majority of Chinese abroad have easily understood and identified with for a long time. Through the community's given or known past, there has been the powerful tradition of reproducing as best as could be done what each first generation of Chinese brought to the foreign land. He, and it was always he until the end of the nineteenth century,[7] was obliged to turn to the family, village or community past in China for the necessary signposts to dignify the new life he had to lead abroad. As traders or working men, the Chinese often travelled together and organized themselves through religious shrines and various forms of fraternal bodies. Most of those with little formal education would have no clear sense of Chinese history as collective national memory. But at the least they would know the names of their villages and be familiar with the family and clan practices of their respective districts. Theirs would have been primarily a male history devoted to the perpetuation of the patrilineal line. Some would have families at home to whom remittances were regularly sent, even if they set up local households of their own abroad. They would normally observe the customary festivals, and respect their dead comrades in strictly conventional ways. Most hoped to return to the familiar past they had left behind and troubled little about local history except when that history impinged on their business activities and their livelihood.

By the nineteenth century, the male society which they built up abroad was enriched by the few who were better educated. They would have brought with them the great stories about heroic men away from home. They would have had a minimum knowledge of the stories of the *Romance of the Three Kingdoms* and the ideals of manhood on behalf of state and society found in that rich and extensive work. No less familiar were the stories of the *Water Margin*, or *All Men are Brothers*, the *Shuihu zhuan*. No young male in China could have missed learning these stories in their youth.[8] They offered not only stratagems of success and models of courage in adversity, but also directly or indirectly set standards of moral values that were consonant with the traditions of Confucianism, Buddhism and Daoism, that is, all the key features of approved behaviour that they would need in foreign lands.

Many of the long-term sojourners married local women and started new families, and some were led to settle. What past should their children have had? Wherever possible, the fathers were obliged to educate them into Chinese ways that they thought were essential to their community and also to their occupations. If they were wealthy, or had the numbers, they would engage tutors for the male children, teach them the Chinese language, and prepare them to live and work as Chinese. We have only fragmentary knowledge of what was taught, but it is clear that the basics of reading and writing would have led to an acquaintance with historical examples of proper behaviour and with Chinese myths, legends and even salient bits of dynastic history, not least versions of the current dynasty and what it demanded of them should they ever go to China. A few who were more privileged, as transportation to China became much improved by the late nineteenth century, could go back there, usually to their fathers' home towns or villages, and reinforce that education. And, for those who did not get enough Chinese skills to learn through the original texts, they had the classic stories retold in the local languages which they grew up with, whether it be Vietnamese, Thai, Cambodian or Malay. In that way, each generation tried not only to transmit parts of their mythologized history to the next, but the community could also introduce Chinese literature to local readers and pass on some understanding of their traditional values. The volume of essays on *Literary Migrations* edited by Claudine Salmon has provided us with ample evidence of the extent of successful cultural maintenance achieved in this way.[9]

All this minimal knowledge of the Chinese past was to change with the rise of modern nationalism in China at the beginning of the twentieth century. This was specially true of areas where Western colonial powers openly discriminated against both indigenous peoples and the Chinese, but also wherever the Chinese communities were large enough to support the establishment of modern schools based on models in nationalist and republican China. Tensions between China and the Powers, including Japan, helped to focus Chinese minds and pinpoint their new-found loyalty to the Chinese state. That it was no longer the hated Manchus who ruled the country, but Chinese who hailed from familiar provinces, like Guangdong and Fujian, helped to speed up the process of national identification (whose aspirations the majority of the overseas Chinese as *huaqiao* could empathize with and understand). The successive regime failures, whether under the warlords or under the Nationalists, sharpened the commitment of some of those whose idealism led them back to fight for China. Others, however, were deterred from supporting what was corrupt and chaotic. But even as the divisions widened among various Chinese overseas who were prepared to be patriotic, the immersion in Chinese history remained significant for almost everyone who wanted to identify with it.

For half a century, during the first half of the twentieth century, as more Chinese schools were established and were invariably modelled on those in China and used the textbooks published in China, the Chinese past was propagated with great effect among those who studied in these schools. Here and there, local authorities insisted on including bits of local history in the textbooks, but the main thrust of Chinese history, biography, poetry and romance, dominated the lives of the communities abroad. And this included the history of recent humiliations suffered by China, events which were deeply shared by the Chinese abroad, especially those who had long been treated as inferiors because of China's weakness. The past, however partially and selectively, was well integrated in the consciousness of most Chinese of at least two generations. The Chinese newspapers established overseas not only reproduced articles written in China, but also began to carry locally written essays which projected visions of a stronger and more prosperous China that every Chinese could be proud of.[10]

There were, of course, contesting histories for those who were locally educated. For example, the royal histories of the Chakri dynasty (1782–) in Thailand had to be taken into account by those Chinese who lived in Thailand. The Chinese who had settled in Western colonies and studied in colonial schools were expected to absorb a fair amount of the histories of Britain, France, the Netherlands and the United States, if not a smattering of local indigenous history as well. But, among those Chinese who felt deeply about the subject, these foreign histories were subordinated to the grander claims of China's new consciousness of its glorious past. The Chinese-educated, in particular, showed their admiration for the intellectuals, the leaders, the writers and artists in China who were not only reviving the Chinese past, but were creatively making a new dynamic present to respond to modern needs. What was exhilarating to them was that the modernizing forces were able to re-shape Chinese history. This could then help the next generation of young Chinese to discard what was obsolete and superstitious in their traditional past and lead them to embrace what was progressive and scientific.

For some 50 years, most overseas Chinese could, if they wished to, contribute to the uplifting of China by scouring its great past for a new vision of China's future. The peak of this came with the Japanese invasion of China. Although most could do little when Southeast Asia itself was occupied by the Japanese, the record of overseas Chinese support for the national salvation movement was one that they could be proud of.[11] The Chinese past, whether modern or ancient, had thus become their own past. With this sense of history, their confidence in themselves was never greater. It is well to note that this sense of the Chinese past and present was transmitted within the home by parents, relatives and leaders of the community, and then formalized and reinforced through school textbooks monitored by their teachers. While we should not underestimate the strength of oral tradition in the transmission, it was formal schooling, particularly through highly politicized teachers, that became the main medium for Chinese history to sink deeply into minds of the young. In this way, there was a reliving of a given or known past of one's own community through repeated telling. Added to other features of economic networking based on Chinese education, and the social and cultural forces of genealogical identification with ancestral homes and districts, at least two generations of Chinese were able to reproduce that which the community approved and considered desirable for its future growth and development.

The adopted country's past ("other people's past")

The love of China's past was seriously challenged in recent decades, most of all by the internal turmoil of the first three decades of the People's Republic of China, but also by the demands of local nationalisms and a changing modernizing world. Ethnic Chinese everywhere were expected to make different choices. The most immediate in many cases was to identify themselves with the new national pasts that were being constructed from local indigenous histories.

By this time, it had become clear that the immersion in the Chinese past had serious ramifications for those who were so fascinated by China that they did not pay attention to the local indigenous past. This may have been understandable to the temporary sojourners who had every intention to return to China after a short stay in the region. But for those who were prepared to settle, the political and cultural reasons which induced them to give their full attention to the Chinese past often caused them to neglect local history totally. They would have time only for local matters which directly affected their daily lives, but the past that meant much to the local people was of little interest to them, and may have even been considered quite irrelevant.

When circumstances in the region changed radically, after the rise of local nationalisms and the withdrawal of the colonial powers, and after the communist victory on the Chinese mainland, the new states expected the Chinese who settled locally to identify with their national pasts. I have already mentioned Thailand, where over time the ethnic Chinese seemed to have had little difficulty accepting Thai dynastic history as integral to their own history.[12] This has not been so straightforward for those who settled in the colonized territories. Colonial schools taught British, Dutch, French or American national histories together with general histories of Europe. Where this was well done, it injected another view of the past among both local and Chinese students. As a result, the image of a triumphant Western civilization, together with a reviving Chinese civilization, combined to leave little room for local histories and even less respect for the past achievements of indigenous peoples.[13]

The source of such neglect of the indigenous past stems from a very important point in history. While successful merchants may work closely with local political and economic elites in the search for wealth and other benefits for their country, mere trading and narrow economic interests do not lead to any identification with their past. It is entirely possible, as is obvious even today, that rich and powerful companies (like many multinational companies) which bring much wealth to the country can remain, and will always be seen as foreign, aloof and alien. Economic investments alone, however much they contribute to the country's development, cannot make up for the lack of political and cultural participation of these investors. True involvement in a country's history requires much more than wealth-making. It demands that the people concerned take on that history as their own.

This is the background to the state of confusion and indecision among most Chinese at the beginning of the nation-building era in Southeast Asia. There has been the hope, which many Chinese had, that economic activity and financial contributions were enough to win the acceptance, if not the gratitude, of the local peoples. Furthermore, for those who were educated solely in Chinese schools, there had been virtually nothing to prepare them to understand how to approach the indigenous past. But even for those who had gone to colonial schools with the children of local elites and merchant classes, there were not many who paid attention to the parts of the local past that were specially meaningful to their local school friends. If anything, what they all shared was a common understanding of the European past, and possibly also a common resentment of European domination. But there was no opportunity to place what they might have known about indigenous and Chinese histories into a perspective that they could all share.

There were only two ways the ethnic Chinese could identify with local indigenous history. One was through common action during the course of national awakening, including siding with the anti-colonial movements that were led by the new generation of nationalists. The other was through education in the new national schools in which the curriculum included strong emphasis on identifying with the local past.

The first was specially significant. It happened in countries where there were violent rebellions against the departing colonial powers. Very early on, we know of examples of such involvements in local politics in the Philippines at the turn of the century.[14] After 1945, we can point to some examples of ethnic Chinese who fought with, or actively assisted, Indonesian forces against the Dutch.[15] But, when military action turned against the Chinese, this did not continue. Elsewhere, Malayan Chinese (including those of both Malaysia and Singapore), and those Chinese of French Indo-China, found it difficult to separate their anti-colonial rhetoric and activities from the anti-imperialist slogans of the nationalist and communist movements in China itself. This was compounded by the fact that these powerful movements represented also an international anti-capitalist force that claimed to be a major stage in the evolution of world history. Thus, ethnic Chinese participation in the historic changes of the local anti-colonial and nationalist countries was uneven and varied considerably from time to time.

What was clear, however, was that where there was active participation, the identification of ethnic Chinese with local history came more easily when it became clear that it was in their interest to do so. The best example of this was, of course, in Thailand where there had not been colonial governments intervening in the relations between the Chinese and the local peoples. But, even where the colonial authorities did encourage Chinese separation from the locals, there were always some Chinese who were sufficiently integrated with their indigenous friends and neighbours to act together with them in times of troubles. Some examples can be found in Burma, Vietnam and Cambodia, and they underline the fact that when the Chinese have consciously participated in the making of modern history for their country of adoption, they are ready to identify with that country's total history.[16] As a result of acting together with local political and cultural organizations, they are likely to be sympathetic with the ups and downs of the people's past lives as well as being willing to share in their future.

For the rest of Southeast Asia, the Philippines had its present borders determined for it much earlier than the other two countries of the Malay archipelago, Malaysia and Indonesia. Its consolidation by the Americans at the turn of the century gave it an historical focus which was greatly assisted by the valuable collection of documents edited by Emma Blair and James Robertson, completed in 55 volumes about 90 years ago.[17] That focus was easy to identify with, also because of the unitary foundations laid down by the powerful Catholic Church for some 400 years. Most of the earlier Chinese communities in the country succeeded in finding their place in that environment. It ensured that the Chinese mestizo enjoyed recognition which, in turn, eased their acceptance in the newly independent country. Newer generations of Chinese immigrants met with greater difficulty because of Chinese nationalism and the application of American exclusion laws to the new colony, but there were at least clear precedents for accepting the Filipino past among even these Chinese.

The picture was more complicated, for quite different reasons, with countries like Malaysia and Indonesia. Perhaps the most important single factor that made it difficult for ethnic Chinese was the fact that these countries were new and did not have a continuous history as distinct polities, with clear and firm boundaries, until the last half century. In the case of Indonesia, nation-building began with the revolutionary war of independence in the late 1940s, but it is relevant that the national borders were not finally settled until after the incorporation of West Irian in 1963 (if we consider East Timor, this came even later, in the 1970s).[18] For

Malaysia, the borders were finalized only in 1965 after the ejection of Singapore from the federation.[19] This was but a generation ago. In both these countries, the second way of identifying with indigenous history was vital, that is, through education in national schools where the country's history is taught, and learning this history together with the indigenous peoples themselves. This way, of course, takes time, in some cases a generation or more, before the national symbols are shared and internalized, so that the ethnic Chinese can address all issues in accord with local sentiment.

But one distinct difference remains between the two countries. In Malaysia, ethnic Chinese participation beyond simple economic activities had been there from the start.[20] The British encouraged this and most Chinese saw the importance of active involvement in political affairs. By so doing, the country's brief history as a united country of thirteen federated states was shared by the Chinese from the beginning. And this sharing enabled them to look back on earlier periods of a more fragmented history with a large degree of recognition and pride. They could then see their economic contributions as an inseparable part of the country's evolution. Thus, despite complaints against certain discriminatory policies, most Chinese seem willing to see their community's history intertwined with that of the country as a whole.

This has not been true of Indonesia. Some Chinese had supported Indonesian nationalism since the 1930s and 1940s, for example, Lim Koen Hian and his colleagues of the Partai Tionghua Indonesia (Party of the Indonesian Chinese). Others fought alongside the nationalists during the revolutionary war, including those described by Pramoedya Ananta Toer; among them were those who followed the nationalist leaders into high national office. By the beginning of the 1960s, most Chinese had been prepared to see themselves as part of the Indonesian nation, including the leader of the Baperki,[21] Siauw Giok Tjan.[22]

But the complex relations involving the governments of Indonesia, the People's Republic of China and the Nationalists in Taiwan between 1949 and 1965 slowed down the process of participation. And then, after 1965, the policies of leaving Chinese largely out of all political and military office, and the encouragement to confine themselves to economic activities, all hampered ethnic Chinese identification with the Indonesian past. It would be over-simple to say that this was one of the causes of their tragic experiences in 1998, but the lack of participation as full citizens certainly contributed to the ethnic Chinese being marginalized where the future of their country is concerned. This has made most of the ethnic Chinese a people without a Chinese past, and with but an imperfect and incomplete local Indonesian past. And that in turn invites the unfair accusation of a lack of commitment to the country. It might even push them back to a sojourning mentality again, to an unwelcome rootlessness.

The news from Indonesia must be discouraging to all those who care for the country's future. Perhaps the only bright note that has emerged out of the post-Suharto period has been the news that ethnic Chinese are now determined to involve themselves in local affairs at all levels. If this is also translated into a deliberate accepting of the Indonesian past and joining their fellow citizens of different cultural and historical backgrounds in seeking to define that past, it may not be too late for the ethnic Chinese to find a new place for themselves consonant with that of the Indonesian nation as a whole. But much will depend on how the ethnic Chinese are recognized as a legitimate *suku* (ethnic) community in the country.[23]

I should add that, looking at the experience of the ethnic Chinese distributed around the world, Indonesia does seem to be an exceptional case. Elsewhere, again and again, Chinese communities have proved that they are willing to participate in local affairs when they have stayed long enough to understand the prevailing social dynamics. This has been true whenever there were opportunities to exercise their civic rights.

A common human past

The two choices I have described have created great tensions between ethnic Chinese and the local communities, and even among the ethnic Chinese themselves. This has been so largely because the choices have to be made in terms of exclusive categories, invariably each in contradiction with the other. But they have created difficulties also because they have been perceived as acts involving whole communities.

I shall now turn to the two inclusive ways of seeing the past that have become more feasible in modern times, one among smaller groups and the other largely by individuals. The first of these concerns groups of ethnic Chinese who seek to reach out beyond national borders to embrace a common human history, as befitting an era of globalization. They have been open to educational and professional networks that emphasize the commitment to scientific progress and a common experience on the road to modern civilization. What this means is that, while everyone can identify with national history and/or one's own ethnic history, this does not preclude simultaneous loyalty to the history of human progress and to the hope that we can all become better than our forefathers. The assumption here is that all references to the past are not exclusive but can co-exist. It helps, of course, if the problems of defining a national past are settled and the national identity is secure. In particular, it would be ideal if the ethnic Chinese communities are not in turmoil but have gained their autonomy in their respective countries. In this way, much of one's own national past can be taken for granted and attention can be given to a larger human future.[24]

I suspect that very few minority peoples in the world are in this happy position in their respective nation-states. Certainly, those in Southeast Asia at an early stage of nation-building have still to complete the primary task of shaping their identity and common destiny. It may seem premature to speak of their future in terms of the progress of mankind. Nevertheless, it would be short-sighted for countries to think always in narrow nationalist terms. It is in the enlightened self-interest of each country to encourage its talented people to look beyond their borders and think in wider global terms. Southeast Asian nations, and their ethnic Chinese minorities, should be no less ready to do their part for modern development. I suggest that there are at least two reasons why such a goal is consistent with enlightened national self-interest.

First, the task of defining a national past that the dominant majority and the minorities can all share should ensure that the country's talents are more fully utilized. It has been shown that the varied talents of the ethnic Chinese can contribute significantly to human as well as national development. Such talents should not be wasted just because of their foreign origin. Instead, their talents should be more broadly harnessed, and the ventures of such ethnic Chinese towards the frontiers of knowledge and the acquisition of valuable rare skills should be systematically encouraged. Eventually, their achievements can be channelled to advance their adopted country's interests as well. The ethnic Chinese loyal to their adopted countries everywhere who have tapped the global sources of scientific and intellectual wealth have been known to bring back their contributions to their respective countries. Such groups among the ethnic Chinese in Southeast Asia are no different. They can be loyal and simultaneously identify with the history of human progress. The benefits they can bring are not merely the economic wealth they can create, but also the enriching human capital they can make available to their adopted countries at key stages of development.

Second, identifying with a larger human past does not contradict more specific loyalties to country or community. The products of modern education are capable of viewing the world at many levels. Thus while the ethnic Chinese in Southeast Asia might be asked to give greater priority to participation in national affairs than to their own communal concerns, there should also be considerable openness for those among them who are active in learning and working beyond the country's borders. In any case, for many of them, even if there is no official endorsement, they will seek other ways of responding to the challenges of modernization. This will include identifying with that part of world history that leads them to the mainstream of human progress. The reality is that globalization will make such an identification easier and more desirable for the ambitious and enterprising. If national governments fail to appreciate this, the risk of losing such talents because groups of ethnic Chinese would prefer the larger human past to their narrower national pasts would become ever greater.

Personal choice

I have moved away from ethnic communities to speak of smaller ethnic groups with shared intellectual and professional interests. Let me go further to talk about personal choices. In the world of modern education and rapid communications technology, it is now possible for individuals to weave their own personal pasts in an inclusive way. There are many ways this can be done. They can concentrate on their personal memories and be very flexible in choosing which of the pasts available to them to include in their own personalized pasts. Among ethnic Chinese in Southeast Asia, this could include bits of their cultural past as Chinese, including select parts of Chinese history, but also those parts of local national history that they can accept. It could extend to the history of other countries and other continents, and the criteria as to why each is chosen can be highly varied. For example, it could be primarily an aesthetic response to a particular feature of the human past, it could be wonderment at a scientific discovery, or admiration of an act of unbelievable courage, it could even be a remarkable flowering of another country's national history. The point is that a personalized and inclusive past could be enlightening and liberating without threatening one's prior loyalties to community and nation-state.

This choice is not an easy one. It may even be tragic, especially if it is not understood by others. Because we are meeting in Manila, I am reminded of something that suggests how difficult it is to have a personalized past. About 50 years ago, I was told the story of a young Chinese-Filipino poet and artist named Homero Chiong Veloso. I never met him, because he had cut his wrists and bled to death in the YMCA building before I arrived in Manila in 1950. I understood at the time that the poet did this to relieve himself of the need to adapt his memories to new realities, that he did it as a way of leaving a message about the pains of his private life being unendurable on the eve of great changes to his community and his country. It was a transitional period when, coming out of the Pacific war in 1945, new Filipino and Chinese nationalisms were challenging the identities of the peoples around him. I have never forgotten the story and still wonder sometimes what made him do that.[25] What was in his personal past that he could not face?

Traditionally, the people of China are not renowned for their reflective moods as individuals, and I believe this has also been true of the Chinese overseas. There is no great literature of remembering one's own past in autobiographies or memoirs. There is no tradition of getting up to tell an audience what one really felt about one's personal life, except when desperate for public redress and a chance to seek justice. More highly respected was a stoic silence about what one did, especially if one were successful. And it was wise not to bore people with accounts of one's failures. From the few available writings about the personal past coming from the ethnic Chinese communities in the region for the past 200 years, one cannot but feel that ethnic Chinese have carried this practice with them overseas.

This is changing, albeit still slowly, as education opens up the literature of other people, especially through the power of the modern media.[26] All Chinese have been exposed for some decades to people who are more open and speak freely about their personal lives. That modernity not only stresses the worth of the individual and what is interesting about the unique features of each life. It also brought in Freudian psychology to explain the universality of each individual's needs, the "I" in poetry and fiction which is far more penetrating and self-analytical than anything in the Chinese past. In addition, the freedom that is claimed in modern law, the protection of individual rights, and the myriad kinds of calls for democratic institutions have all helped to release the younger generation of Chinese from their inhibitions about their personal past.

This kind of personal release depends on the environment in which the ethnic Chinese live. In Southeast Asia, there is a general reticence that has been reinforced by the suspicions and sensitivities of indigenous peoples and governments. And this has discouraged even modern ethnic Chinese from exploring their personal pasts in creative ways.

But times have changed. Communities and countries have to be more open. People as individuals can reach out. More ethnic Chinese want to choose their futures, and their choice of futures can be helped by knowing the various pasts available to them. And this leads me to link these pasts with their futures.

There is natural sentiment about the community's own Chinese past, and following the community's natural inclinations is both healthy and understandable. But it can be overdone. There can be too much of this past, so much so that the community depends on China for everything. The community then loses its ability to adapt, to learn on its own, to be creative and innovative under new and different conditions, like those rapidly changing conditions in each Southeast Asian country. If this happens, there is no autonomous future for the community. The danger is to become wholly passive and dependent, and increasingly alien in the adopted country.

It need not necessarily be so. A community can be independent in what it chooses from Chinese history and culture, which values are needed and how they can be improved. How to be modern as ethnic Chinese among non-Chinese cultures and peoples is a worthy challenge. If successful, it can demonstrate what such Chinese have to offer their adopted country, and to the Chinese in China and elsewhere as well.

Of course, in the long run, learning and caring for the past of one's adopted country (that is, the past in each of the countries in Southeast

Asia) is itself a natural historical process. If the process leads gradually, harmoniously and voluntarily to assimilation, it is one to be welcomed especially when the adopted country grows rich and strong in an atmosphere of equality and freedom. Ultimately, the community's own past will be integrated fully with the adopted country's past – and both Chinese and Southeast Asians could be thereby enriched.

In those societies that have found the desired balance between the individual and the society, there is room for personal autonomy. For the ethnic Chinese to enjoy that, they need to participate actively in all aspects of life around them. Only by so doing can they determine where the limits are, what they can do within those limits, as well as what they can do to extend the limits. At each step, they would have to choose which bits of the past they want and need.

When I travel around and meet ethnic Chinese living in different historical conditions in various parts of the world, I am often struck by the number of them who have made their personal choices – not like Homero Chiong Veloso when he decided to end it all, but more like Lime Koen Hian and Siauw Giok Tjan, and those described by Pramoedya Ananta Toer who fought in the Indonesian revolution. Their motives today might be different, their fates will certainly not be the same. But all of them are, in one way or another, better placed to choose their personal pasts to help them find their future. Ethnic Chinese, not only in Southeast Asia, but everywhere, are likely to have more choices than any of those in the past ever had. With new and better education opportunities available to them, they should certainly do more for their futures than any of their predecessors could have done.

Notes

1 This is a revised version of the Keynote Lecture given at the International Conference on Ethnic Chinese held in Manila in November 1998.

2 Early accounts of what the Chinese experienced may be found in various essays collected in Geoff Forester and R. J. May, eds, *The Fall of Suharto*, Crawford House, Bathurst, 1998. For an assessment 6 months after the May riots, see Jamie Mackie, "Tackling 'the Chinese problem'", in Geoff Forester, ed., *Post-Suharto Indonesia: Renewal or Chaos?*, Canberra: Research School of Pacific and Asian Studies and Singapore: Institute of Southeast Asian Studies, 1999, pp. 187–197.

The Conference on Ethnic Chinese was organized by the International Society for the Study of the Chinese Overseas (ISSCO) and held in Manila on 26–28 November 1998.

3 On the 60th anniversary of the Rape of Nanjing, Chinese scholars produced a large number of books that brought out the gruesome details of that event, notably the two volumes of pictures and documents edited by the Second National Archives and the Nanjing Municipality Archives, *Qin Hua Rijun Nanjing datusha tuji* (the Nanjing massacre and the Japanese invasion of China), and *Nanjing datusha dangan* (the Nanjing massacre archives), Jiangsu

guji chubanshe, 1997. Another volume of documents (*shiliao*) edited by the Nanjing Library and a draft history (*shigao*), published by Jiangsu guji, are also noteworthy.

In English, James Yin (edited by Shi Young and Ron Dorfman), *The Rape of Nanking: An Undeniable History in Photographs*, Chicago: Innovative Publishing Group, 1997; Iris Chang, *The Rape of Nanking: The Forgotten Holocaust of World War II*, New York: Basic Books, 1997. This account has been further heightened by the publication of John Rabe's diaries, *The Good Man of Nanking: The Diaries of John Rabe (1882–1949)*, edited by Erwin Wickert, translated by John E. Woods, New York: Knopf, 1998.

4 Pramoedya Ananta Toer (b. 1925) is famous for his novels, the best known of which being the Buru Quartet (*This Earth of Mankind, Child of All Nations, Footsteps* and *House of Glass*, all translated by Max Lane), which he wrote when he was a political prisoner (1965–1979). The new edition of his *Hoakiau di Indonesia* was published by Penerbit Garba Budaya in Jakarta in 1998. It was first published in 1960 in Jakarta, by Penerbit Bintang Press.

5 The significance in the application of the term Huaqiao to the Chinese overseas is examined in my essays "The Origins of Hua-ch'iao", in Wang Gungwu, *Community and Nation: China, Southeast Asia and Australia*, St Leonards, NSW: Asian Studies Association of Australia, with Allen and Unwin, new edition, 1992, pp. 1–10; and "Patterns of Chinese Migration in Historical Perspective" and "Southeast Asian Huaqiao in Chinese History-Writing", in Wang Gungwu, *China and the Chinese Overseas*, Times Academic Press, Singapore, 1991, pp. 3–21 and 22–40.

6 Reliable figures for the number of ethnic Chinese are hard to get for Southeast Asia, except for Singapore, Malaysia and Brunei, where they are about 75 per cent, 28 per cent and 15 per cent of their respective populations. The other countries use nationality figures, and those still identifiable as Chinese range from 0. 5 per cent to 3 per cent of the populations. The figures quoted of between 25 and 30 million Chinese in Southeast Asia, mostly originating from sources in China and Taiwan (and often repeated uncritically elsewhere), are no more than rough projections based on pre-war early census reports and later estimates. Figures for North America and Europe do not concern us here, but the numbers there are growing yearly and they are more or less accurate; for careful estimates, see the chapters on various countries and regions in Lynn Pan, ed., *Encyclopedia of the Chinese Overseas*, Richmond: Curzon, 1998.

7 In Southeast Asia, a small number of Chinese women did manage to leave China towards the end of the nineteenth century. For example, see Lim Joo Hock, "Chinese Female Immigration into the Straits Settlements, 1860–1901", *Journal of the South Seas Society* (*Nanyang Hsueh-pao*), vol. 22, 1967, pp. 58–110. Also Joyce Ee, "Chinese Migration to Singapore, 1896–1941", *Journal of Southeast Asian History*, vol. 2, no. 1, 1961, pp. 33–51.

In most of North America and Australasia, female immigration was stopped before the end of the nineteenth century and not resumed until after the end of the Second World War: Charles A. Price, *The Great White Walls are Built: Restrictive Immigration to North America and Australasia, 1836–1888*, Australian National University Press, Canberra, 1974, pp. 106–109, 215–277.

8 The two translations into English of these two novels are: *Water Margin*, translated by J. H. Jackson, Hong Kong: Commercial Press, two volumes, 1963; and *Three Kingdoms: A Historical Novel*, translated by Moss Roberts, Berkeley: University of California Press and Beijing: Foreign Languages Press, 1991.

9 Claudine Salmon, ed., *Literary Migrations: Traditional Chinese Fiction in Asia*

(17th–20th Centuries), Beijing: International Culture Publishing Corporation, 1987; parts III and IV cover Mainland Southeast Asia and Insular Southeast Asia. Of particular interest are the three essays by Claudine Salmon, pp. 375–498. Many of the stories are also found in Vietnamese, Thai and Cambodian and their influence spread beyond the Chinese communities. Their wide availability in Malay can be attested by Claudine Salmon's 1981 bibliography: *Literature in Malay by the Chinese of Indonesia: A Provisional Annotated Bibliography*, Paris: Editions de la Maison de l'Homme, 1981 (Editions Insulindiennes-Archipel, no. 3). For Thailand, Craig Reynolds, "Tycoons and Warlords: Modern Thai Social Formations and Chinese Historical Romance", in Anthony Reid, ed., *Sojourners and Settlers: Histories of Southeast Asia and the Chinese*, St Leonards, NSW: Asian Studies Association of Australia, with Allen and Unwin, 1996, pp. 115–147.

10 The experiences of Malaysia and Singapore illustrate the more complex issues of education and political loyalty in the region. The origins are clearly traced in Victor Purcell, *Problems of Chinese Education*, London: Kegan Paul, Trench and Truber, 1936; and Philip Loh Fook Seng, *Seeds of Separation: Educational Policy in Malaya, 1874–1940*, Kuala Lumpur: Oxford University Press, 1975. They are more systematically pursued after the Second World War by Tan Liok Ee, *The Politics of Chinese Education in Malaya, 1945–1961*, Kuala Lumpur: Oxford University Press, 1997. Three essays on later developments, by Sally Borthwick, Tan Liok Ee and Sharon A. Carstens respectively, may be found in Jennifer Cushman and Wang Gungwu, eds, *Changing Identities of the Southeast Asian Chinese since World War II*, Hong Kong: Hong Kong University Press, 1988, pp. 35–59, 61–74 and 75–95.

11 Wang Gungwu, "The Limits of Nanyang Chinese Nationalism, 1912–1937", in Wang Gungwu, *Community and Nation: China, Southeast Asia and Australia*, St Leonards, NSW: Asian Studies Association of Australia, with Allen and Unwin, 1992, pp. 142–158; Yoji Akashi, *The Nanyang Chinese National Salvation Movement, 1937–1941*, Lawrence, Ka.: University of Kansas Center for East Asian Studies, 1970; and Stephen Leong Mun Yoong, Sources, Agencies and Manifestations of Overseas Chinese Nationalism in Malaya, 1937–1941, PhD dissertation, University of California Los Angeles, 1976.

12 G. William Skinner, *Chinese Society in Thailand: An Analytical History*, Ithaca, NY: Cornell University Press, 1957.

13 Victor Purcell, *The Chinese in Southeast Asia*, second edition, Kuala Lumpur: Oxford University Press, 1965 (first published, 1951); Douglas Murray, "Chinese Education in Southeast Asia", *The China Quarterly*, no. 20 (1964), pp. 67–95; Francis Wong Hoy Kee, *Comparative Studies in Southeast Asian Education*, Kuala Lumpur: Heinemann Educational Books, 1971; Chai Hon Chan, *Education and Nation-building in Plural Societies: The Malayan Experience*, Canberra: ANU Development Studies Centre, 1977.

14 Antonio S. Tan, *The Chinese Mestizos and the Formation of the Filipino Nationality*, Asian Center, University of the Philippines Occasional Paper, Manila, 1983; Teresita And See and Go Bon Juan, *The Ethnic Chinese in the Philippine Revolution*, Manila: Kaisa Para Sa Kaunlaran, 1996; Isagani R. Medina, "Chinese Mestizos and the Ethnic Chinese in Cavite During the Philippines Revolution, 1896–1902", in *The Ethnic Chinese as Filipinos*, part two, edited by Teresita Ang See, *Chinese Studies Journal*, vol. 7, 1997, pp. 54–66.

15 Li Xuemin and Huang Kunzhang, *Yinni huaqiao shi* (History of the Chinese in Indonesia), Guangzhou: Guangdong Higher Education Publishers, 1987, chapter 7; also Twang Peck Yang, *The Chinese Business Elite in Indonesia and the Transition to Independence, 1940–1950*, Kuala Lumpur: Oxford University Press, 1998.

16 Assimilation through intermarriage in these countries occurred in similar ways to those in Thailand. This has enabled many Chinese to participate in local

nationalist activities without being identified as Chinese, but detailed monograph studies to establish the extent of this phenomenon are lacking. For Cambodia, W. E. Willmott, *The Chinese in Cambodia*, Vancouver: University of British Columbia Press, 1967; and *The Political Structure of the Chinese Community in Cambodia*, London: The Athlone Press, 1970, provides valuable background. Some general comments are found in Victor Purcell, *The Chinese in Southeast Asia* (note 13) and Lynn Pan, *Encyclopedia of the Chinese Overseas* (note 6).

17 Emma H. Blair and James A. Robertson, *The Philippine Islands, 1493–1898*, Cleveland: Arthur Clarke, 1903–1907, in 55 volumes.

18 For the early period, John O. Sutter, *Indonesianisasi: Politics in a Changing Economy, 1940–1955*, four volumes, Ithaca, NY: Cornell University Southeast Asia Program. Also, Merle C. Ricklefs, *A History of Modern Indonesia since c.1300*, second edition, Stanford: Stanford University Press, 1993, parts V and VI.

19 James Ongkili, *Nation-building in Malaysia, 1946–1974*, Singapore: Oxford University Press, 1985; Lee Kuan Yew, *The Singapore Story: Memoirs of Lee Kuan Yew*, Singapore: Times Editions, 1998.

20 K. J. Ratnam, *Communalism and the Political Process in Malaya*, Kuala Lumpur: Oxford University Press, 1965; Gordon Means, *Malaysian Politics*, second edition, London: Hodder and Stoughton, 1970.

21 The Indonesian Citizens Consultative Body, a socio-political organization formed in 1954 to protect members of the Chinese minority who were Indonesian citizens [eds].

22 For Lim Koen Hian (1896–1952) and Siauw Giok Tjan (1914–1981), see *Political Thinking of the Indonesian Chinese, 1900–1977*, edited by Leo Suryadinata, Singapore: Singapore University Press, 1979. Pramoedya Ananta Toer, in his *Hoakiau in Indonesia*, acknowledges Chinese support for Indonesian causes in his 5th letter (pp. 141–170), and mentions Injo Beng Hoat (Goat) (1904–1962), editor of the daily newspaper *Keng Po*. Elsewhere, he praises the early contributions of Lie Kim Hok (1853–1912) to the Malay language. Biographical information about these men and others who were active in local affairs may be found in Leo Suryadinata, *Prominent Indonesian Chinese: Biographical Sketches*, Singapore: Institute of Southeast Asian Studies, 3rd edition, 1995.

23 I first discussed this issue in Wang Gungwu, "'Are Indonesian Chinese Unique?': Some Observations", in *The Chinese in Indonesia*, edited by J. A. C. Mackie, Melbourne: Thomas Nelson, 1976, pp. 199–210.

24 For this and the following section, see Wang Gungwu, *The Chinese Overseas: From Earthbound China to the Quest for Autonomy* (the 1997 Reischauer Lectures), Cambridge, Mass.: Harvard University Press, 2000.

25 Subsequent to this lecture, I learnt that some of the art and poetry of Homero Chiong Veloso (d. 1950) has been recently published. I have so far not been able to obtain a copy of his work.

26 Two recent examples of intimate writing about one's family or oneself in Southeast Asia are Lien Ying Chow, with Louis Kraar, *From Chinese Villager to Singapore Tycoon: My Life Story*, Singapore: Times Books International, 1992, and Hsuan Owyang, *The Barefoot Boy from Songwad: The Life of Chi Owyang*, Singapore: Times Editions, 1996. The records based on oral history collected by the Singapore National Archives are more revealing than the conventional Chinese biographical collections compiled this century in various parts of Southeast Asia. For examples of these records, see the work of Chan Kwok Bun and Claire Chiang See Ngoh, *Stepping Out: The Making of Chinese Entrepreneurs*, Singapore: Centre for Advanced Studies, National University of Singapore and Prentice Hall, 1994.

16

THE CHINESE REVOLUTION AND THE OVERSEAS CHINESE[1]

Wang Gungwu

It does seem timely today to reflect on the impact of the Chinese revolution on the *huaqiao* (overseas Chinese). By overseas Chinese, I refer to those Chinese not living in territories traditionally regarded as part of China, that is, not in the People's Republic of China (hereafter the PRC), Taiwan and the territories of Hong Kong and Macau. For example, Hong Kong and Taiwan Chinese are not overseas Chinese although they lived for a while under foreign jurisdiction.

Last year was the 50th Anniversary of the establishment of the PRC in 1949. For most Chinese living outside China at the time, this would have been their second or third experience of Chinese revolution. Many of the older *huaqiao* had been through the excitement of the 1911 republican revolution when the Qing dynasty was overthrown. Many others would remember the struggle to implement Sun Yat-sen's revolution against various warlords, and the founding of the Guomindang's nationalist government in Nanjing in 1928. And many more would have been active in the civil war and the patriotic task of saving China from the Japanese, a series of momentous events which ended in communist victory. Thus the Chinese abroad were no strangers to revolution in China. It may seem to have been a series of different revolutions but, to most of them, it was one continuing revolution striving to bring China into the modern world. What is important to stress is that these Chinese had always been divided by that revolutionary cause, by the different definitions and perceptions of revolution and by the leaders and the parties that claimed to represent it. In addition, some of these overseas Chinese were further divided by the policies of host governments outside China which were increasingly suspicious of the Chinese living in their territories and who actively engaged in the politics of China.

Are these experiences of the overseas Chinese different from those of other diasporic peoples? One should note that revolution is really a very modern phenomenon; thus the link between diaspora and revolution could only have happened in recent history. Among Europeans who had left their homelands to go overseas, some also saw revolutions in their respective countries, notably the French, the German and the Young Italy revolutions. But, before the twentieth century, there was little evidence of direct involvement in revolutions by those residing abroad: a few restorationist Frenchmen and some risorgimento Italians. It was not until this century that the politics of the diaspora became significant. Most dramatically, there were the Zionist movement for the return to Palestine of European Jewry and the overseas Irish support for independence from Britain, but also, there were the anti-communist politics of some Russians after 1917, of German sympathizers of Hitler, and then, after the Second World War, among anti-Soviet Czechs and Poles, the anti-Russian Baltic peoples and some anti-Yugoslavia Croats. Closer to China, there were diasporic Arabs, Kurds and Iranians who felt that their peoples had suffered unjust humiliation at the hands of the West, or at those of the Turkish and Israeli governments. Others were politically engaged because they had been displaced by dictatorial regimes at home, regimes which they desperately wanted to overthrow. We know how active these diasporas have been. But most of these examples became important only after the end of the Second World War.

Some other overseas Asians have had experiences more comparable to those of the Chinese, for example, the Indians in former European colonial territories, the Japanese in North America and, more recently, the Vietnamese in the United States and Australia. This is not the place to make detailed comparisons. I mention them only to remind us that similar links between diasporas and revolutionary changes at home can be found. The major differences, however, lie in that China alone has had an ongoing revolution for the greater part of the century, one that was accompanied by civil wars and foreign invasion, and that its *huaqiao* overseas had been involved with them all from the start. In addition, China was the largest country to accept communism during the Cold War and it is still demonized by large numbers of anti-communists among whom the overseas Chinese still have to live. These circumstances gave the relationship between the Chinese revolution and the *huaqiao* some exceptional features. In this lecture, I propose to outline some of the most important of those features during the past half century.

I have been using the word *huaqiao*, usually translated as 'overseas Chinese' and meaning sojourners, that is, those Chinese who are temporarily living abroad and who intend to return to China. This is deliberate, for it is among them that the Chinese revolution has meant the most, as seen in the famous saying attributed to Sun Yat-sen, "*huaqiao* is the mother of revolution". The term came into common use at the beginning of this century and has carried political connotations ever since, especially when linked with patriotism, as in *aiguo huaqiao* (patriotic overseas

Chinese). But, strictly speaking, despite its common usage, not all Chinese outside China considered themselves *huaqiao* even before the Pacific War. For example, Chinese who became subjects of the Siamese king, many Catholic Chinese in the Philippines, and some of those who became British, Dutch or French subjects in their respective colonies. Since the 1950s, the numbers of such Chinese have grown, especially among those in Southeast Asia who have found it necessary to distance themselves from the term *huaqiao* as one that is both inaccurate and outdated. Instead, words like *huaren* and *huayi* have been substituted for it. These reflect recent political and social changes in the region. If *huaqiao* are sojourning Chinese, *huaren* would be ethnic Chinese, and *huayi* those "descendants of Chinese" who consider themselves politically integrated with their adopted countries if not culturally assimilated as well. (There is some argument about how many generations must transpire before one may be called a *huayi*, but today it really represents the attitudes of those who, while being proud of being of Chinese origin, do not see themselves primarily as Chinese.) Of the three terms, the first is clear and the third is self-defined. The second (*huaren*), however, remains difficult to pin down and can still be a source of misunderstanding. The greatest difficulty lies in the fact that the literal meaning of the word is "Chinese" while usage has made it apply to ethnic Chinese minorities who are citizens or nationals of non-Chinese countries. It is commonly used together with *haiwai*, thus *haiwai huaren*, which confusingly, actually translates as "overseas Chinese". And it does not help when many writers make no distinction whatsoever and still use "overseas Chinese" to cover everyone outside China who is identifiably Chinese, to the extent at times of applying racial criteria.

I have dwelt on the three terms here because their distinctive use may be seen as a product of the impact of the Chinese revolution and, certainly in Southeast Asia, is the result of the region's international politics pertaining to the PRC during the last 50 years. These distinctions are less understood in North America, but I suggest that they might eventually be useful there as well. For my purposes, I shall use shorthand references for the three in this lecture, as follows: sojourners for *huaqiao*, ethnic Chinese for *huaren*, and local nationals for *huayi*. By doing this, I make two points immediately. First, there were already internal divisions within overseas Chinese communities dating from the first half of the century which determined their different responses to China politics during the second half. Second, in their varied responses to the Chinese revolution, the Chinese in Southeast Asia were, and still are, significantly different from those in North America. These two points provide a general background to the impact of the revolution as represented by the 1949 victory of the Chinese Communist Party on the China mainland.

To speak of the impact since 1949, we need to ask what numbers of overseas Chinese were involved. There has been no accurate count of the number of Chinese outside the PRC, Hong Kong-Macau and Taiwan when the PRC was founded. Good estimates would place the total in 1950 somewhere between 8 and 9 million around the world, of which some 90 per cent were resident in Southeast Asia. Today, the figure for *haiwai huaren* (the ethnic Chinese overseas), or the preferred term in the PRC, the *huaqiao-huaren* (the sojourners plus the ethnic Chinese), is not much more accurate. Most estimates suggest that the figure should be about 22–25 million, with about 80 per cent living in Southeast Asia and the bulk of the remainder in the English-speaking world of North America and Australasia. During the past 50 years, the number of Chinese overseas has nearly trebled but, because of the rate of integration and assimilation in some areas, not all those with part-Chinese blood can be described as Chinese, and many would reject such an identification. On the other hand, given changing conditions, for example, a stronger and more prosperous China or a national leadership more sympathetic towards the PRC, local nationals of Chinese descent have been known to re-identify as Chinese, even though only for specific purposes. This does not help us determine accurate figures, and we have to be content with gross estimates.

For our purposes, however, the total figure is not important. We are primarily concerned with those sojourners and ethnic Chinese distributed all over the world who have looked to China for their cultural and political needs and who could clearly be called *aiguo huaqiao* in 1949. From China's point of view, all overseas Chinese would qualify, but my own estimate would be that, at the end of the Pacific War, following the defeat of Japan and the elevation of China to membership of the United Nations Security Council, all the sojourners and the majority of all others would be prepared to be described as patriotic (*aiguo*). This did not mean that they would return to serve their country. Most would continue to live abroad and be ready to support their families and countrymen to the best of their ability. But the communist victory in 1949 did dampen the enthusiasm of those who had long been nationalistic and were wary of the PRC's alien commitments to the internationalist Marxist bloc. Guomindang followers, in particular, remained hostile to the PRC. Among younger Chinese, however, most were proud of a strong and united China and many were genuinely sympathetic with the cause of revolution. Of course, there were also those who were simply so disgusted with the corrupt regime in Nanjing that had moved to Taiwan that they embraced the new Beijing government.

There are no reliable figures as to how the overseas Chinese divided on this subject. What became obvious quite early on was that the divisions were influenced by the political leanings of the countries in which they were resident. In Southeast Asia, the end of colonial rule produced a totally new environment for the overseas Chinese there. There were now independent governments newly embarked on their own nation-building programmes. Thus, in countries which recognized Beijing, most Chinese would look to the PRC and, where the governments withheld recognition, there was the political space to support the government in Taipei. In this way, local Chinese commitment to the power politics in China was subject to the policies of the new regimes under which they had to live. The prime concern of most overseas Chinese was pride in a China that was respected by foreign states, respect that could translate into respect for them as ethnic Chinese and make the majority peoples in these states refrain from discrimination against them. They did not bargain for the global ideological division which local governments could use as a weapon to discriminate against them in other ways. This was particularly true of countries where the Chinese formed a small minority. For example, Sukarno's Indonesia leaned towards the PRC and the PRC embassy officials protected the Chinese who looked to them for help, while the Philippines followed the United States in recognizing the Guomindang government in Taiwan and could, if they wished, punish local Chinese who were thought to be sympathetic to Beijing. These examples explain why, in the 1950s, the majority of the Chinese in Indonesia turned towards the PRC and the majority of those in the Philippines backed Taiwan.

A position similar to that in the Philippines could also be found in North America, especially in the United States, but for perhaps somewhat different reasons. In the 1950s and 1960s, the Chinese there were not under pressure to naturalize and they remained Chinese nationals far longer than in Southeast Asia. US society as a whole was greatly hostile towards revolutionary ideology, and communism in particular. The Cold War was a sharp divide and there was little room for neutrality or ambiguity, especially if most Chinese were not even American citizens. Of course, this did not stop some patriotic sojourners from working on behalf of the new regime in Beijing in educational bodies, international institutions and the media. But they received little help from the larger overseas Chinese community who tended to sympathize with US policies. The fact that the Republic of China was represented in the United Nations in New York for more than 20 years was enough to ensure majority support. Over time, dismay over Chiang Kai-shek's dictatorial ways towards the Taiwanese, and some progressive and romantic representations of the revolution in China, did lead to changes in attitudes among the younger generation, but the overseas Chinese response had to be muted until other young Americans began to change their views about the PRC. The best example would be that of the Cultural Revolution of the late 1960s which evoked sympathy among the rebellious young for a few years. This played a part in arousing the activism of younger Chinese in the vigorous Diaoyutai movement against Japanese claims on tiny islands in the East China Sea. The movement provided a focus for patriotic feelings under conditions which deterred Chinese from openly and directly identifying with the PRC and opposing the government in Taiwan. It also marked a significant change of national mood on the eve of a major shift in US policy towards the PRC.

In short, for the first 20 years, Guomindang officials in North America were effective in claiming that it was the ROC that represented the Chinese revolution and the PRC was a betrayal and an aberration in allowing China to be subordinated to an alien Soviet revolution. Ultimately, as US national interests led to new China policies, other views surfaced to counter that Guomindang claim. Increasingly, the view that the Guomindang had become reactionary and anti-revolutionary became more acceptable. This was reflected not only in the writings of the sojourners themselves, but more so in the national and ethnic Chinese media. Perspectives began to change towards the revolution itself, so much so that the destructive excesses of the Cultural Revolution were played down as the US government moved towards the diplomatic recognition of the PRC. Instead, by the early 1970s, the contradictory sentiments aroused included, on the one hand, a mixture of admiration and disgust for the actions of revolutionary youth and, on the other, a readiness to welcome young Chinese to study in America, accompanied by a new missionary zeal to bring enlightenment to the spiritually impoverished in China.

As most of you know, the situation changed again in the 1980s. But the pattern of overseas Chinese response is not all that different. The ethnic Chinese attitudes towards the Chinese revolution continue to reflect the concerns of the host country. For example, just as US politicians, academics and the media are divided on how to cope with China, so are the various Chinese communities in the country. This is particularly true on issues like the future of Taiwan and political reform. With the former, there are residual questions of which is the more constructive revolution for China, the 1911 or the 1949 revolution, or whether the PRC today has turned away from revolution to become a force for conservatism as compared with the leaders in Taiwan who stand for democracy and freedom. The divisions among the ethnic Chinese are clearest on what the US government ought to do. Should it encourage the current economic reforms because, at this stage, a true Chinese revolution will come only through peaceful evolution? Or, should every effort be made to contain a stronger China, even to the extent of bringing about a regime change? As long as the host country is divided about what to do, it would appear that the ethnic Chinese there would be similarly divided.

The situation in Southeast Asia where the impact of the Chinese revolution is concerned was quite different. Of the current ten countries (East Timor is likely to be the eleventh, but is a special case whose story need not detain us), three can be separated from the other seven. I refer to the two states that had been British Malaya (that is, Malaysia and Singapore today) and the special case of Indonesia. These deserve fuller treatment here. This is not the place to go into how the Chinese in each of the other seven countries responded to China. Let me give a brief outline to emphasize some common points. These latter communities are relatively small, between 1 and 5 per cent of the total population of each country. There was considerable variety among different groups of Chinese in each of their responses to the Chinese revolution. In these countries, the majority were engaged in businesses large and small. For them, there were few options other than to hide their often ambiguous feelings about China. The tendency was for the majority in each Chinese community to accept the official China policies which their respective governments espoused, that meant, to rejoice when these were pro-China and to keep their heads down when they were hostile. On the whole, as businessmen, they exercised great care not to offend their respective governments, while trying not to miss any opportunity to trade with Chinese agencies (whether based in the PRC or in Taiwan, but best if they operated out of Hong Kong). If they resided in capitalist countries, they knew there would be no sympathy for communist sympathies. If they lived in communist or socialist societies, there was clearly no room for most of their kinds of businesses.

Let me now turn to the remaining three countries in the region. In some ways, Indonesia resembled the other seven: the Chinese population was small, about 3 per cent of the total, and the majority had little choice but to submit to national government policies towards the PRC and Taiwan. But there were exceptional conditions. First, the bulk of the Chinese were visibly better off in the urban centres throughout the country. Second, President Sukarno was clearly on the side of the PRC from 1950 to 1965, while his successor President Suharto radically changed the government's position to one of hostility and suspicion for the next 25 years. That shift marked the Chinese revolution's direct impact on Chinese lives and livelihood in the country. Clearly the impact was neither consistent nor predictable. In a matter of weeks in 1965, a violent local revolution or, in the eyes of some, a murderous reaction turned the world upside down for most Chinese. The results were not all negative. Many of those who had suffered during Sukarno's 15 years did very well because of the change and became wealthy beneficiaries of Suharto's 32 years.

There is evidence that many younger Chinese in the 1950s did admire the ideals of the Chinese revolution. Some became ardent supporters of the Indonesian Communist Party while others chose to return to China to work for the new China. However, it is not clear how accurately the figures of those who were considered Chinese citizens in the mid-1950s, about 1 million out of an estimated 2.5 million, represented those who identified with revolution. Certainly, we know most of them had no choice because they did not qualify as Indonesian citizens. During the 1960s, when choice became possible, the majority applied to be Indonesians. Thereafter, it would have been difficult to find among them any who supported the excesses of the Cultural Revolution in the PRC. By force of circumstances, most Chinese Indonesians were driven to accept business careers and capitalist goals because many avenues of normal employment, for example, in the civil service, were denied to them. Their violent swing from a willingness to go along with communist revolution in China to a grim commitment to market economy ways marked the extreme conditions under which most ethnic Chinese had to adapt their lives. These wrenching experiences have come to distinguish such Chinese from their counterparts elsewhere.

This brings me to the former British territories that have now become the two states of Malaysia and Singapore. There were altogether fifteen such territories at the end of the Second World War: three colonies which were directly under British rule, four sultanates which the British administered on behalf of the Malay rulers, six others of which they were officially only protectors, and two which received special protection from the British, that is, the Brooke family's heritage of Sarawak and the North Borneo Company's territory now known as Sabah. I stress the fragmentary characteristics of the two countries now called Malaysia and Singapore because these multiple origins explain the different degrees of control the British had over the various Chinese communities in each of these states and territories, and also why the differences allowed these communities more freedom to organize themselves than was possible elsewhere in Southeast Asia.

It was not until 1947, on the eve of a communist insurgency on the Malay peninsula, and only 2 years before the communist victory in China, that eleven of the territories on the Malay peninsula came together, ultimately to be called the Federation of Malaya. At this point, about 1,885,000 or some 38.4 per cent of the Federation's population were Chinese, while in Singapore, the 730,000 Chinese constituted about 77 per cent of the total population (see Table 16.1). The preponderance of Chinese in Singapore was the main reason why Singapore was left out and remained a British colony. From the Malay point of view, the fact that the

Table 16.1 Chinese population in various parts of the Federation of Malaya (FOM) and Singapore, 1947

FOM 38.4% [1,885,000]. Cf. 49.2% Malays
Singapore 77% [729,473]. Cf. 12% Malays

Penang	55.4%	Selangor	51.0%
Johore	48.1%	Perak	46.6%
Malacca, Negri Sembilan both over 40%			

Chinese in four of the eleven states already averaged over 50 per cent of each state's total population, and that Chinese constituted over 40 per cent of two other states, made future nation-building a serious problem. Thus the Malay leaders, supported by the British, preferred not to have Singapore as part of the federation.

Leaving out the island of Singapore was a decision that is very relevant to our story. Had Singapore been included, the Chinese population would have outnumbered the native Malay peoples, something the Malay sultans and aristocracy and the new nationalist leaders simply could not accept. They had experienced the rise of Chinese nationalism in response to revolution in China and, during the 1920s and 1930s, saw this nationalism unite most Chinese against the Japanese. After the Pacific War, this had turned into a liberation war against British imperialism and the communist leadership of that war could have placed the Chinese in a dominant position in an independent Malaya. The Malay leaders could not allow this and worked closely with the departing British to prevent it from happening. Thus, the Chinese revolution was the underlying factor why great care was taken to align with anti-communist forces in post-colonial Malaya and exclude local Chinese from key positions in the government and the military.

Herein lies one of the most important manifestations of China's revolution in Southeast Asia, the formation of revolutionary parties largely inspired by a Marxist-Leninist anti-imperialism that began in Europe and spread east spawning communist parties among the overseas Chinese. Where the Chinese were few in number, there was among them no sizeable working-class nor a middle-class intelligentsia. Only in the British and Dutch territories were there the numbers of overseas Chinese to produce a potentially revolutionary base, and only in British Malaya and northern Borneo were there Chinese groups that could be described as acting as a radical proletariat. Not surprisingly it was among these Chinese that the potential for armed revolution was found.

There are now several major studies of the origins of the Communist Party of Malaya (CPM).[2] Clearly, despite the success of British efforts at breaking up the early cells, it was the left-wing idealists driven out of China by civil war during the years 1928–1937 who laid the foundations of the Party, and it was their disciples who sustained it during the war against the Japanese in Malaya. That fact both inspired the notion of revolution and bedevilled it after the Malayan Emergency was declared in 1948. It created the image of the CPM as an import from China which the Party never succeeded in removing no matter how hard its leaders like Chin Peng (Chen Ping) and his few Malay and Indian colleagues tried. The fact that the PRC and all socialist countries, for ideological reasons, gave the Party moral and material support, and Britain, the US and their allies, including Taiwan, gave this support prominence in their propaganda against communism, helped to isolate any drive to revolution.

Thus, while it can be said that the Chinese revolution inspired a similar revolution in Malaya, it also contributed to its ultimate defeat. Given that the Chinese numbers were large, would the outcome have been different if external factors had not played so strong a part in the revolution? Perhaps the 38.4 per cent Chinese population would have ended eventually with less than 38.4 per cent power and more than 38.4 per cent wealth even if the Chinese revolution had not had any influence in Malaya. I shall not speculate on that here. As for other aspects of the Chinese revolution and how they impacted on the region, I shall come to that in the final section of this lecture.

Let me return to the expectation in the 1950s that Singapore should have been part of a single country called Malaya. That possibility had raised hopes among some that revolution was an anti-colonial reality the region had to accept. It was thought that the large number of Chinese would allow them to link their fate with that of revolution in China if they wished to; it certainly helped them claim the political right to determine the kind of country they would want to live in. These hopes coloured thinking about how an independent Malaya should one day include Singapore. Under the glaring light of Indonesia's Confrontation policy, the British made new territorial arrangements that enabled Singapore to join the larger federation called Malaysia, and the merger was achieved in 1963. It did not last long. After more than a year of turmoil in which ethnic Chinese rights were in dispute and race riots left hundreds killed, Singapore was ejected in August 1965. This was a fateful decision. What part did the Chinese revolution play in the drama that unfolded? The PRC had supported President Sukarno in his opposition to the formation of Malaysia. Weeks after the ejection of Singapore, the Indonesian military annihilated the Indonesian Communist Party and greatly strengthened anti-communist and anti-Chinese forces in the region. Most Chinese who had sympathized with revolution in China were removed from the political arena.

For those who survived, there was little room for neutrality or ambiguity. Ethnic Chinese confronted the great divide as revolution in Vietnam backed by the Soviet Union and the PRC broke the region effectively into two. Three-quarters of the Chinese in Southeast Asia were located in the anti-revolutionary half that eventually became in 1967 the members of the Association of Southeast Asian Nations (ASEAN). Many began to vote with their feet to leave the region, not to go to China but to migrant nations in North America and Australasia and any country that would welcome the better educated among them. By then, the PRC was no longer an attraction. Following the failures of the Great Leap Forward, the Maoist economics that led to national famines, and the start of the Cultural Revolution early in 1966, ethnic Chinese had fewer options. They could turn further outwards away from China and the region wherever they could, or make their peace with the new nation-building pressures where they had settled down. In less than 20 years after revolutionary victory, the appeal of revolution was dead for most ethnic Chinese in Southeast Asia.

No one in 1965 could have predicted the outcome of Singapore's independence. The complex circumstances that led to the formation of first Malaya and then Malaysia included the long shadow of the Chinese revolution. But the tide turned in the mid-1960s. Even as the Soviets and the PRC backed the Vietnamese to win their war against the US and its allies, the Chinese revolution was losing the hearts and minds of the Chinese overseas in Southeast Asia. Although the impact of revolution on the Chinese communities had left a profound impression, a new chapter had begun following the deep split within the communist bloc between its largest powers, Russia and China. Early in the 1970s, spectacular diplomatic initiatives led to the PRC's admission into the United Nations at the expense of Taiwan. These led to extensive changes in policies towards China and cleared the way for a different face of revolution to be painted.

Perhaps the most significant of all changes was the exposure of the self-destructive revolution in the PRC itself. Chairman Mao's deadly efforts to remake the Chinese Communist Party opened the eyes of Chinese both inside and outside China. The absurdities of revolutionary rhetoric were so extreme that, by the end of the 1970s, with the return of Deng Xiaoping, the word revolution had totally lost its appeal. The most remarkable turnaround came when most Chinese overseas responded with undisguised relief and pleasure when the word revolution left the present and became a memory and an historical concept.

Have these ethnic Chinese been inconsistent, naive, hypocritical, filled with romance and wishful thinking about the Chinese revolution? Or did they only appear so? We do not have enough detailed studies of their varied responses to answer such questions yet. After all, even the way the Chinese in China embraced revolution and then set it aside has not been fully understood. All I can offer here are some preliminary thoughts about how this vast subject might be approached.

I believe we will always be perplexed unless we start with the rise of nationalist revolution under the aegis of the movements which supported men like Sun Yat-sen. These had ranged from popular associations with anti-Manchu credentials to merchant groups who longed for China to play its rightful role in the world, and to new intelligentsia educated outside the country who admired the revolutions that had modernized the powerful nations of the West. The delight of Sun Yat-sen in 1897 when he saw that he was not merely a *pan-nie* (rebel), but a *kakumeisha* or *gemingzhe* (revolutionary) is well known. That was recognition and legitimation in the eyes of the world, the new image which raised his actions to a higher plane. He never looked back. The word *geming*, revolution, stayed with him until his dying day, and is still the word associated with him among those who remember him today, whether in the PRC, Hong Kong and Taiwan, or among the Chinese overseas.

In short, *geming* had been a heritage of modern China. Its transformation from nationalist revolution to social and economic, and then communist, revolution was far less important among most Chinese than the fact that it stood for a new China, one that would be restored to wealth and power by heroic leaders. The means needed to achieve that desired end would vary and those who found the correct path to bring such a revolution to China deserved great respect. The *huaqiao* or sojourner Chinese believed this no less fervently than those at home. The earliest supporters of Sun Yat-sen in Hawaii, Yokohama and Kobe, San Francisco or Vancouver, provided financial and moral support. Similarly with those in Singapore, Penang, Ipoh, Kuala Lumpur, Saigon or Hanoi, but amongst these were many who returned to fight for revolution and some who died. The connection became legendary. The fact that they had contributed to the revolution's beginnings from outside the country rarely failed to tug at their hearts if not also their purse-strings for decades to come. For people far away from home, this was the least they could have done.

All this continued despite the fact that the revolution did not do well for half a century. Sun Yat-sen's presidency in 1912 was the shortest on record, warlords and local banditry terrorized the country for the next decade and a half, Sun Yat-sen's domestic followers who went among the sojourners began to divide among the nationalists, the communists, the anarchists, the westernized liberals and democrats. Still, they were welcome as long as they stood for different roads towards the same goal of the revolution. Disappointments followed throughout the 1920s and 1930s, but the overseas Chinese were galvanized by the fresh dangers to China when the Japanese invaded the country. Thus the patriotic war, the salvation efforts, the boycotts of Japanese goods, the volunteers to fight on Chinese soil were all part and parcel of the revolution that had long been denied them. No wonder the excitement when the end of the Pacific War was followed by the ultimate victory of Mao Zedong's armies in the name of what was then considered by many the most genuine revolution of them all.

Were the overseas Chinese much interested in the contents of the Chinese revolution? There is early evidence of debate among supporters of Kang Youwei, or the pro-emperor constitutionalists, and those of Sun Yat-sen, or the pro-republic nationalists, before 1911. When the republic was established and needed substance, the newspapers read by the sojourners distinguished between selfish militarists and idealistic patriots who carried the nationalist flag. For 20 years after 1928, most sojourners looked to the Guomindang state as China's only chance for survival. They were saddened by a civil war between nationalists and communists they did not fully understand and did not really approve, especially when it spread the contagion far and wide. The media available to these sojourners did explain the major thrusts of the ideological divide, and many took sides in fierce exchanges.

Among the larger communities of the sojourners where many modern schools were established, politicized teachers brought revolutionary ideas of every complexion to prepare the younger generation for the day when they should return to China, either to study or to work. Precisely how most sojourners placed themselves in China's political baskets is difficult to calculate. The evidence is that most sojourners cared and some were drawn to do battle for their version of revolution. But for the long haul the struggle for livelihood engaged their energies far more, and in each community were increasing numbers who came to care less for China's politics as the party disputes seemed endless and even futile. By the end of the Second World War, sojourners and ethnic Chinese alike longed for peace and reconstruction of a battered country and a devastated economy. The growing disgust at corruption in high places and runaway inflation deterred many sojourners from returning to China. Already, a clear majority had determined that their future lay outside, even that they could help China more by being abroad than in China itself.

Were they more impressed with the focused goals of the communist revolution after 1949? Some radical youth among the Chinese overseas cheered the removal of the corrupt politicians and bureaucrats of the previous regime, the violent land reforms in the countryside, and the dismantling of the old social structures. Others also welcomed the replacement of ancient traditions in favour of a modern and progressive outlook. In any case, for most Chinese overseas, whatever their age and persuasion, they were conscious of living outside the country. The specifics were not relevant. It was not for them to determine what China really needed. What certainly evoked applause amidst surprise was Mao Zedong's spectacular military victory. The fact that this was followed by unification on the mainland, for the first time since 1911, had a strong impact among all of them. Chinese tradition itself encouraged the idea that success was the ultimate proof of truth and greatness. But there were also feelings of longing and hope: this time, may these new leaders give the people the peace and prosperity they have not had for more than a century. Beyond that, it is doubtful if many outside China cared what the new classics of Marx, Lenin, Stalin and Mao contained. There were appealing parts in the ideals they represented. These included the nationalist bits in Mao's speeches and some of the egalitarian rhetoric but, for a while, what attracted most admiration was the strategic thinking that led to his final victory.

Sojourners who could be called patriotic *aiguo huaqiao* would love China anyway. Ethnic Chinese were largely involved in the sinews of competitive commerce and normally shy of politics of any kind. Local nationals identified with what their own governments supported. There is little evidence that communist programmes were in themselves important except to some of the students and proletariat among the Chinese in Malaya and Singapore. Elsewhere, the appeal was greater among the indigenous peoples, and a few idealistic young Chinese did join local communist movements. But the key was always in the presence of China, the image of strength it projected, the respect it aroused and the authority it exuded. On the whole, sojourners could not have enough of that. Ethnic Chinese felt a deep pride to be Chinese and welcomed the help which that presence would give to their safety and their livelihood. As for local nationals, they have always longed for the day when their Chinese ancestry would be an asset and not a liability. Thus, with the return of Deng Xiaoping in 1978 and the substitution of economic reforms for social and political upheavals, there has been a new beginning in which revolution is no longer the magic word. The new convergence between the PRC's major goals and the aspirations of the Chinese overseas has been nothing short of marvellous.

The Chinese revolution has given most Chinese overseas great hope, but has also brought them much grief. What is their verdict today? They would first wonder if the revolution is finally over. If it is, there would be relief accompanied by sadness that it has been such a bitter and painful road to get to where China is now. If, however, the present rejection of the word revolution is but a pause on a yet more tortuous road ahead, it would be unlikely that the Chinese outside would ever embrace yet another Chinese revolution. It has been a long century and the Chinese have endured much in the name of revolution because they had high expectations of the leaders who espoused it. The world itself has changed, in other ways probably more revolutionized than China has ever been. The new generations, whether sojourners, ethnic Chinese or local nationals, can better judge what should lie ahead than any of their forbears could. In the decades to come, they are likely to see the Chinese revolution as history, part inspiring and glorious, part tragic and futile, a subject that evokes awe and tears, but they may well conclude that revolution in China has done its best and worst and we need to move on.

Notes

1 This address was given as a part of the lecture series to commemorate the 50th Anniversary of the People's Republic of China (Stanford University, March 2000).

2 They include C. F. Yong, *The Origins of Malayan Communism* (Singapore: South Seas Society, 1997); Lee Ting Hui, *The Communist Organisation in Singapore, 1948–1966* (Singapore: Institute of Southeast Asian Studies, 1976); and Lee Ting Hui, *The Open United Front: The Communist Struggle in Singapore, 1954–1966* (Singapore: South Seas Society, 1996) [eds].

17

CULTURAL CENTRES FOR THE CHINESE OVERSEAS[1]

Wang Gungwu

The importance of culture has long been acknowledged. But how important one's own culture is for any group of people can vary a great deal, and why it is more precious for some people and less for others has been a controversial subject. How vital are questions about culture among the Chinese in China? Is it of such great interest to the Chinese diaspora as has been suggested by the idea of "Cultural China" (Tu Wei-ming, 1991)? In the context of this conference, one may ask, has it not been equally significant for the Indian diaspora? Indeed, the open manifestations of appreciation today of the various religions of the sub-continent, and music and dance, among Indian communities overseas suggest that traditional culture may be more alive among them than among their Chinese counterparts. Yet, among the Asian diasporas, it is the Chinese attitudes towards China and its cultures that have attracted more research and debate. Underlying that interest is the idea that Victor Purcell thought was commonly believed among non-Chinese observers: "once a Chinese, always a Chinese" or, as the Chinese themselves might have preferred, "where there are Chinese, there is China" (Purcell, 1965: xi). What did that mean? Was it true and was it more true for the Chinese than a similar statement about the Indians?

This chapter does not try to answer the question for the Indian diaspora. It has been stimulated by the belief that external perceptions of the two communities are different, and that is because Chinese diasporas respond to the idea of Chinese cultural centres very differently from the way their Indian counterparts do. With the Chinese, there is ample historical evidence to show that the local culture that Chinese traders and sojourners brought with them helped to bond together in alien lands as well as with their families and native places in China. Because this was crucial to their lives abroad, they believed that this culture should be transmitted to their descendants, wherever possible through cultural centres represented by their home towns back in Guangdong and Fujian provinces.

Later, during the twentieth century, when national consciousness grew among all Chinese, they identified with the culture that became a strong expression of nationalism. Great efforts were made to make this culture an integral part of the modern education their children abroad would receive. In this way, culture was often politicized and was associated with new concepts of race and nation-states. Here the anti-colonial national movement in India probably had a similar impact on the diaspora. But when China became the battlefield between nationalists and communists between the 1920s and 1950s, patriotic Chinese abroad had to decide whether to be drawn into Chinese politics and risk being deported to China, or to settle down locally and adapt to other people's national loyalties. Those who chose the latter had then to re-evaluate the issues of race, politics and culture for their lives in their adopted countries. And as issues concerning Chinese race and Chinese politics became locally controversial, and in many cases unacceptable to both colonial and native governments, many concluded that only a depoliticized cultural strategy could ensure the ethnic identification of those who expected to live abroad for generations. In that case, they needed to find new cultural centres to assist them in that task.

For the Indians overseas, we can also distinguish between national and local responses. Like the Chinese, there were many levels at which different communities related to their cultures. We might also ask, did Indians overseas identify more with secular India or seek a closer bond among themselves through their respective religions (Hinduism, Sikhism, Jainism, Islam, Buddhism and Christianity)? Is it meaningful to speak of cultural centres in India for different groups of people, for example, Chennai for those from Tamilnad, Mumbai for the West coast, Kolkohta for Bengal, or the national capital of Delhi itself? Or, Benares for Hindus, Allahabad for Muslims, and Amritsar for Sikhs? What about the special case of the Sindhis, whose lands were lost to Pakistan and who have no historical home to return to or identify with? The essays collected in the authoritative volume on the Indians in Southeast Asia, edited by Kernail Singh Sandhu and A. Mani, give many examples that show the variety of responses. The story that struck me most was about those Tamil families in Java who valued their earlier connections with Sumatra, and others who look to their larger communities in Malaya (West Malaysia), rather than look directly to India (Sandhu and Mani, 1993). There have certainly been Chinese families in Southeast Asia whose links were largely with their relatives and friends in another part of the region rather than with those in China, and there are many more today for whom similar links are intercontinental, even global. I shall not attempt any direct comparisons between the Indians and the Chinese, but merely hope that my focus here on the attitudes towards cultural centres inside and outside China among the Chinese overseas will invite contrasts with Indian experiences.

China has been a civilization that encompassed many cultures. That civilization served as the basis of an empire that asserted a feudal relationship over all lands under its control and, in turn, all the cultures within the empire have been deemed to be variants of a single entity. An abstract notion of a cultural centre like the *zhongyuan* (Central Plains) could be seen as one that represented all Han Chinese. Or the imperial capital, wherever it was located, could be taken to symbolize such a centre. Those living within the empire would be identified as Chinese. Those resident outside, however, would not necessarily be so unless they chose to orient themselves towards that centre. The difference was traditionally expressed in the concepts of *nei* and *wai* (inside and outside), or Chinese and non-Chinese. Would that still be true today? For the people within, could their culture be taken to mean anything and everything that Chinese people accept, follow and normally practise? For those outside, if they maintained some features of Chinese culture and behave as sojourners only temporarily away, would they not always be seen as some kind of Chinese?

China, of course, is no longer seen as a civilization or an empire. For a modern China that is expected to behave like a nation-state, the ground rules of international behaviour have changed. New concepts like *zhongzu* for race and *minzu guojia* for nation-state have entered the Chinese vocabulary from Western languages. Today, a Chinese national does not only include all those who are considered racially Chinese, but may include the fifty-five official minorities most of whom clearly do not share the culture of the Han majority. If culture remains important for the Chinese overseas, is China the only centre for that culture, or are there several centres? It may be that the Chinese overseas identify with culture in quite different ways from the Indians, for example, more through political structures than through cultural institutions. This chapter explores some of the variations among the Chinese.

At several recent conferences on the Chinese overseas, papers were presented which touched on the new relationships between recent immigrants, mostly from Taiwan, Hong Kong and the People's Republic of China (PRC), and established Chinese migrant communities in towns and cities where they had settled (Zhuang, Huang and Fang, 1998; Ang See, 2000). Although greater attention was paid to the commercial and technological possibilities in these relationships, there has also been renewed interest in issues like political involvements and cultural linkages. A feature of some of the reports concern the future of Chinese culture in the diaspora and the role of "China" in defining that culture. In particular, there is concern that globalization will impact on the way Chinese culture will be transmitted. How well will that culture survive the changes to come, including the question how much will it be "localized" or "westernized"? Will there always be one Chinese culture or could there be many Chinese cultures? With this background in mind, I offer some preliminary ideas about cultural centres among the Chinese overseas during the twentieth century.

As background, I shall take the following three developments as given. The first is that a gradual process of "globalization" has been going on for some 500 hundred years. The pace and scale of that process have grown immensely during the past century and Chinese migrations have been global since the middle of the nineteenth century. The Chinese are not new to globalization and have been working out strategies to cope with its changing shape and intensity for at least 150 years. Throughout that period, their ideas about their culture have undergone severe trials. The cumulative evidence suggests that there was nothing essentialist about the Chinese responses even though some of the elitist rhetoric may suggest that this was so. Most Chinese have been adaptable and pragmatic about which aspects of that culture need to be preserved and which they could afford to discard.

The second is that the primary cultural centre or reference point for most Chinese is China itself. It is to China (whether imperial Confucian or republican nationalist) that they would begin to look for guidance about their cultural heritage. Such a China is largely an abstraction, and attempts are made to essentialize its cultural components for easier identification, but to think that this would impress all Chinese would be misleading. On the one hand, China itself has been open to many influences, and cultural formation in China has been a dynamic process. On the other, we could point to the major sub-cultures that have been specially relevant for any understanding of the Chinese communities abroad. These are the areas from where most Chinese overseas originated, for example, the Pearl River delta of Guangdong, the south Fujian or Minnan districts, or the inland valleys that were the homes of the Hakka people. An examination of these sub-cultures would lead us to basic structures of village and county level practices which include pre-Chinese expressions that have enriched these cultures over the centuries. That would also enable us to unravel the rich variety that underlies what we call Chinese culture. But, outside China, with notable exceptions, these differences rarely mattered in the eyes of foreign administrations. For immigration officials, the main category under which the immigrants were registered would be as Chinese, even when these officials were conscious of some of the bewildering variations among them. It is in the eyes of foreigners that Chinese are most essentialized if not caricatured. For the immigrants themselves, depending on when and where they had chosen to settle, alternative new cultural centres might have acquired significance, and this is a question I wish to pursue.

The third is that these relationships, whether we accept the idea of one cultural centre or can identify several cultural centres, went through many changes. For this chapter, I shall make comparisons for three periods:

a the last decades of the Qing dynasty (notably the turn of the twentieth century);
b the decade immediately before and after the Second World War; and
c the past decades of renewed migrations.

The first period was one in which there was one main centre and several subsidiary ones; the second was when there was a concerted effort through a newly discovered nationalism to create one primary *national* cultural centre; and the third represents an opening up to the world, especially among the Chinese overseas, in which there are divisions into primary, secondary and tertiary cultural centres. It is these changes I want to emphasize.

Last years of the Qing (the first period)

Before the rise of modern nationalism, the idea that China was the cultural centre for the sojourning overseas Chinese would be misleading. These Chinese looked only to their home towns and local counties to support their religious and customary practices. How they met their various family obligations and structured their social organizations depended on their maintaining connections with their respective native places, their *jiaxiang*. These were the only places that mattered to them, and they served as their cultural centres, very specific areas on which they could anchor their deeper sentiments and sense of identity.

Before the twentieth century, although described as sojourners, relatively few such Chinese could afford to return to China on a regular basis. Instead, some looked to cities and towns closer by where there were concentrations of Chinese living as large communities. For example, Singapore was such a concentration for most of the Nanyang or Southeast Asian region; and San Francisco for parts of North America. Cities like these were transit or dispersion centres for the Chinese when they went to Southeast Asia or to North America. Because of their large communities, these cities also became the distribution centres for news from home, and later on, also for magazines, books, educational resources and films. For smaller groups who lived in relative isolation, there might be other cities that could perform these functions as well, like Manila for the Philippines and the eastern archipelago, and Batavia for Java and the western part of the Malay archipelago. None of them, however, were seen as reliable sources of Chinese tradition nor as significant centres for original cultural practices and activities. They could not replace native places in China as cultural centres, nor did they claim to serve as new external *huaqiao* centres that could satisfy the cultural needs of Chinese living far away from home.

From the official point of view, there was an obvious centre for Chinese culture. That would have been the symbol of Confucian orthodoxy, represented by the imperial court in Beijing. But it was recognized that only the local and provincial manifestations of that culture were what the Chinese abroad could identify with. Official culture at the court and among the mandarins and literati had little relevance for contract labourers who did not aspire to a higher social status. On the other hand, it was important to the new classes of merchants produced during the Ming and Qing dynasties, men who had a growing familiarity with the Confucian hierarchical system. Through past experiences, these merchants appreciated the value of acquiring some degree of official recognition through their purchases of imperial titles. For them, China meant learning the Confucian classics and seeking as many direct links with the gentry classes as possible. The actual physical centre that facilitated such contacts was less important than understanding the idea of a cultural orthodoxy that could be used to raise one's social status in the eyes of Chinese and foreigners alike.

In reality, since most early sojourners originated from the two provinces of Fujian and Guangdong, these two provinces were, to all intents and purposes, their China, their Tangshan (*tong-shan* or *dng-sua*). Prior to the advent of modern nationalism, that was enough to satisfy their sense of being Chinese. Such a notion of Chineseness could be further extended so that any part of the two provinces could be seen as representing China. Some might even have thought that one's own part of China might be more Chinese than others, but such perceptions did not really count because most Chinese would agree that it was imperial authority that laid down the criteria for what was genuinely Chinese. These criteria were too abstract for most ordinary people but, if they were transmitted by their local mandarins, their legitimacy was not in question. In the end, the criteria for the Qing dynasty even included alien styles of tonsure and dress forced on the Chinese by the Manchus at the time of conquest. By the nineteenth century, these had been taken as normal because they were officially authorized (Wang Gungwu, 2003).

In short, for the *huaqiao*, there were already two kinds of cultural centres: the mandarin-led primary centre (representing what the court recognized) for the few who were highly literate, and the subsidiary local centres which provided models directly for the majority. Apart from the few successful merchants who might have ambitions for their offspring to rise above their class and aspire to join officialdom, most Chinese abroad were satisfied with their respective local centres.

This began to change during the last years of the Qing. The rise of Shanghai as the most successful of the Treaty Ports caught the imagination of all those in search of a new China. This trend was accelerated with the growth of national consciousness, especially the attention given to the contradictions between Han Chinese and the minority Manchus who formed the core of the ruling elites. The Chinese overseas, mostly southerners, most resented Manchu rule, and took the opportunity to express their nationalism. Most gave their support to reformist and revolutionary movements which finally led to the fall of the dynasty and the establishment of the Republic in 1911 (Yen Ching-hwang, 1976)

The impact of these changes on the idea of a cultural centre was immediate for the young generation of radical activists in China. On the one hand, the changes led to the search for a national culture that all Chinese could accept as their own. On the other, they helped to remove the Confucian state, the dominant source of authority for their millennia-old culture of Confucianism and Sino-Buddhism, but failed to replace it with a credible Republican source of cultural authority. All at once, there were too many claimants for attention among the social and political philosophies, largely inspired by the West, offered up to the new generation of politicians and intellectuals. This brought considerable confusion to the Chinese overseas. Who should they turn to for their cultural models?

Between 1911 and 1949, the political centre shifted back and forth between Beijing and Nanjing and, for some during the Sino-Japanese war of 1937–1945, the national centre was located in Chongqing. The economic centre throughout the first half of the twentieth century, however, was Shanghai, supported to a lesser or greater extent by Hong Kong and other Treaty Ports along the China coast. What did the Chinese abroad feel about this phenomenon? Did Shanghai become the cultural centre for the diaspora?

By the 1920s, most Chinese within China looked to Shanghai for new Chinese culture. The reasons are complex and need not be detailed here. Suffice it to say that Beijing was identified with warlords, and the other coastal cities were too singularly commercial to develop rival cultural identities. Nanjing did not become the new national capital until 1928 and, with the political obsessions that hung over it during all the 9 years it served as capital before the Japanese attack in 1937, the city had little to offer the development of modern culture. In contrast, Shanghai had developed rapidly not only to become the most commercial and industrialized city in the country but also the liveliest place for modern education, political debate and a whole range of modern cultural activities of both foreign and national origins (Wei Peh-t'i, 1987; Yeh Wen-hsin, 2000).

This new culture, symbolized by the success of the May Fourth movement among young Chinese after 1919, also embodied the nationalism which was transmitted to the Chinese overseas through textbooks published in Shanghai. The liveliest magazines came from there. The latest books were published there, and also the most exciting artistic, literary and scientific ideas emanated from that most cosmopolitan city in Asia. For most of the *huaqiao*, Shanghai represented the most progressive and advanced features of modern Chinese culture. In less than two decades, it had become the virtual national centre that began to displace the local centres represented by the *huaqiao* home towns and villages and, in some cases, even their provincial capitals.

In short, during this first phase, the cultural centre that was China changed for the Chinese overseas from the combination of imperial Beijing (for the high culture of the Great Tradition) and home town and village culture (of the Little Tradition) to the beginnings of national culture. This happened in two stages. The uncertainty about the political centre had moved the cultural centre away from Beijing and, for a while, the *huaqiao* only had their native place to serve as cultural centres. But national fervour intensified and this demanded that they should look at the larger picture. There were some *huaqiao* who turned to Guangzhou and others who were content to seek their centres at Xiamen or Shantou. This local focus was, however, brief.

There was simply no denying the rapid development of modern schools that used the national language and this soon challenged the cultural claims of the Cantonese, Hokkien and other southern traditions for national attention. By the time the Guomindang government was established in Nanjing in 1928, the need for a national cultural centre was widely accepted. However critical the older elites might have been about the alienness of some of the developments in Shanghai, the lead over the rest of China that the city had already achieved was so great that its dominance was taken for granted.

Before and after the Second World War

The start of the Sino-Japanese War of 1937–1945 saw the tide of nationalism reach its peak, not only political and economic nationalism, but also cultural nationalism. Most overseas Chinese responded to this tide with varying degrees of enthusiasm wherever they were permitted to do so. More importantly, this was a period when there were no new large-scale emigrations from China. On the contrary, the Great Depression led many countries and colonies, in both Southeast Asia and the migrant states of the Americas and Australasia, to repatriate unemployed Chinese labour. They allowed only a few family members and small numbers of businessmen to immigrate and, into areas where there were sizeable Chinese communities, also a few professionals, notably teachers and journalists. It was a time less of people movement than of community consolidation. Because of the hiatus in Chinese emigration, the question of new immigrants relating to settled communities was not a serious one. The few immigrants adapted themselves to local conditions that were, in any case, more congenial when the Chinese who were already there had come to identify themselves closely with patriotic causes. The significant difference from earlier conditions was the fact that nationalistic links with a China that needed to be saved from Japanese imperialism had become a shared value.

Because of Japanese ambitions, the desire among the *huaqiao* to keep up with developments in China was heightened and Shanghai remained the main channel through which the newest ideas and trends of modern Chinese culture reached the Chinese outside. Transportation to and from Shanghai was more direct and efficient for people who could afford it. New forms of communications perfected in Europe or the United States were quickly introduced and used to reach out to scattered communities of Chinese in the strong migration arc that fanned out from the China coast and the Nanyang (Southeast Asia) across the South and East China Seas to the further shores of the Americas and Oceania. The latest media and artistic skills were used to foster patriotism and these products were marketed far and wide wherever the Chinese were. There is little doubt that, during this period, China as a cultural centre for all Chinese was largely transmitted from Shanghai and national culture, to all intents and purposes, was represented by Shanghai.

There were obvious contradictions here. How could Shanghai be taken seriously as a national cultural centre when it was still a city in which foreigners enjoyed extraterritoriality, where most of its most successful enterprises were owned by non-Chinese? How could a city with a deadly variety of politics dominated by opponents of the national government serve as a national centre for anything? The issues are too many to be examined here. The point is that, among most *huaqiao*, the local Chinese language schools used textbooks supplied from Shanghai, most of its teachers looked to the cultural life in Shanghai for inspiration, and the latest scientific and technological knowledge entered China through Shanghai before being transmitted to the rest of the Chinese world. If the *huaqiao* schools did not want to be left behind, and teachers who aspired to have their pupils ultimately return to study in China certainly could not afford to see that happen, then plugging into the ever up-to-date culture of Shanghai was necessary. In fact, no other city could match what Shanghai had to offer.

This was a new phenomenon for China. That one city, and not the capital at that, could become so dynamic and dominant was something that had never happened in the past 2,000 years of China's history. That it was the dragonhead of a national modernization process helped it become so, and this was unique for China. Thus, it was not surprising that the *huaqiao* who faced modernizing pressures outside China would also look to Shanghai to see how they, as Chinese patriots, should best learn new knowledge in the national interest, and acquire skills which their local indigenous or colonial rulers did not encourage them to have. Nevertheless, the fact that so many of them saw Shanghai as the cultural centre marked a major change in Chinese ideas about the salience of centres that could lead the way towards a modern and progressive future for China.

But more changes and uncertainties were yet to come. The Japanese attack on Shanghai in 1937 led to a reduced role for Shanghai as an "isolated island". When China's capital was moved into the interior to Chongqing, followed by the virtual collapse of Shanghai's economy during the Pacific War, there was a hiatus when China had no firm and acknowledged centre to speak of. No city could replace Shanghai during these years. The people, in any case, faced too desperate a struggle for survival to worry about cultural centres. Temporarily, the centre might have been wherever the capital was. But for most *huaqiao,* Chongqing was too remote, and any access to their homes in Guangdong and Fujian depended more on the Japanese than on the national government. Then for 3 years and 8 months, most *huaqiao* in Southeast Asia came under Japanese rule and the idea of a national cultural centre became irrelevant, if not downright dangerous.

What this meant was that the Chinese both at home and abroad learnt to live in a chaotic period without any cultural centre. Instead, the abstract idea of China as the name of the new nation was enough. That was the symbol of Chinese culture. It called for essentializing the elements that stood out in that culture so that all Chinese could have a set of norms for their activities to be measured by. Thus two developments occurred at the same time for the *huaqiao.* One was for them to identify their modern culture with China as a nation in the abstract, and the other was to begin to see culture as an organic force, something that could free them to seek new cultural lives in dynamic situations. This latter was where some of the Chinese overseas began to part company from their compatriots inside China. Whereas those within would still be bound and grounded by China's heritage and new modifications, those abroad could redefine their own Chineseness, keeping what they wanted and releasing what they no longer needed. They might even look for cultural centres elsewhere to replace those in China that they could no longer rely on. Such a loosening prepared them to redefine their cultural perimeters for even more uncertain times which followed the end of the Second World War.

The last two decades of renewed migrations

After a break from about 1930 to 1945 when there were few new emigrants from China, and a break from 1937 to 1945 when few *huaqiao* could return to China, a great flow was expected of people stranded in China ready to return to their homes abroad and migrants anxious to visit their families in China after years of separation. But this was largely a one-off back-log of people who had been immobilized one way or the other. There was no renewal of steady emigration from China because no country was prepared to open its doors to the Chinese. The victory of the Chinese Communist Party and the advent of the Cold War made emigration even more difficult. The exceptions were refugees into Hong Kong in the 1950s, notably from Shanghai and the Pearl River delta, and the few who were admitted into parts of Southeast Asia, North America and Australia on compassionate grounds and a small trickle of students from Taiwan and Hong Kong who were granted university places abroad. For these few, the relationships between immigrants and settled communities posed no problem.

This brings me to recent trends in Chinese global migrations which became significant with the steady flow of immigrants from Hong Kong into Canada during the 1970s. Unlike the students from Taiwan who went to the United States, the businessmen and professionals from Hong Kong emigrated to Canada as families and set up chain migration links. In this way, a steady rate of new immigration was sustained that grew in number through the 1980s and early 1990s. With the reforms in Deng Xiaoping's China, there followed a growing stream of students and intellectuals from the mainland who set out for the United States, Canada and Australia. During this same period, emigration from Hong Kong and Taiwan to the Americas and Australasia remained steady. Small numbers also chose to go to Southeast Asia, notably to Singapore, the Philippines and Thailand.

With renewed emigration, relationships between immigrants and the settled have attracted fresh attention. This takes me back to the questions asked at the beginning of this chapter, questions like political involvements and cultural linkages, the future of Chinese culture in the diaspora, and the impact of globalization on how Chinese culture or cultures might change. They are all linked to the issue of cultural centres.

I earlier outlined the shift from an era of abstract imperial tradition accompanied by concrete dependence on local native place centres to one of national cultural centres. But, in the absence of a stable political capital, the latter did not materialize except as an abstract patriotic ideal. The real centre was located in Shanghai and most young Chinese were drawn to it by its vitality. As the most vibrant cultural centre of modern China, it was the focus of attention among the Chinese overseas as well. What of cultural centres today?

During the past 50 years, two generations of Chinese overseas have grown up for whom China did not provide any kind of cultural centre. More and more of them consisted of the new local-born (*peranakan* or *baba* in Malay, *lukchin* in Thai, and ABC's in the United States and Australia). Whether forced to or by personal choice, they have chosen careers and life-styles consonant with those of their compatriots in their newly adopted countries and few have the Chinese language skills that their parents had. Among them, especially in North America and Australasia, have come immigrants from native Chinese areas like Taiwan and Hong

Kong and more recently mainland China. For these newer immigrants, it is still meaningful to speak of Chinese culture and the centres to which they could turn for reference and fresh nourishment. The bulk of them are mindful that, as Chinese, their primary cultural centre would have to be located in China, at least the historic idea of China or the abstract ideals associated with Chinese civilization, if not the physical entity of the China mainland. Certainly, most Chinese on the mainland would be surprised if anyone of Chinese descent abroad thought otherwise. Those who have recently emigrated from China may also assume that this is accepted by all Chinese.

For them as for the Chinese in China, the idea that China is the primary cultural centre for all Chinese is taken for granted. It is one of the givens I outlined earlier. Backed as it is by some 1.3 billion Chinese, the potential for the PRC to be that China and, therefore, to be always such a centre, need not be challenged here. From the point of view of most Chinese overseas, however, this is no longer self-evident. What can be observed among the diasporic communities is that, during the past half century, secondary cultural centres have emerged in Hong Kong and Taiwan, and there is even the possibility of tertiary centres forming.

Hong Kong as secondary centre

For recent immigrants from Hong Kong in cities like Toronto, Vancouver and Sydney, there is no doubt that they look to Hong Kong for their cultural needs (Hamilton, 1999). Daily newspapers, music, television news, videotapes of films and shows produced in Hong Kong, weekly and monthly magazines and all variety of books and reference materials are awaited with eagerness. They provide enjoyment and a rich diet of lively debates. They even provide the school textbooks for the new Chinese schools that some of these communities try to maintain, although these may not be as welcome or acceptable to the children who were born abroad. In such ways, Hong Kong now performs the role that Shanghai used to play for the *huaqiao* of earlier generations. And like Shanghai in the past, this culture is an amalgam of many sub-cultures of China, both north and south, with a dose of British and American (even some other European) cultures, and even elements of the life-styles the Chinese overseas had brought to the former colony over the past century. Also like Shanghai, the unique mix this has produced distinguishes Hong Kong culture from that of any other primary centre one might look to elsewhere on the mainland. The mix is seen as being as modern as that of Shanghai when it was at the peak of its greatness as a cosmopolitan city.

The interesting point to make is that this modern culture appeals to more than just the immigrants from Hong Kong and their families. It has attracted many of the young local-born just as much as it has won adherents within the PRC and set standards of modernity there. And this is not confined to the communities which the Hong Kong immigrants had joined. It has also occurred among the local-born ethnic Chinese in Southeast Asia for whom Hong Kong as cultural centre is most accessible. After Hong Kong returned to the mainland in 1997, there have been fresh inputs of the cultures of China into the city. In time, an enriched Hong Kong culture could be expected to articulate Chinese culture for the Chinese overseas in new ways. And as Hong Kong culture becomes an integral part of modern Chinese culture, it will act as a secondary cultural centre, not only for the Chinese overseas but also for the Chinese within China itself.

Taiwan as secondary centre

Taiwan has a different cultural history. Having been the political base for a former government of China, it had seen itself as a bearer, or at least an alternative bearer, of the grand historical heritage of China. But its appeal has been mixed among the Chinese overseas. For older *huaqiao*, the political position as legitimate China was primary, but that group is diminishing. For others, now citizens of their adopted countries, Taiwan has provided for some an invaluable source for education and tradition. Their children are able to get a good university education there in Chinese, one that is still mildly nationalistic without being involved with radical ideologies. However, there are others who have been disappointed with the Chinese culture Taiwan now represents. In their eyes, this has drifted away from the modern national culture as represented by Shanghai before the war. By failing to build on that progressive development, and by allowing a growing cultural localism that emphasizes its Taiwan identity, Taiwan has allowed Hong Kong to seize the mantle from Shanghai as the flag-carrier for a Chinese modernity.

The position is not simple. Taiwan still has the capacity to stand for the primary Chinese heritage and could remain the major secondary centre for all things Chinese if it wanted to. The contributions of Taiwan scholars, teachers and cultural officials to the persistence and enrichment of that heritage during the past five decades have been outstanding. The quality of the writings and research of their best work on Chinese philosophy, history and cultural change is widely recognized. Among Taiwan emigrants, mainly those to North America and Australasia, there is hope that the reunification issue across the Taiwan Straits be not limited to the political sphere but might give greater attention to aspects of culture. For some, there is the need to reunify Chinese culture, to restore confidence in its unity in order to remedy the destructive forces unleashed by the Cultural Revolution on the mainland. For them, the idea of "one China" should not concentrate so much on political unification. The greater and more urgent need is cultural reunification.

Tertiary centres? Sub-cultures?

I mentioned earlier the possibility of tertiary cultural centres and even new centres representing smaller sub-cultures. If cultural reunification becomes the victim of politicization, what would the Chinese overseas do? There would be many who will abandon the idea of being culturally Chinese. These ethnic Chinese loyal to their adopted countries as members of multicultural states would tend to embrace a mix of cultural values that suits the local environment. Will these in turn be recognized one day as forming sub-manifestations of Chineseness? How would that development affect the question of a specific Chinese identity through China, Hong Kong or Taiwan?

In time, three developments are possible. One is that the numbers of such Chinese overseas would grow and where they are located becomes a matter of strategic significance in their respective regions. Eventually each of them could be recognized as an ethnic centre in its own right, one to which all smaller Chinese communities in the region turn for sustenance in cultural matters. These tertiary centres would become specially significant when, for a variety of reasons, dependence on the cultures of PRC, Hong Kong or Taiwan is not practicable, and minor groups look to them to measure their own expressions of Chineseness.

The second is that each group of local ethnic Chinese would breed a sub-culture that others regard as sufficiently Chinese to deserve the name. If their numbers remain relatively small and their locations remote, avoiding assimilation by the majority group and attaining the status of a sub-culture would itself be something of a triumph. Whether this sub-culture looks directly to the primary and secondary cultural centres of China, or could thrive on close relations with a tertiary centre closer by, may be a matter of choice or convenience and would be a decision to be made by the community's leaders. But it may not be necessary. The sub-culture could feed off all three, the primary, secondary and tertiary centres, depending on what they need at any one time.

The third possibility is that the group's numbers become too small and their location too remote to sustain their ethnicity. They could then choose to give up and merge into the majority group or, as individuals, either vote with their feet to join larger ethnic communities or seek to identify with the most viable tertiary centre or sub-culture that they could reach.

How large is large enough for any group to establish a tertiary cultural centre? If both size and location are taken into account, the city-state of Singapore and the Bay area in California are likely candidates to play that role for the two regions of Southeast Asia and North America, while the Sydney–Melbourne axis might one day have large enough ethnic Chinese communities to play that role in Oceania. One could speculate on other urban centres like Toronto and Vancouver, New York, Penang and Kuala Lumpur, and even some city in Western Europe one day, but for the moment I shall leave it at the two: Singapore and the Bay area.

What criteria would serve to identify such tertiary centres? A key ingredient would have to be that the ethnic Chinese in that centre would be able to sustain large-scale cultural activities on a regular basis. These activities need not be exclusively Chinese, nor need they always draw from the primary and secondary centres for help, but would be expected to include activities that are spearheaded by people who readily admit to being Chinese in their own ways. In addition, although these cultural activists may also be inspired by cultures that are clearly not Chinese, their creative efforts should be able to win admiration from ethnic Chinese in the region, if not from Chinese everywhere. In particular, those in the region would normally turn to these activities for cultural sustenance and the cultural leaders in the primary and secondary centres would be proud to recognize their achievements. By those standards, both Singapore and the Bay area would qualify. Whether or not they will provide such tertiary cultural centres for their respective regions, of course, would depend on their willingness to take on that burden of cultural leadership.

Finally, the issue of cultural centres must bring us back to the point of view of China and the issue of the oneness of Chinese culture. That culture today, unlike some other cultures, is not in any way defined by adherence to religion. With the weakening of its historical civilization in the twentieth century, it has now become more closely tied to the twin concepts of nation (with its ethnic and racial connotations) and state (defined in terms of sovereignty and territory). For the Chinese overseas, however, cultural identity is often the only option, and economic action the only road to cultural freedom. This is a position which political China, whether based in Beijing or in Taipei, might find difficult to accept.

To put the issue in perspective, two trends since the end of the Second World War need to be considered. The first concerns the oneness of China. In political terms, this is widely accepted by most governments. In economic terms, it is expressed through the concept of a "Greater China" that includes PRC, Hong Kong and Taiwan. But in cultural terms, there are as many centripetal as centrifugal forces at work. China as the primary centre can be matched by Hong Kong and Taiwan as secondary centres for most Chinese overseas. In both the secondary centres, the deep structure of the earlier civilization is accepted. The current versions emanating out of Beijing, Shanghai and other cities, however much appreciated, are regarded as supplementary, and at best complementary, to what Hong Kong and Taiwan already offer. Both these secondary centres have their own clientele among the Chinese abroad and can satisfy needs which the primary centre cannot.

The PRC has a legitimate claim to project the key standards of Chinese culture. When it has the wealth and power to do so systematically, the Chinese outside are likely to pay it more attention. In the meantime, alternatives provided by secondary centres are welcome. Whether they can be satisfactory substitutes for long is not clear. The dilemmas for the PRC are two. First, how should it deal with these centres without tying it too closely to the political struggle with Taiwan that is going on at the same time? Second, how should it admit Hong Kong culture in its present form into the fold as an integrated part of the future culture of China? An even greater dilemma is, what is the best strategy to achieve the goal of eventual reunification of Chinese culture? Here the PRC may find the response of the Chinese overseas a valuable index of success. If these Chinese outside Chinese jurisdiction altogether can be persuaded that ultimately all Chinese culture must be related to the heritage of China and, therefore, that they should acknowledge the cultural centres in the PRC as primary, that would be a major step towards a larger and enriched future for Chinese culture. Despite this acknowledgement of primacy, the PRC authorities may nevertheless find it wise to recognize the secondary centres in Hong Kong and Taiwan as integral and legitimate to China's future cultural growth. They would then also see that the need for Chinese overseas in their respective localities to identify their own tertiary centres could be invaluable to their communities' cultural survival. Nothing, of course, is for ever. But an open approach towards cultural centres outside China may be the best way for a single reinforced modern culture eventually to emerge.

Ultimately, it would depend on what culture remains important for the Chinese overseas. If future generations of such Chinese are fully accepted locally and develop firm loyalties to their adopted countries, their attitudes may change and cultural assimilation will follow. But, if globalization continues to give prominence to pluralist and multicultural communities, identifying with inherited cultures is likely to keep its value in the eyes of diasporic peoples, whether they are Chinese, Indian, Japanese, Thai, Javanese, Arab or sub-Saharan African. If that happens, a cultural heritage would be depoliticized, away from racial, national and tribal loyalties. If the Chinese overseas then wish to preserve their culture in any way, they will have the choice of looking to primary, secondary or tertiary centres for inspiration. In any case, that would affirm the proposition that culture, however you approach it, will always be important.

Note

1 Keynote address at the Conference on Chinese and Indian Diasporas, the University of Hong Kong (24–25 February 2000).

References

Teresita Ang See, ed., *Intercultural Relations, Cultural Transformation, and Identity: The Ethnic Chinese*, Manila: Kaisa Heritage Center, 2000. (Essays by Khua Kun Eng and Wong Siu-lun, Tan Chee-Beng, and Mely G. Tan, pp. 226–235; 284–300; 441–456.)

Gary G. Hamilton, ed., *Cosmopolitan Capitalists: Hong Kong and the Chinese Diaspora at the End of the 20th Century*, Seattle: University of Washington Press, 1999.

Victor Purcell, *The Chinese in Southeast Asia*, London: Oxford University Press, second edition, 1965.

K. S. Sandhu and A. Mani, eds, *Indian Communities in Southeast Asia*, Singapore: Institute of Southeast Asian Studies and Times Academic Press, 1993. (Essays by A. Mani, pp. 46–97 and 98–130.)

Tu Wei-ming, "Cultural China: The Periphery as the Center", in *Daedalus: Proceedings of the American Academy of Arts and Sciences* (Spring 1991), republished as *The Living Tree: The Changing Meaning of Being Chinese Today*, edited by Tu Wei-ming, Stanford: Stanford University Press, pp. 1–34.

Wang Gungwu, "Questions of Identity During the Ch'ing Dynasty", in Jiang Bin and He Cuiping, eds, *Proceedings of the Third International Sinology Conference: Anthropology (2000)*, two volumes, Taipei: Academia Sinica, vol. 1, 2003.

Betty Peh-t'i Wei, *Shanghai: Crucible of Modern China*, Hong Kong and New York: Oxford University Press, 1987.

Yeh Wen-hsin, ed., *Becoming Chinese: Passages to Modernity and Beyond*, Berkeley: University of California Press, 2000. (Essays by Yeh Wen-hsin, and Leo Lee Ou-fan, pp. 1–30; 31–61.)

Yen Ching-hwang, *The Overseas Chinese and the Chinese Revolution: With Special Reference to Singapore and Malaya*, Kuala Lumpur and New York: Oxford University Press, 1976.

Zhuang Guotu, Huang You and Fang Xiongpu, eds, *Shiji zhi jiao di haiwai huaren* (Ethnic Chinese at the turn of the centuries), two volumes, Fuzhou: Fujian renmin chubanshe, 1998. (Essays by Guo Yucong, Tan Tianxing and Franz Schurmann, vol. I, pp. 22–32, 33–43; vol. II, pp. 8–25.)

18

NEW MIGRANTS

How new? Why new?[1]

Wang Gungwu

The International Society for the Study of Chinese Overseas (ISSCO) normally holds its official conference once every three years. At each Conference, the significance of Chinese migrations during the past half-century has been commented on, albeit in different thematic contexts. At the first in San Francisco, it was in the context of settlement, *luodi shengge*,[2] at the second in Hong Kong, it was set in migration history over the past 50 years;[3] and at the third in Manila, the context was that of intercultural relations.[4] Today, at the fourth ISSCO Conference held at the Academia Sinica in Taipei, I would like to reflect on the phenomenon of *xin yimin* or new migrants. The bulk of these are immigrants from Mainland China. Officials dealing with Overseas Chinese affairs had previously lumped them together with the *huaqiao* or *huaqiao-huaren*. The new term is attracting increasing attention, especially in Europe and North America where most of them are to be found. Does the new term reflect new thinking about the Chinese overseas? Or simply new practice? Or is it largely a euphemism for the old term, *huaqiao*?[5] If so, it is one way of capturing the essence of that older term without using the very clumsy idea of *huaqiao-huaren* to imply that nothing much has changed. It will avoid having to increase the number of family members within the PRC who would have expected to be treated like *guiqiao* (returned overseas Chinese) or *qiaojuan* (relatives of returned overseas Chinese). And it would satisfy the settled Chinese populations abroad who deny that they are *huaqiao* and who are also not new migrants.

What are the long-term implications of separating the new migrants from the older ones? For example, how would the term affect the relationships of the established Chinese communities with China? Will there be any impact on their place as privileged Chinese overseas, and on the treatment of their families back home? I note that some of the papers presented at this conference will be examining specific issues that have arisen. I shall only offer some thoughts on how these new migrants might be studied.

The point to stress here is that there are new kinds of Chinese migrants, and the new term, *xin yimin*, was introduced by the authorities in the PRC to address their own recent emigrants. It does not as yet replace *huaqiao-huaren* but seems to be a subset of the larger grouping. It would be interesting to see if this term is accepted for and by other new migrants who have recently moved from Hong Kong, Macau and Taiwan, or for and by those re-migrants who have moved from Southeast Asia to various Western countries during the past three decades. If the term comes to be generally used, it alerts us to the way Chinese living abroad today respond to what the PRC does, and this may tell us something about the Chinese overseas in decades to come. On the other hand, if it is not generally accepted, but used only for those recent immigrants who originated from the PRC, that also would be significant. It suggests that the time may come when those of Chinese descent outside Chinese territories may eventually be identified separately according to their actual country of origin, especially if they do not hail directly from the mainland.

The changes are new and the situation is fluid. Nothing has yet been settled. This may be a good time to consider how we might study the various groups of new migrants, whether called *xin yimin* or not. I shall suggest that the following key issues should be freshly re-examined:

1 territories from where recent Chinese migrants originate;
2 receiving countries targeted by new migrants;
3 check-list of certain recurrent themes;
4 re-visit the theme of assimilation in a new context.

Territories from where recent Chinese migrants originate

The PRC is the source of most of the new migrants to the distant countries of Euro-American cultures. These are only a small minority of all the Chinese overseas, but they invite comparison with those who left China in earlier periods. There have been brief comparisons made with those, also from the mainland, who first went to Taiwan and Hong Kong before becoming overseas Chinese. In the 1950s and 1960s, these latter could only go to the very few countries that were prepared to have them. Only the businessmen-investors were welcome, and later also increasing numbers of students going to the United States. These numbers remained very small until the three major English-speaking migrant nations, the United States, Canada and Australia, changed their immigration policies from the mid-1960s onwards. Those directly from the PRC only joined the migration flow after 1978. Beginning with the PRC students who stayed on in the US and Australia after graduation, there were also family reunion programmes which admitted the relatives of earlier groups of immigrants.

Finally, with the success of the enterprising illegals, new PRC Chinese migrant numbers swelled beyond expectations.

Most of these new migrants, especially those who went to the US, faced three difficult problems. First, the political connections of the old *huaqiao* communities who had been loyal to the Guomindang and, therefore, by extension, to the ROC in Taiwan. Many of them were fiercely hostile towards the PRC. Second, the temptation for them not to be sojourners as expected, but to move quickly to stay on as settlers, especially in countries like Canada and Australia that encouraged immigrants to take up citizenship. And, third, the urge in many to remain as conscientious Chinese who care for the future development of China, and the deep-seated wish in most to transmit their Chinese values to their children.

Equally, the PRC officials assigned to these countries to deal with the greater variety of Chinese there would have to face their own set of difficulties. How are they to treat all Chinese alike when many different political loyalties confront the several different Chinese communities? They would be expected to persuade the new Chinese elites abroad to remain sympathetic if not committed to the PRC. To do that successfully, they would have to move away from the mistakes associated with older *huaqiao* policies. A very important task would be to help the new migrants establish new kinds of communication lines with their families and homes back on the mainland. Here, I believe that merely perusing the many official policy documents put out by the PRC authorities would not be enough.[6] We need to know what actually happens on the ground among the new migrants themselves, what they now do and what they think about their current condition. Also, the actual experiences that their families at home now encounter because of, or despite, the new policies, would be of particular relevance.

As for Taiwan, there have only been recent, or relatively recent, emigrants. The earliest, during the 1950s, left Taiwan mainly to study in the US. Those who did not return became Chinese sojourners in the eyes of the government, even those who obtained American citizenship, for whom the old word *huaqiao* seemed appropriate. Since the 1990s, many of the older migrants, especially those who had opposed the Guomindang, have returned to Taiwan. With a more liberal and democratic regime in Taiwan, fewer people now wish to emigrate in the old way, that is, there is less interest in going abroad as students and then staying on to settle. There are fewer new migrants of that kind now, nothing comparable to the *xin yimin* from the PRC.

It is still easy to distinguish Chinese permanent residents with Republic of China passports from those who hold PRC passports. If the latter group are the only ones being called *xin yimin*, we might soon have to consider how to study them quite separately from the former, and even whether we can still speak of them all as Chinese in the conventional way. And, should a category of *taiqiao* (Taiwanese overseas) become popular usage, what will that do to the study of the Chinese abroad? There may be some who are striving for a transitional stage here. If this happens, such a process would deserve sensitive attention.

Hong Kong is different again. Although not exclusive, the terms that local communities abroad use to differentiate Little Hong Kong from the traditional Chinatown may be indicative of future changes. The strong presence of Hong Kong centres in several cities in Canada make them behave more like old migrants than like the new ones from the PRC.[7] This is also true for their growing numbers in some cities in Australia and New Zealand,[8] and there are a few pockets of them in California and Hawaii.[9] So far, *xin yimin* does not seem to apply to them. It probably does not matter. With the return of Hong Kong to China, those who identify with the PRC may not ultimately mind being called *xin yimin* by the Beijing authorities, or whatever, as long as they can continue as a separate identifiable sub-group calling themselves Hong Kongers. And, as long as they do that, they will provide interesting contrasts with other Chinese migrant groups, especially in North America.

We need also to distinguish one other kind of migration source, the source from where re-migrants depart to find safer havens or to go to countries with greater opportunities. I refer mainly to those of Chinese descent who decided to leave their homes in Southeast Asia to go to the West, especially to the migrant states of North America and Australasia.[10] The countries are Indonesia, the Philippines, Malaysia, Singapore and Thailand and, after the Vietnam war, the three Indo-Chinese states that produced hundreds of thousands of refugees. But there are several others in this category, countries like Mauritius, Fiji and Papua-Niugini, South Korea, the Caribbean and some countries in Latin America. These re-migrants are practised migrants and clearly not *xin yimin*. I mention them here to remind ourselves that we already have large numbers of Chinese re-migrants whose homelands are not any part of China. When they say that they are Chinese, or of Chinese descent, each of their claims may well be distinctive, if not uniquely linked to an ancestral home in Southeast Asia, or elsewhere in former colonies and new nations. The introduction of the new term *xin yimin* is unlikely to affect the relations of these re-migrants with the settled Chinese communities that they have recently joined. On the contrary, the new term might underline the differences between them and those who have come directly from the China mainland. More significantly, their presence highlights the many varieties, if not layers, of Chinese overseas and helps us appreciate the richness in the Chinese migration experience.

Receiving countries

I turn to the receiving countries. For the *xin yimin*, the key countries are in the Americas, Australasia and Europe. What a difference from the anti-Chinese attitudes at the end of the nineteenth and the first half of the twentieth century when these countries admitted very few Chinese, and only European colonies and semi-colonies of Southeast Asia received new immigrants from China.

Since the late 1960s, the US and Canada have received the largest numbers of Chinese. The former has admitted them mainly from Taiwan and the mainland, while the latter began with immigrants from Hong Kong, but also now welcome those from the mainland.[11] It is widely agreed that these migrants are valuable new citizens who have contributed to the pool of trained and specialized skills in both countries. But, unlike in the past, both governments have been highly selective.[12] Also, Chinese immigrants are but a part of a much larger flow of new immigrants from all over the world.

In the spirit of newly enlightened migrant nations, new laws have been enacted that are more humanitarian. At the same time, these laws are also more demanding, and Chinese migrants are expected to conform and behave like other immigrants. There is now less patience with any kind of Chinese exceptionalism which previous racially discriminatory laws and practices had actually encouraged. The legal systems today are more transparent and anti-Chinese behaviour can be openly challenged. These, on the whole, make the receiving countries more attractive to the new migrants. What is less clear, especially in the US, are the long-term implications of the current debate between assimilation and multiculturalism that continues to trouble the settled populations and the new Chinese Americans alike. I shall re-visit this issue later.

Similar developments are found in Australia and New Zealand where multiculturalism is more consistently the official policy and confrontational race and civil rights issues are less prominent than in the United States. Also, unlike in North America, there are greater varieties of people of Chinese descent arriving from Southeast Asia who are, to their immense relief, not caught up in, and fiercely divided by, the internal politics of both Taiwan and the Chinese mainland.

As for Europe, the numbers of Chinese there have always been very small. Thus, many European countries find it remarkable how many Chinese have been arriving from the PRC during the past two decades. In particular, the new arrivals overland via Russia and Eastern Europe represent a truly new *xin yimin* phenomenon. Unlike in the established migrant states of the New World and Australasia, European authorities are unaccustomed to the large numbers involved. Also, Europeans face several new conditions at the same time. It is unprecedented to have both an increasingly borderless community of nations in Western Europe at the same time as ineffective and porous borders in Eastern and Central Europe. Thus, the policies and attitudes of the receiving countries there are often contradictory and confusing.

The breakdown of the draconian controls of a decade ago, leading to eastern and central Europe becoming the favoured route for illegal immigrants from China, could not have been anticipated. The dramatic and unprecedented phenomenon of all kinds of desperate migrants passing through to get to Western Europe has led to alarm and consternation, and this is obvious in the new studies initiated in Europe. The new research being conducted there makes valuable comparisons possible with other parts of the world but, until we know more about the new Chinese communities being formed there, it may be wise to treat these *xin yimin* as rather exceptional products of an unusual set of circumstances for the time being. It is already clear that earlier studies of Chinese migrations elsewhere do not help us much to understand this new phenomenon. The patterns of Chinese migration emerging in Europe seem to be unique, although some of the new dimensions discernible there might well be relevant for studies elsewhere in time to come.

I shall be brief about countries in Asia. Relatively few Chinese have been admitted into Southeast Asia since the 1950s. A highly selected small number have come to Singapore, and others have managed to enter the Philippines, Burma and Thailand. Compared to earlier figures, the new ones are minuscule and the *xin yimin* phenomenon may be described as insignificant. Similarly, Chinese migration elsewhere in Asia, for example, the Russian Far East and the Muslim states of Central Asia, is limited, and has not attracted study. The one exception is Japan which has attracted new migrants from mainland China as a developed country that is short of labour. But their experience does not resemble either the experience of the migrant states of North America and Australasia or that of Europe. As an East Asian country with traditions in common with China and Korea, and historical links with Southeast Asia, Japan has always encountered different problems.[13] It had long been closed to immigration. Admitting labour migrants during the past decades, even on a limited scale, has been a taxing issue for the authorities. For an understanding of the place of Chinese new migrants, it may be more relevant to examine the Korean communities in Japan than Chinese experiences elsewhere.[14]

Check-list of recurrent themes

Let me now come to a check-list of recurrent themes. What are the questions facing new migrants that are specially important now? I have selected for brief mention here five common and persistent themes, and will end with some reflections on the theme of assimilation.

Immigration checks and controls

Procedures are more elaborate but also more transparent. Receiving countries are more caring towards immigrants than ever before. There have been signs of humanitarian progress towards migrants who come through approved ways. Below the surface, however, there is another picture arising from efforts to stop illegal immigrants coming from the Chinese mainland. This phenomenon itself is not new. Methods to counter these developments have been steadily upgraded to keep their numbers to a minimum. But the plight of these illegals is easy to sensationalize and they often embarrass the settled Chinese communities. Globalization has now made these struggles more public. I am not sure scholarly studies are possible at this stage, but it would be a pity to leave the subject to the media.

Family

The new migrants, as in the past, include both those who travel as families and those who migrate singly, but it is not clear if, overall, the latter still outnumber the former as in the past. Many new migrants move as families, especially the middle-class professionals from Hong Kong and the remigrants of Southeast Asia. But reports suggest that, from mainland China, singles are still numerous, and the differences between family migrants and the majority of these single migrants may intensify the divisions between PRC Chinese and others of Chinese descent. If it is true, the established family-based communities could be expected to dictate the terms of settlement in the adopted country for a long time to come. They will ensure continuity and set the social parameters for new single migrants to follow. But we need more studies here.

Equally important is the evolving status of women as more women emigrate, especially when single women independently relocate and find careers in modern institutions. They are a far cry from the poorly educated women in the past who were brought out of China, or followed their husbands without preparation and with much trepidation. Today, they could outshine their brothers and husbands and earn the professional respect that they deserve. Their successes, particularly in North America and Australasia, are already being studied, often as breathtaking contrasts to the lives of their earlier sisters.[15] Their future roles in the family await closer attention.

Work

The new migrants are clearly more urban than the pioneers who worked the mines and plantations in tropical Southeast Asia, and those who built the railroads and produced vegetables for North American markets. This makes the new experiences more like what was historically normal for migrants from Europe. At one level, they would be more like the Europeans who went to North America and Australia to work in cities and factories. At other levels, they may be compared to the European scholars and professionals who were recruited to large enterprises, laboratories and universities. This suggests that new migrants do not have peculiarly Chinese features, but may be better studied as examples of modern migration. Does this mean that the generalizations about all migrants in the West could now be easily applied to these new Chinese ones? This seems increasingly likely and studies of the new phenomenon would focus on common migrant experiences and minimize the references to their special Chinese characteristics. Will this lead to the emergence of sharp class differences among the Chinese communities? As long as Chinese remain less than 3 per cent of the population in each receiving country, this is unlikely to be an issue.

Education

The new migrants have gone to developed societies in which education facilities are invariably better than back home. Unlike in the past, most are familiar with the cultures of the receiving countries. Many admire the meritocratic features of education there and the opportunities offered to those who perform well in their studies. Clearly, these conditions would be very important for their children. This has been a well-studied topic in North America and Australasia, and little more needs to be said about it here. But specific comparisons between different migrant layers, that is, between the new migrants and those settled for decades or longer, and those who have re-migrated from Southeast Asia and elsewhere, deserve attention. They could tell us more about the qualities that migrants coming directly from China bring, especially those coming from a post-revolutionary China that seems to be struggling to find its way. I shall come back to this again when I re-visit the theme of assimilation.

Religion

Unlike those from Hong Kong and even those from Taiwan, and unlike most re-migrants from Southeast Asia, the new migrants from mainland China very rarely arrive with strong religious faiths. They are more likely to have the secular outlook that the several Chinese revolutions of the twentieth century have inculcated in most Chinese on the mainland. Most are admirers of the developments in science and technology in the West since the Renaissance, and identify with the ideas of the Enlightenment and the ideals of the French and American, if no longer the Russian, revolutions.

How they respond to the lifestyles of the local Chinese families who practise various religions would be interesting, especially after they have been in the receiving countries for many years. Also, has there been any interest in the religions found in these countries independently of other Chinese? Is there a readiness to seek new faiths? An understanding of their responses may help us understand those who prefer to follow something new but recognizably Chinese like the Falun Gong rather than the established religions spurned by the secular education they had received.

Re-visiting the theme of assimilation

Let me now go to re-visit the theme of assimilation. Like the concept of identity, for which there has not been an exact Chinese equivalent, assimilation or *tonghua* is a modern word that also captures something the Chinese have long felt but never fully articulated. That the word envisages the possibility of Chinese undergoing *tonghua*, or assimilated by others, has been a matter of concern since the beginning of the twentieth century.[16]

As you know, throughout Chinese history, the fact that alien peoples acknowledged China's power, or adopted Chinese customs and practices, or accepted Confucian and other values and, in some cases, identified themselves or were identified as Chinese (that is, *guishun*, or *guihua*), affirmed for the Chinese the superiority of their civilization. Some Chinese did move the other way and choose to identify with other polities or cultures. They were politically regarded as traitors to the emperors and, more significantly, accused of betraying their cultural roots, their parents and their ancestral homes. At times of China's weakness, feelings ran strong about such behaviour, and these people were condemned as *Hanjian* (traitors). Given the number of times the central regions of China were invaded and conquered, and millions were forced to live under foreign rule, such loyalties were repeatedly tested. The fact that Chinese civilizations seemed always to have survived and to have been enriched by the experiences led to deep convictions about the power of traditional Chinese values, however defined. Ideas akin to that of assimilation, therefore, were mainly applied to examples where other peoples became Chinese.

Nevertheless, most Chinese understood that culture, especially in its public display, was not an absolute, but changed according to circumstance. For example, when forced to do so, Han Chinese wore the queue as a mark of subservience to the Manchu conquerors. They wore it for so long that when asked to remove it after 1911 as a symbol of liberation, many older Chinese resisted. But times changed. Most Chinese have not only embraced modern science and accepted all new knowledge but have also adopted other forms of dress and haircuts. Being modern has replaced many of their earlier secular faiths.

This is where the new migrants today are most different from their predecessors of the nineteenth century. The two revolutions of Sun Yat-sen and Mao Zedong have educated them for the modern world. No longer do migrants need to feel that they have to defend received traditions against foreign cultures. Chinese efforts at internal modernization for the past 90 years on both sides of the Straits, and in Hong Kong, and among the Chinese overseas, have made this new generation of migrants thoroughly ready for the pressures of further change when they move abroad. In short, the cultural gap between the new migrants and the people in the receiving countries has been much diminished. Although some still go out blindly, desperate for a new life, most of them know where they want to go and why. Some not only do not fear assimilation, but actually seek it. What then does the process of assimilation mean to these new migrants today?

There are many different kinds of responses. To begin with, there is the other meaning of assimilation which is the key to modern education. This refers to the ability to absorb new learning, the new ideas necessary for further progress in China. That is clearly something to be desired for those who want to learn and then ultimately return to benefit the Chinese people. Then there is the question of what is left for them to defend in the civilization of their forefathers. Very few of the new migrants are devoted to the kinds of tradition that earlier sojourning Chinese cared about. Instead, they are more likely to defend China as a modernizing country, or China's honour and long-term interests as a sovereign nation, or their personal dignity as Chinese, or all three at the same time. If they could do that abroad in relatively free and tolerant countries, that would be ideal.

There is, of course, a price to pay. Their children will benefit from education systems that lead to excellent universities and colleges. There can be no assurance that they will share the same feelings of their parents. What the cultures and policies of the receiving countries have to offer could make all the difference. Here the best example for close study is the United States. Their migration scholars have been studying the topic of assimilation most carefully since before the Second World War. Their pioneer studies have been about assimilating the Amerindian tribes in the country. These were followed by the melting pot theory for immigrant peoples from non Anglo-Saxon countries in Europe, and there were numerous examples of how they became Americans within one or two generations. Similar studies were done by their counterparts in Canada and Australia. We know that all three countries before the 1960s did not want Chinese migrants and gave the fact that Chinese would not assimilate as a major reason why they did not want them. Now, ironically, these are the same three countries that have taken in the largest numbers of new Chinese migrants. At the same time, these migrants are now better prepared to deal with the cultures, politics and economic systems of the three countries. They are more ready than Chinese have ever been before to assimilate what they want to learn and accept the political culture and lifestyles they have found there. For the reasons I have outlined, they not only have less reason to resist being assimilated but also want their children to be educated as Americans, Canadians or Australians.

There is, of course, a lively debate being conducted in all three countries about problems of assimilation and multiculturalism. Will multiculturalism be a permanent characteristic of all three societies? Or is it but a measured phase towards assimilation? The new migrants have arrived in the midst of this important debate, the first generation to be part of an experiment to deal with large-scale migration in an era of globalization. Why these migrants are truly new is that the new ground rules of global migration are still being set and they are well equipped to cope with future changes. And as these rules are being shaped, the new Chinese migrants are joining their settled compatriots, and many others, in making sure that their multiple voices are heard. Unlike in the past, their new voices include those that are educated, gender-equal, professionally secure, politically savvy, and globally connected. This may be a matter of assimilating the earlier Western European migration patterns, but for the Chinese, that is indeed a new experience.

Concluding remarks

ISSCO members are well placed to study this experience around the world. Those in Southeast Asia, the cradle of Chinese migrant populations, have observed Chinese communities in the various stages of assimilation and cultural maintenance. They have noted that re-migrants from the region to North America and Australasia seem content to seek assimilation with the local elites. Other members find themselves living among, and ready to study, the new migrants who are self-consciously seeking their place in varied conditions. Yet others are themselves new migrants who are perhaps best positioned to record their own experiences as they unfold. Theirs is a unique opportunity under conditions never before as favourable. They are not merely new migrants. They are in a position to help earlier generations of scholars, both within and outside the Chinese world, to re-write the histories of migrant Chinese. With that, they could also bring new theoretical insights to the study of migration itself, a field so far dominated by the experiences across the Atlantic and ready to be compared to those across the Pacific.[16]

Notes

1 This article is a revised version of the keynote speech delivered at the fourth ISSCO conference in Taipei, 25–28 April 2001.

2 The first ISSCO conference was held in 1992 in San Francisco. Selected Conference papers were published in 1998 by Times Academic Press in Singapore

under the title *The Chinese Diaspora: Selected Essays*, vols. I and II, jointly edited by Wang Ling-chi and Wang Gungwu.

3 The second ISSCO conference was held in Hong Kong in 1994. Selected essays were published by Hong Kong University Press in 1998 under the title of *The Last Half-Century of Chinese Overseas*, edited by E. Sinn.

4 The third ISSCO Conference in Manila in 1998. The proceedings were published by Kaisa Para Sa Kaularan in 2000 under the title *Intercultural Relations, Cultural Transformation, and Identity*, edited by Teresita Ang See.

5 For a discussion of the term *huaqiao*, see Wang Gungwu, "A Note on the Origins of Hua-Ch'iao", in Wang Gungwu, *Community and Nation: Essays on Southeast Asia and the Chinese*, Singapore: Heinemann Educational Books (Asia) and Sydney: Allen and Unwin Australia for ASAA, 1981, pp. 118–127. (Note that the article was first published in 1977.)

6 For instance, Mao Qixiong and Lin Xiaotong, eds, *Zhongguo fawufagui gaishu* (A brief account of China's Overseas Chinese laws and regulations), Beijing: Zhongguo huaqiao chubanshe, 1994.

7 For a brief study of Hong Kong recent migrants in Canada, see Lawrence Lam, "Migration and Settlement: Hong Kong Chinese Immigrants to Toronto, Canada", in Wang and Wang, eds., *The Chinese Diaspora*, vol. II, pp. 181–197; Peter Li, "Chinese Canadians in Business", in *Asian and Pacific Migration Journal*, vol. 10, no. 1, 2001, pp. 99–122.

8 For a brief study on Chinese recent migrants in Australia and New Zealand, see Manying Ip, ed., *Re-examining Chinese Transnationalism in Australia-New Zealand*, Canberra: CSCSD, Australian National University, 2001; Manying Ip, "The New Chinese Community in New Zealand: Local Outcomes of Transnationalism", in *Asian and Pacific Migration Journal*, vol. 10, no 2, 2001, pp. 213–240.

9 For some recent studies on the Chinese in the US, see Timothy P. Fong, "Monterey Park and Emerging Race Relations in California", in Wang and Wang, eds., *The Chinese Diaspora*, vol. II, pp. 167–180; Hoover Wong, "The North American (US) Chinese Experience", in Zhuang Guotu, ed., *Ethnic Chinese at the Turn of the Centuries*, pp. 353–397; Amy L. Freedman, *Political Participation and Ethnic Minorities: Chinese Overseas in Malaysia, Indonesia, and the United States*, London: Routledge, 2000, pp. 137–182.

10 I have discussed this issue in my earlier article, "Sojourning: The Chinese Experience", in Wang Gungwu, *Don't Leave Home: Migration and the Chinese*, Singapore: Times Academic Press, 2001, pp. 54–72. (Originally published in 1996.)

11 For instance, Li Zong, "Chinese Immigration to Vancouver and New Racism in Multicultural Canada", in Zhuang, ed., *Ethnic Chinese at the Turn of Centuries*, pp. 443–463.

12 For a new American immigration policy and its impact on Chinese Americans, see Bill Ong Hing, *Making and Remaking Asian America through Immigration Policy, 1850–1990*, Stanford: Stanford University Press, 1993.

13 He Ruiteng, *Riben Huaqiao shehui zhi yanjiu*, Taibei: Zhengzhong, 1985; and Luo Huangchao, *Riben Huaqiao shi*, Guangzhou: Guangdong gaodeng jiaoyu, 1994.

14 George Hicks, *Japan's Hidden Apartheid: The Korean Minority and the Japanese*, Aldershot: Ashgate, 1997.

15 For instance, Guida Man, "Hong Kong Middle Class Immigrant Women in Canada: An Investigation in the Social Organization of Work", in Zhuang, ed., *Ethnic Chinese at the Turn of the Centuries*, pp. 464–485.

16 Wang Gungwu, "Tonghua, Guihua and Overseas Chinese History", in *Overseas Chinese in Asia Between the Two World Wars*, edited by Ng Lun Ngai-ha and Chang Chak Yan, Centre for Contemporary Asian Studies, Chinese University of Hong Kong, 1989, pp. 11–23.

INDEX